Discourses of Crisis and the Study of Religion

NAASR Working Papers

Series Editor: Emily D. Crews, University of Chicago Divinity School

NAASR Working Papers provides a venue for publishing the latest research carried out by scholars who understand religion to be an historical element of human cognition, practice, and organization. Whether monographs or multi-authored collections, the volumes published in this series all reflect timely, cutting edge work that takes seriously both the need for developing bold theories as well as rigorous testing and debate concerning the scope of our tools and the implications of our studies. NAASR Working Papers therefore assess the current state of the art while charting new ways forward in the academic study of religion

Founding Series Editor: Brad Stoddard, McDaniel College in Westminster, Maryland

Published

Constructing "Data" in Religious Studies: Examining the Architecture of the Academy
Edited by Leslie Dorrough Smith

Hijacked: A Critical Treatment of the Public Rhetoric of Good and Bad Religion
Edited by Leslie Dorrough Smith, Steffen Führding, and Adrian Hermann

Jesus and Addiction to Origins: Towards an Anthropocentric Study of Religion
Willi Braun
Edited by Russell T. McCutcheon

Key Categories in the Study of Religion: Contexts and Critiques
Edited by Rebekka King

Method Today: Redescribing Approaches to the Study of Religion
Edited by Brad Stoddard

On the Subject of Religion: Charting the Fault Lines of a Field of Study
Edited by James Dennis LoRusso

"Religion" in Theory and Practice: Demystifying the Field for Burgeoning Academics
Russell T. McCutcheon

Religious Studies Beyond the Discipline: On the Future of a Humanities Ph.D.
Edited by Russell T. McCutcheon

Remembering J. Z. Smith: A Career and its Consequence
Edited by Emily D. Crews and Russell T. McCutcheon

Thinking with J. Z. Smith: Mapping Methods in the Study of Religion
Edited by Barbara Krawcowicz

Discourses of Crisis and the Study of Religion

Edited by
Lauren Horn Griffin

SHEFFIELD UK   BRISTOL CT

Published by Equinox Publishing Ltd.

U.K.: Office 415, The Workstation, 15 Paternoster Row, Sheffield, South Yorkshire S1 2BX

U.S.A.: ISD, 70 Enterprise Drive, Bristol, CT 06010

www.equinoxpub.com

First published 2025

© Lauren Horn Griffin and contributors 2025

All rights reserved. No part of this publication may be reproduced or transmitted in any form or by any means, electronic or mechanical, including photocopying, recording or any information storage or retrieval system, without prior permission in writing from the publishers.

ISBN-13 978 1 80050 530 8 (hardback)
         978 1 80050 531 5 (paperback)
         978 1 80050 532 2 (ePDF)
         978 1 80050 653 4 (ePub)

British Library Cataloguing-in-Publication Data
A catalogue record for this book is available from the British Library.

Library of Congress Cataloging-in-Publication Data
Names: Griffin, Lauren Horn, editor.
Title: Discourses of crisis and the study of religion / edited by Lauren Horn Griffin.
Description: Sheffield, South Yorkshire : Equinox Publishing Ltd, 2025. | Series: NAASR working papers | Includes bibliographical references and index. | Summary: "This volume, focusing on discourses of crisis during a time that is constantly mediated as "in crisis," shows us ways of doing religious studies that are up to the challenge of reflecting on the problems, strategies, and political structures through which we construct our social worlds"-- Provided by publisher.
Identifiers: LCCN 2024038232 (print) | LCCN 2024038233 (ebook) | ISBN 9781800505308 (hardback) | ISBN 9781800505315 (paperback) | ISBN 9781800505322 (pdf) | ISBN 9781800506534 (epub)
Subjects: LCSH: Religion--Study and teaching (Higher) | Religion and social problems.
Classification: LCC BL41 .D58 2025 (print) | LCC BL41 (ebook) | DDC 200.71/1--dc23/eng/20240924
LC record available at https://lccn.loc.gov/2024038232
LC ebook record available at https://lccn.loc.gov/2024038233

Typeset by JS Typesetting Ltd, Porthcawl, Mid Glamorgan

Contents

Introduction

Don't Call it a Crisis, It's Been Here for Years: The Uses and Abuses of Anomaly 1
Lauren Horn Griffin

Part I Critiquing "Crisis" in Higher Education

1 Crisis, What Crisis? The Study of Religion Is Always in Crisis 11
   Aaron W. Hughes

2 The "Discipline" of Humanities: Rhetorics of Interiority, Discourses of Crisis, and Contemporary Nationalist Ideology 21
   Lauren Horn Griffin

3 "I Went to the Crossroads, Fell Down on my Knees": On the Rhetoric of Crisis and Academic Labor 35
   James Dennis LoRusso

4 Theology and Religious Studies: A Relationship in Crisis? 45
   Suzanne Owen

5 Scholars Are People Too: The (Sometimes) Difficult Shift to the Discourse of Crisis 50
   Russell T. McCutcheon

Part II Language: Crisis as a Turning Point

6 Profit and Loss: The New Time of Crisis 63
   Zoe Anthony

7 Black Fires: Crisis as Nadir and the Memory of Racial Violence in the South 69
   Aaron M. Treadwell

8 Force of Law: Resources in Derrida for Rethinking Policing 82
   Karen Zoppa

9 When Is a Crisis a "Turning Point"? 97
   Andrew Durdin

Part III Lexicon: Crisis as Method in the Study of Religion

10 The Crisis of World Religions and the Critique of Essentialism 105
    Michael P. DeJonge

11 Enlarging Religious Studies, Wither-ing Neoliberalism 114
    Matt Sheedy

12 Pop Goes the People: Populism, Panics, and Pandemics 130
    Carmen Celestini

Part IV Locus: Landmarks in Religious Adaptations in the Face of "Crisis"

13 "Social" Church and "Pragmatic" Relationship with the State: The Wager of the Roman Catholic Church in Mexico and the Orthodox Church in Russia in Response to Discourses of Crisis 145
    Xochiquetzal Luna Morales

14 Yoga's Flexibility in Brazil during the COVID-19 Pandemic 156
    Gustavo H. P. Moura

15 Compounded Crises: How the Principle of Subsidiarity Informs Catholic Responses to Critical Issues in North America 165
    Ben Szoller

Part V Locution: Upending the Discipline

16 World Society: Upended? 179
    Adrian Hermann

17 Competing Economies in Studies of Identity and Religion 190
    K. Merinda Simmons

Afterword

Hey, What About Me? 197
Aaron W. Hughes

Index 203

Introduction

Don't Call it a Crisis, It's Been Here for Years
The Uses and Abuses of Anomaly

Lauren Horn Griffin

Paul Fairie, a researcher and instructor at the University of Calgary, has produced several viral Twitter threads in which he compiles newspaper clippings to demonstrate the antiquity of arguments we cannot seem to quit trotting out (e.g., "nobody wants to work anymore," "men aren't manly," and "kids these days ...").[1] This turned into a book for Unbound titled *The Press Gallery*, which compiles over 500 historical newspaper clippings into a "coffee table book that offers reassurance that the past made as little sense as the present."[2] It turns out, people really enjoy reading about how our concerns and crises are not at all new. Altogether, the clippings help reveal the construction of certain problems (like the crisis of masculinity), which has proven comforting for many. As one Twitter user responded: "This is helpful. If masculinity has always been in crisis, was it ever in crisis? Is this just its normal state?"[3] Others asked why femininity is never framed as in crisis. In other words, questioning the framework of crisis in relation to gender served as a useful reminder that debating it actually creates the thing itself.

On the other hand, realizing that some dangers have long haunted us can also feel deeply distressing. In reading accounts of sexual abuse committed by Catholic clergymen, scholar of Catholicism Robert Orsi put it like this:

> My disgust with Catholicism has been growing for a long time. For the past ten years or so, I have been immersed in the sheer horror of the Catholic clergy sexual abuse crisis. "The sexual abuse crisis" refers to the sexual violation of Catholics by their priests, first of all, and, second, to the protection of these priests by their bishops and religious superiors, who were quite often themselves involved in illicit sexual activities. The word "crisis" for this moment in Catholic history is a mischaracterization, if what is meant by "crisis" includes any notion of the exceptional, unforeseen, or unusual nature either of the abuse or its cover-up.
> (Orsi 2019)

---

1. He posts as @paulisci at https://x.com/paulisci.
2. See the book description at https://unbound.com/books/thepressgallery?utm_campaign=thepressgallery&utm_medium=AuthorSocial&utm_source=AuthorActivity.
3. Following the guidelines laid out by Buck and Ralston (2020), I am not citing or directly quoting tweets from unverified users. I have paraphrased this post in order to protect the user.

Like the Twitter user above who explained how continuity makes a "crisis of masculinity" by definition not, indeed, a crisis, Orsi began to understand this dark picture of sexual behavior as the norm in Catholic communities. "This is not a crisis," he argues, but rather "the modern Catholic normal, finally disclosed for all to see clearly" (Orsi 2019). What does the framework of crisis accomplish in this case? It helps portray clerical abuse as new, rare, and unforeseen when, as Orsi demonstrates, it is ongoing, an open secret, and tragically common.

"Crisis" rhetoric, then, often quarantines particular moments in such a way as to preserve the comforting illusion of anomalousness. In relation to religions and things we call religious, this often works hand in glove with the good religion/bad religion binary that has proven resilient in the field despite sustained critique. We see good religion rhetoric in support for religious studies programs in colleges and universities; a quick scan of department websites will result in various articulations of "richness and mystery," "human flourishing," and "personal fulfillment." Bad religion rhetoric, as we have seen time and again, justifies derision, surveillance, and violence.[4] Like the judgments implicit in terms such as "fundamentalist" or "extremist," the implications of labeling something a "crisis" can prove far-reaching. This framework of crisis and turning point can make "repugnant others" out of particular social actors and it can, on the other hand, maintain the perception that a problem was an aberration rather than the rule (Harding 1991). Historicizing "crisis" and its opposites—calm, continuity, comeback—in relation to religion can provide another vantage point from which to forcefully challenge the enduring formulation of good/bad religion. Examining discourses of crisis, rather than taking at face-value the crisis itself, can underscore how social and political interests animate the crisis/continuity dichotomy.

So we may well ask, does "crisis" overemphasize the particular inflictions of the moment, masking what came before? There is no shortage of news articles calling our time (particularly the 2020s) a "time of crisis."[5] But are things really worse? Where? For whom? In what ways? Crises may fall out of the headlines or, on the other hand, replicate like a virus. Whether or not we are living in "a time of crisis," the nature of our all-encompassing digital hyperconnectivity makes us feel like we are. As comedian Bo Burnham sings in "Welcome to the Internet" (2021):

> Could I interest you in everything?
> All of the time?
> A little bit of everything
> All of the time
> Apathy's a tragedy
> And boredom is a crime
> Anything and everything
> All of the time

---

4. See for example Mamdani (2004), Johnson and Weitzman (2017), and Evans (2020).
5. See for example Parikh (2020).

Highlighting the role of hyperconnectivity is certainly helpful, but even the crisis of information overload is not necessarily new. In her book *Too Much to Know*, Ann Blair examines the ways people have responded in eras of new technology and exploding information, from ancient and medieval Europe as well as the Islamic world and China (Blair 2010). From premodern times to now, people have had to deal with the feelings of discombobulation that comes with too much information. Thus, even with ye olde information overload, we can examine those interests, structures, and technologies that make it feel like a crisis in the first place.

Of course, this is not to say that problems, difficulties, and dangers do not exist. The point of analysis is not to determine whether or to what extent bad things happen, but rather to examine when discourses of crisis become mobilized, by whom, and to what social ends. To echo what Orsi argued about modern Catholicism, this may challenge some colleagues in religious studies to take a step back from the usual framework of religious respectability (e.g., look how religion helps in times of crises) and to think twice before we speak authoritatively about good/bad and crisis/peace. The promise of such a "disgusting" (to follow Orsi's affective theme) example like the clerical abuse crisis to destabilize the anomaly/continuity distinction exists not only for the study of Catholic history, but for religious studies in general. While the reader will be intrigued by the range of topics in the chapters that follow (from analyzing discourses of crisis in the humanities to the U.S. history of race relations to the Roman Catholic Church in Mexico), the larger principles we engage with go beyond our sub-disciplinary limits. The contribution of this volume, then, is to demonstrate the frequency, power, and mechanics of discourses of crisis in the study of religion.

This is not to argue that we should abandon crisis as a term or as an analytical concept. Indeed, crisis is a useful heuristic for several chapters in this volume (in particular, the chapters in Part IV); these authors use the framework of crisis to bring together particular examples (e.g., to compare Mexico and Russia) or to think through the impact of a particular event (e.g., quarantine and the increase of virtual activities). But what we *can* do is offer a reflection on the ways in which the field of religious studies continues to construct "religion" as an object of study vis-à-vis popular binaries like good/bad and crisis/normal. Just as Jean Baudrillard acknowledged that the violence of what has been called the Gulf War took place, he also asked if the events that took place could be called a war, why, and to what social ends (Baudrillard 1995). The point is to expose how our acts of classification, identification, and signposting perform a significant amount of work in creating particular narratives. In contrast to other studies that view "crisis" as a self-evident object of study, the contributors of this volume add case studies that will serve as larger examples of how the discourse on crisis serves the goals of specific social actors in particular social contexts. How is "crisis" constructed and depicted in the academic study of religion? How is a crisis for some an opportunity for others? How do scholars of religion, given our expertise on discourse and ideology, still have blind spots when it comes to applying our critique of categories in religion to other terms and classifications?

Over the last decade or so, the North American Association for the Study of Religion's (NAASR) annual conference has been dedicated to unpacking the primary assumptions that underlie the academic study of religion. After analyzing concepts like theory, method, data and their attendant political functions, NAASR programs examined the construction and deployment of key categories in the study of religion (King 2022) and revisited the fabric of the field itself, interrogating how we construct, teach, and fund religious studies in the contemporary university (LoRusso 2022). The 2021 program, which is the basis for this book, was the second NAASR meeting to take place completely online (the first being the 2020 meeting during the initial year of the COVID-19 pandemic), and COVID was still an overwhelming part of daily life for many. Academic conferences were of course focusing their themes on the pandemic, examining various lenses through which to conceptualize what had happened and what was still happening after a year of living with the threat of the virus and all it had entailed. As Aaron Hughes noted in his keynote (which is now the opening chapter to this volume), a presentation at the American Academy of Religion (AAR) might examine how religious people act in times of crisis, or ask what religions around the world teach us about persevering through crises. "We might then engage in some sort of interfaith exploration of the world's religions and spiritual traditions," Hughes predicts, "all with the aim of offering us some sort of antidote to our present crisis and, in so doing, help alleviate our collective suffering" (Chapter 1, this volume).

A quick glance through the 2021 AAR call for proposals and the resultant program reveals that Hughes was correct in his projections; we find panels that investigate how a particular tradition "provides means of responding to the COVID-19 crisis," "spiritual responses to the current global environmental crisis," and how "religion can address the contemporary immigration crisis." Regarding the COVID pandemic specifically, panels reflect on "Muslim responses," "responses of megachurches," "South Asian religious responses," and the list could go on. Admittedly, no one can historicize everything at once, and while these questions may yield interesting data, we can still ask how that data was produced, understood, and used to construct concepts of religion, particular religions, and stuff we label religious or spiritual. Thus, with the COVID-19 crisis still very much in view, the goal of the NAASR program and this present volume is to remain in line with NAASR's focus on a rigorous self-consciousness.

Throughout the first several years of the 2020s, the experience of a global pandemic had further exposed and exacerbated what we might call existing crises, including racial injustice and economic inequality, the collapsing of higher education, and the breakdown of so-called democratic norms and institutions. As seen in the AAR themes above, religion often figures prominently in public and scholarly discourse surrounding these issues. Rather than ask how religious people may handle a crisis or what religion can offer people who feel they are in crisis, this volume asks what happens when we classify something as a "crisis," and what is at stake in linking these "crises" to "religion." In his chapter "The Uses of Anomaly" (echoed in the subtitle of this introduction) in *Discourse and the Construction of Society*, Bruce Lincoln reminds us that "there is nothing that is intrinsically, inherently, and automatically anomalous. Rather there are only things that appear anomalous within the framework of a given taxonomic system" (Lincoln 2014, 165). With this in mind, the goal of the present volume, *Discourses of Crisis in the Study of Religion*, is to continue to investigate how our terms and categories, though seemingly neutral, do real political work.

To accomplish this goal, the volume is organized into five parts. Part I focuses on higher education, asking how discourses of crisis function in the field of religious studies (Hughes and Owen), in the humanities more broadly (Griffin), in academic labor (LoRusso), and for scholars themselves (McCutcheon). The rest of the book structures the critical approach to the category of crisis through four distinct sections on language, lexicon, locus, and locution (Parts II–V respectively).

Part II examines the various rhetorical and theoretical frameworks for "crisis." Zoe Anthony investigates the construction of "unprecedented" events to force radical decision through the work of Walter Benjamin and Reinhart Koselleck, while Aaron M. Treadwell interrogates the "Nadir" as a concept in the memory of race relations in the United States. Karen Zoppa asks how framing something as crisis can destabilize its authority. Taking these together, Andrew Durdin reflects on the functions of theorizing crisis as "turning point."

Part III considers the question of method in the study of religion, interrogating the ways in which perceived crises mark shifts in how we do our work. DeJonge looks at a major shift in methodological framework, Sheedy reconsiders the goals and identity of the discipline, and Celestini rethinks teaching religious studies during times constantly framed as unprecedented.

Part IV takes up the concept of data for religion and crisis, analyzing examples of how the construction of "crisis" can force moments of decision, adaptation, and reaction. These examples compare instances from North America (Szoller), Brazil (Moura), Mexico, and Russia (Morales), highlighting how religions are not fixed entities but fluid ideas constructed and reconstructed in social contexts.

Finally, Part V brings together two senior scholars, Merinda Simmons and Adrian Hermann, to assess the stated aim of the American Academy of Religion's Annual Meeting in 2021 (i.e., "thinking about the actual human implications of religion in a world upended") and explain how we might provide an alternative to that use of crisis in the field of religious studies. The volume closes with an afterword by Aaron Hughes, who considers what happens when theorizing cuts too close to home.

The title for this introductory chapter is a play on the opening lines of LL Cool J's title track for his fourth studio album, Mama Said Knock You Out. In that single, which dropped in 1990, he famously raps "Don't call it a comeback / I've been here for years." Historicizing "crisis" necessarily involves its opposite: "coming back." The return to normal/stasis is the other side of the coin. LL Cool J's previous album (released just a year prior in 1989) was a flop both critically and commercially, and reviewers were claiming that his career was waning. Appearing at the 1989 Stop the Racism rally in Harlem—a response to the racially motivated murder of Yusuf K. Hawkins, a black youth who was killed in the Bensonhurst section of Brooklyn—LL was booed. To encourage him, his grandmother told him to "knock them out" with his next album. Some critics initially panned Mama Said Knock You Out. Writing in Melody Maker in November 1990, Jon Wilde said it showed LL Cool J "struggling hopelessly to resurrect his career ... with more of the same bilious rubbish." In the same month, in response to LL's demands that we not refer to this album as a comeback, David Quantick from New Musical Express retorts, "I don't think we need go as far as that." Nevertheless, the single went on to reach number 17 on the Billboard Hot 100, was certified platinum by the RIAA, and won the Grammy award for best rap solo performance. It is consistently ranked among the best hip hop tracks of all time.[6] In picking apart the idea of the "comeback" and whether or not LL had one, fans and critics have analyzed the song, the album as a whole, LL Cool J's career as a rapper, the past and future of hip hop, and broader issues in American culture from the late 1980s to the present. However one wants to depict his career, it amounted to something much different than it was before his crisis in 1989. Over 30 years later, LL Cool J and this song in particular serve as a milestone in narratives of hip hop history, standing between the golden age of hip hop and the emergence of gangsta rap and hardcore hip hop. The comeback and the preceding crisis it implies, it seems, has served as a useful heuristic to historicize the broader cultural history of hip hop.

The promise of interrogating concepts like "crisis" and its attendant "comeback" has been to destabilize the solidity of distinctions like good/bad and continuity/turning point; once a destabilizing concept is brought out into the open, the broader field around it must also be addressed. This volume, focusing on discourses of crisis during a time that is constantly mediated as "in crisis," demonstrates ways of doing religious studies that are up to the challenge of reflecting on the problems, strategies, and political structures through which we construct our social worlds—a move that, as disclosed in several chapters in this volume, is not always easy to make, even for scholars committed to critique.

Lauren Horn Griffin is assistant professor in the Department of Religious Studies at Louisiana State University. She is the author of *Fabricating Founders in Early Modern England* (Brill 2023). Her research and teaching focus on religion, politics, media, and technology.

References

Baudrillard, Jean. 1995. *The Gulf War Did Not Take Place*. Bloomington, IN: Indiana University Press, 1995.

Blair, Ann. 2010. *Too Much to Know: Managing Scholarly Information Before the Modern Age*. New Haven, CT: Yale University Press.

Buck, Amber M., and Devon F. Ralston. 2020. "I Didn't Sign Up for your Research Study: The Ethics of Using 'Public' Data." *Computers and Composition*, 61. https://doi.org/10.1016/j.compcom.2021.102655

Evans, Richard. 2020. *MOVE: An American Religion*. Oxford: Oxford University Press.

---

6. For example, see "50 Greatest Hip-Hop Songs of All Time" (*Rolling Stone*, December 5, 2012) and "The 500 Best Pop Songs: Staff List" (*Billboard*, October 19, 2023).

Harding, Susan. 1991. "Representing Fundamentalism: The Problem of the Repugnant Cultural Other." *Social Research*, 58(2): 373–393.
Johnson, Sylvester A., and Steven Weitzman (eds.). 2017. *The FBI and Religion: Faith and National Security Before and After 9/11*. Oakland, CA: University of California Press.
King, Rebekka (ed.). 2022. *Key Categories in the Study of Religion: Contexts and Critiques*. Sheffield: Equinox Publishing.
Lincoln, Bruce. 2014. *Discourse and the Construction of Society: Comparative Studies of Myth, Ritual, and Classification*. Oxford: Oxford University Press.
LoRusso, James Dennis (ed.). 2022. *On the Subject of Religion: Charting the Fault Lines of a Field of Study*. Sheffield: Equinox Publishing.
Mamdani, Mahmood. 2004. *Good Muslim, Bad Muslim: America, the Cold War, and the Roots of Terror*. New York: Pantheon.
Orsi, Robert A. 2019. "The Study of Religion on the Other Side of Disgust." *Harvard Divinity Bulletin*, 47(1–2): 21–30. Retrieved from https://bulletin.hds.harvard.edu/the-study-of-religion-on-the-other-side-of-disgust (accessed April 19, 2022)
Parikh, Nish. 2020. "The Importance of Living in the Present During Times of Crisis." *Forbes*, April 18. Retrieved from www.forbes.com/sites/forbeshumanresourcescouncil/2020/04/18/the-importance-of-living-in-the-present-during-times-of-crisis/?sh=5469c82f6715 (accessed June 19, 2022).

Part I

Critiquing "Crisis" in Higher Education

Chapter 1

Crisis, What Crisis?
The Study of Religion Is Always in Crisis

Aaron W. Hughes

If this were an American Academy of Religion (AAR) keynote address, I would most likely say something very different from what I propose to say here.¹ Most likely such an AAR keynote address on crisis would fall along the lines of "let's look at religious people in crisis." Or, perhaps better, "What do the religions of the globe teach us about persevering in the midst of crises, all with an eye towards overcoming them with equanimity and our spiritual lives intact?" After all, the so-called founders of the so-called world's religions overcame their own respective so-called crises—so, following their models *in illo tempore*, why should we not be able to do the same? Or, perhaps even better yet, let's look at crises in the world, of which the one that has put us all online for yet another year is certainly a part, and see how religion—as a special category that exists somehow immune from the mundane or quotidian—can actually help to solve them and make all our lives better in the process. What are Buddhist responses to COVID-19? How have Muslims tried to overcome the pandemic, and so on and so forth? All the while probably ignoring why certain religious people are more prone to be anti-vaxxers than their secular counterparts. We might then engage in some sort of interfaith exploration of the world's religions and spiritual traditions, all with the aim of offering us some sort of antidote to our present crisis and, in so doing, help alleviate our collective suffering.

I want to reframe—I trust in typical NAASR fashion, or at least the NAASR with which I am historically familiar—the very nature of the term in question. This will hopefully allow us to turn the torch back a little further than is traditional or customary and, in the process, try to illumine some otherwise dark or cavernous corners. I think that is the *raison d'être* of NAASR—at least it has been and continues to be for me. Crisis, using NAASR as my guide, is not something real that exists naturally in the world and as something we can simply point to. This is a crisis, for example, or that is a crisis over there. Instead, a crisis becomes, like anything we

---

1. I have opted to keep the oral tone and nature of the keynote for my chapter here. It is also the exact same format to which the following set of chapters respond. To my complete surprise, some in the Q&A session after I delivered my initial paper took exception to my theorization of "crisis" as opposed to talking about their actual crises. I will have more to say about this in the Afterword to this volume.

study, a term that we impose on our unruly social worlds to make sense of them. When we call something a "crisis," in other words, we articulate a set of interests—our own, perhaps those of others—that have come under threat in some place, and for some reason. This is why it seems to me, we should not look just at so-called actual crises, especially our own, but instead examine those interests, structures, and ideologies that go into what we call crises in the first place.

What's in a Word?

Before we examine crises, both large and small, academic and nonacademic, personal and collective, it might be worthwhile examining some of the semantic shifts that the actual term in question has undergone over the centuries. I think if Russell McCutcheon and I have done anything this past very productive year, it has been to try to reframe the field and nudge certain conversations along with our two co-written volumes—*Religion in 50 Words* (Hughes and McCutcheon 2022a) and its cheekily named sequel *Religion in 50 More Words* (Hughes and McCutcheon 2022b). If these two books do anything, and I do think they do quite a lot, they show us that the terms we have inherited and that we use, often so nonchalantly and without proper attention to where they came from and what they are doing, actually come from somewhere and that they do have, often rather complicated, genealogies. Taking such words at face-value or as natural markers, I submit, have brought us, collectively, to a crisis point. Due attention to their genealogies—to the work they have done and purport to still do—provide us with some potential to aid us in overcoming this crisis.

These are not innocent words that simply reflect the natural world that so many of our colleagues tend to assume just self-categorizes and that we are then supposed to spend our academic lives simply trying to reflect and describe such self-categorization accurately. And knowing where these words, terms, categories, tropes—and, of course, the narratives they have structured—come from—how they got from there to here and sometimes back again, when their meanings changed, where, and by whom—ought to be an activity that is incumbent upon all of us. That many of us do not do this or simply write it off as a form of intellectual masturbation, I might suggest, has only further exacerbated the crisis that exists deep at the heart of our collective field.

Our terms, after all, have undergone changes, semantic shifts, and all sorts of other twists and turns. Indeed, the noun "crisis," it would seem, is little different from words that more commonly fill up our collective field-wide toolbox, such as "secular," "prayer" or "experience." From the Latin crisis, itself from the Greek κρίσις, the *Oxford English Dictionary* informs us that the word seems to have originally connotated a "discrimination" or a "decision." We first encounter the term in English in the middle of the sixteenth century, where it was initially used within the domain of pathology to refer to the point in the progress of a disease when an important development or change takes place which decides recovery or, alternatively, death. A crisis, at least originally, in other words, refers to the turning-point of a disease for better or worse; something that could, by extension, also be applied to any marked or sudden variation occurring in the progress of a disease and to the various phenomena accompanying it.

We read, for example, in Edward Hall's 1548 work with the title *The vnion of the two noble and illustrate famelies of Lancastre [and] Yorke*, the following description of Henry V: "When the crisis of his sicknes was past and that he perceiued that helth was ouercome" (f. lxxx). Or, again, in a curious work by James Hart, a Northamptonshire physician, published in 1625 with the rather strange and lengthy title: *The Anatomie of Urines. Containing the Conviction and Condemnation of them. Or, the second Part of our discourse of urines. Detecting and unfolding the manifold falshoods and abuses committed by the vulgar sort of Practitioners in the judgement of diseases by the urines onely: together with a narrow survey of their substance, chiefe colours, and manifold contents, joyning withall the right use of urine*. Indeed, the title is longer than the quotation I wish to procure here: "Then shall the sicke ... by the vertue and power of a happy Crisis, saile forth into the hauen of health" (I.ii.21). A happy crisis. Imagine that. Not all crises, in other words, need be bad or conceived of in negative terms. The crisis can, in other words, effect positive change and even end positively for all concerned. There is, in other words, potential light and the potential end of the potential tunnel.

Coinciding with the notion of sickness, we also see early usages of the noun "crisis" used synonymously with a decision or the decision-making process. Thus in the Preface to the English theologian and scholar of Patristics, William Cave's (1637–1713) *Ecclesiastici, or, The history of the lives, acts, death & writings, of the most eminent fathers of the church, that flourisht in the fourth century*: "We have not made ... a Crisis and Censure of every single Tract." Like its synonym, decision, then, a crisis functions as a crossroads, the point at which we have two (or more) often stark alternatives with often radically different repercussions for ourselves, for our careers, for our families, and even for the health of our planet.

It is only when these meanings are transferred onto a more figurative register that we begin to see something that we today mean by the term in question—and I assume the one I have been asked to speak about here. About a century or so after the meanings just recounted, we now begin to see the term deployed in a manner that refers to a vitally important or decisive stage in the progress of something. Once again, with the idea that a "crisis" is a turning-point, a state of affairs in which a decisive change, for better or worse, is imminent. Only now do we see the term applied to times of difficulty, insecurity, and suspense, often in the domain of politics or commerce, often known by their aliases ideology and power. Thus, in his 1659 *Historical Collections of Private Passages of State*, John Rushworth, the English historian and politician, could write of the tension between king and government: "This is the Chrysis of Parliaments; we shall know by this if Parliaments live or die" (501). I like this quote because it retains both meanings of "crisis": security or lack thereof and health or lack thereof. Such crises need not just be human-manufactured and occur in the human realm, however. We also read of natural crises, as when, for example, John Tyndall writes in his 1860 *The Glaciers of the Alps*, and I quote, "The layer of snow had been in a state of strain, which our crossing brought to a crisis" (202).

What happens when we append the adjective "religious" to the noun "crisis." Well, for one thing, and a quick perusal of the literature in question reinforces this, it would seem to mean that every era has been, is, and will continue to be in some state of religious crisis. In his 1868 *Practical Suggestions Appropriate to the Present Religious Crisis*, Octavius Winslow—a nineteenth-century English evangelical preacher, also known as "the Pilgrim's Companion"—is concerned with the fact that the true religion, to wit, his own, has "been assailed by an overwhelming cataract of error and superstition, threatening the destruction of every vestige of those sacred principles which have left the moulding and enduring impress of their genius and character upon all the great institutions of the land" (6). And what is this threat? To what possible cause does he locate the crisis that besets "the sacred ark of our Christian faith and national Protestantism" (6)? Since I always enjoy a good footballing metaphor (the real football, not what passes for it in North America), he informs us that they are threatened by "the football of the sceptic and the sport of the Papist" (6).

Even as late as 2007, we witness in Hugh McLeod's *The Religious Crisis of the 1960s*, published by Oxford University Press, that the long 1960s—why is everything long these days?—that witnessed Christianity face challenges from what he calls "Eastern religions," Marxism, and feminism, and something that he vaguely refers to as "new affluent lifestyles." In his quantitative analysis McLeod seeks to explain what happened, again in his own words "to religion in the 1960s, why it happened, and how the events of that decade changed the rest of the 20th century." Though not nearly as rhetorical or alarmist as "the Pilgrim's Companion" noted previously, he nonetheless works with a normative idea of what religion is and it is a generic religion, moreover, one that, like Octavius Winslow's, sounds remarkably close to Protestant Christianity. Or again, in his 2007 *God's Continent: Christianity, Islam, and Europe's Religious Crisis*, also published by Oxford University Press, Philip Jenkins seeks to examine the tensions—or the so-called crisis—between the religion of Islam and the secular and progressive values of Europe.

Every age, to reiterate, would seem to be smack dab in the middle of not only a crisis (e.g., ecological, social, economic, intellectual), but also smack dab in the middle of a religious crisis.

Now we might well ask ourselves: What has this genealogy of the term showed us? What do these urine-soaked, medical quotations, football metaphors about the problems besetting so-called "true religion," and the threat that radical Islam poses to the health of Europe's body politic tell us? Well, for one thing, a crisis is not necessarily a crisis to everyone. Some people do well—even very well—by crises. They profit from them and, indeed, increase their social and other capital in the process. Think of the "Pilgrim's Companion," or all those who seek to put an end to so-called European or Western values from Muslims in their midst, those who are imagined to want to subvert such values, often from within. We are, after all, in a constant state of crisis. And calls or threats of a crisis are meant to goad us into action and/or encourage us to be self-reflective in the process. But a crisis in the Conservative Party of Canada is not the same thing as a housing crisis or a crisis in higher education, though they may, of course, be intimately related to one another. Crises are manufactured to protect certain interests, just as they can be invoked to subvert others. We are, to repeat, in a constant state of crisis. We hover between life and death, health and sickness, and, to paraphrase the aforementioned James Hart, between heaven and hell.

We are a curious species. Though each generation always likes to think that it is somehow special, that its own state of crisis is more pressing or dearer than that of its predecessors, be it in other times in the past or in other places at the current moment, it is, of course, rarely the case. Crises, not unlike their doppelgangers, so-called Golden Ages, after all are never full-scale episodes that effect all in equal measure, at least not yet prior to the impending ecological Armageddon. Instead, they tend to pertain only to some social groups and not others. Elites, of course, whether of the religious or the socio-economic variety, are often protected from crises, even though they might very well cause them or, at least, contribute to them. In the current moment, for example, Jeff Bezos and those like him are certainly not in a state of crisis—they are flourishing financially and flourishing, moreover, in ways that they never did before this damned pandemic.

What Crisis?

These musings bring me to the title and topic of my talk: "Crisis, What Crisis? The Study of Religion Is Always in Crisis." It is, isn't it? To those who see the academic study of religion as the "queen of the humanities," and I use this phrase intentionally as the modern incarnation of theology as the "queen of the sciences, and to those who think it is little more than theology recalibrated, the study of religion has always been a problem. It would seem to occupy a place at the decision-making crossroads where it attempts to ascertain where it was, what it should be, and, most importantly, where it should go moving forward. What is the study of religion good for? Why do we engage in it? How is it different from theology and other fields and/or disciplines? It is, after all, why we have NAASR. It is why we have IQSA (or the International Quranic Studies Association). It is why we have all those other organizations that meet concurrently with the AAR every year, at least until last year. We talk about this crisis, even if we do not call it such. We at NAASR pride ourselves on the fact that we do not do what the AAR does. We pride ourselves on the fact that we do not do theology, but—perhaps for lack of a better term—social theory or the like.

But we never address this crisis. We acknowledge it, but then there is a tendency just to paper over it and move on, and then every couple of years draw attention to it again. And then repeat the same process all over again. And we have been doing this for decades, on and off and then off again. The academic study of religion, it seems to me was predicated on the idea of crisis. In one generation back in the late 1800s and early 1900s a group of individuals, some known to each other and others working in isolation from one another, decided that the study of religion had to move in new directions and, in the process, shed its traditional theological and biblical skin. Theological and largely textual study began to transform, for some, to ethnographic and anthropological study—no doubt encouraged by the heyday of colonialism and empire administration, all of which took place against the backdrop of changes brought about by the Victorian era.

Were they effective? It depends whom you ask. Certainly, some were naive to think that they could just switch, willy-nilly, to academic study after some 2 millennia of (largely Christian) theologizing. But others did the best they could and tried to pave a new way of thinking about religion in a manner that was inconceivable only a generation prior. New institutions were formed, new positions were created, new journals founded—all of which led directly to what we do here, for better or worse, today. Is it their fault that their reductionist and functionalist initiatives were hijacked by phenomenology in the 1960s? Were they to blame for subsequent excesses that led to a primacy put on interfaith relations and interreligious dialogue? I seriously doubt it.

I think we spend too little time on that "crisis"—used now in the sense of decision and the decision-making process—that they faced, that they tried to respond to, and that, in many ways, created the space for what we try to do here at NAASR. It might be helpful to focus on their crisis, if for no other reason that it gives us clarity and, perhaps just as importantly, it might prevent us from repeating old mistakes and falling into old patterns.

Allow me to use an example. While it has become in vogue during our current virological crisis to speak of coronaviruses that have jumped species or variants that constantly mutate, I want to focus on another set of species jumping, variations, and mutations. But this time in the academic study of religion. Now, it is a fairly conventional story, one that we do not necessarily have to paraphrase here, that the academic study of religion began in earnest roughly one hundred and fifty or so years ago. We could point to the usual suspects in, e.g., Marburg (Rudolph Otto), Cambridge and Oxford (E. B. Tylor and Friedrich Max Müller), Amsterdam (Cornelis Petrus Tiele), Vienna (Sigmund Freud), Paris (Émile Durkheim), even here in Canada (Louis Henry Jordan) and the U.S. (e.g., Morris Jastrow).

Many of us can name these people, or at least most of them, and we can also write them off, as many tend to do, as "old white dudes," invested in and upholding the colonial and colonialist project, as Orientalists, as engaged in empire maintenance, and so on and so forth. But, like virologists who want to understand COVID-19 and public health officials who want to understand its community spread through, among other things, contact tracing—it might be worth looking a little more closely at the origins of our own field. We can do this, moreover, by engaging in our own set of contact tracing. I always find it interesting, for example, that the work that William Robertson Smith was engaged in on totemism caught the eye of Durkheim in France and that Robertson Smith's *Lectures on the Religion of the Semites* (first published in 1889) led Durkheim to think about sacrifice in his 1912 *The Elementary Forms of Religious Life*—just as it did on Freud's *Totem and Taboo*, a book published the following year. Indeed, Durkheim encouraged his nephew Marcel Mauss to spend a year abroad, in Leiden and Oxford, in order to broaden his intellectual horizons. In the Netherlands, Mauss met the historian of religion Cornelius Petrus Tiele, and in England the anthropologist Edward

Burnett Tylor and the classicist and folklorist James George Frazer (see the important comments in, e.g., Stroumsa 2021: 224). How is that for contact-tracing?

While we certainly witness the cross-over of what were, for all intents and purposes, Christian theological terms and categories to understand the religions of the globe. Where does the word "totemism," for example, come from? Or sacrifice? Here, I again draw your attention to the two volumes—*Religion in 50 Words* and *Religion in 50 More Words*—that Russell and I have published this year. But there is also another story at work here, one that also needs to be told, and one that I am currently in the process of beginning to explore in more detail. If there is cross-over, there is also resistance. And there are also mutations and variations. There are, for example, many dates and events that we simply overlook in our dominant narrative of religious studies. I think, for example, of:

1851	First world's fair/the so-called Crystal Palace Exhibition.
1859	Publication of Darwin's *Origin of Species*.
1873	Founding of ethnologisches Museum in Berlin.
1878/1937	Founding of Musée de l'homme (but a heir to Musée d'Ethnographie du Trocadéro).
1879	Collège de France establishes its first Chair devoted to the history of religions (held by Jean Réville).
1879	founding of *Revue de l'Histoire des Religions*.
1884	Founding of Pitt Rivers Museum in Oxford.
1893	World parliament of religions in Chicago.
1868	Founding of the École Pratique des Hautes Études (ÉPHÉ), and the establishment of the Fifth Section, devoted to the "Sciences Religieuses" in 1886.
1890	First International Congress for the History of Religions (in Paris).

What do all these dates and events have in common? Well, for one thing, we usually forget them or, if not—like the Parliament of World Religions in Chicago—mention them and then quickly pass them over as if the very mention of it makes it significant. But I think we ignore them at our own peril. Not only does it mean we are blind to the creative dialectic between individual scholar and institutional support, we risk in the process trying to reinvent the wheel every ten years or so without learning from the breakthroughs, tensions, and controversies of earlier generations. Finally, though all these dates are all but ignored in the academic study of religion despite the fact that, for all intents and purposes, they created said study. I think we have misread many of them in our desire to write them off as outdated precursors to the ostensibly "real" work that we engage in today. And this is the crisis I wish to draw attention to here.

While we have been quick to write off the early study of religion as too this, that, or the other thing, what happens when we instead situate the field within the broader framework provided by growing secularization, colonialism, the flowering of the missionary movement, and the rise of the modern university. When were the first academic Chairs created? Where and by whom? What journals and conferences were devoted exclusively to the new field? How exactly did the study of religion extract itself from anthropology and ethnography and Victorian museums? It is, after all, only in the nineteenth century that scholarship moves from the personal adventures and studies of idiosyncratic individuals into the modern university and institutionalized systems of knowledge. Indeed, it was this dialectical interaction between individual thinking and institutional spaces that was responsible for the transformation of many disciplines and fields at this time.

As theology gave way to an interest in praxis, as anthropology replaced philology as the primary method for studying religion, new vistas opened up. New ways to think about monotheism. New ways to think about Christianity. New ways to think about the category of religion. And, all of these new ways have left their mark on what we do here in NAASR. What we are trying to do with the phenomenological approach—despite the fact that it today goes by different names in different guises—is precisely what our phenomenological predecessors did with their Victorian ancestors. We cannot move forward, in other words, without going backwards and trying to understand previous crises that, in their own ways, have led us to the present one. I am always struck by how many of the founders associated with the early study of religion tried to differentiate their enterprise from the theological—both in what they studied and how they went about studying it. It was not perfect, by any means. Far from it. We all can rehearse their assumptions about religion and where and how to find it. They were in a moment of crisis and they tried to work their way out of it. That they did not, of course, is not necessarily their fault as they did not possess the skills to do it. But I am intrigued by how they conceptualized it and the various artistic, intellectual, cultural and social contexts against whose backdrops they plied their trades.

It is incumbent upon us to understand these crises and, just as importantly, to understand why people name them as such. Only by understanding them—and their naming—are we able to confront our own crisis, one that conceptualizes the study of religion in the most unacademic of terms, one that puts a pride of place on ecumenicism, one that encourage interfaith dialogue, one that focuses on interreligious freedom, and so on and so forth. But then again, and reinforcing my point, many of our colleagues in the AAR would not even call this a crisis!

Conclusions

It is now time to move towards a conclusion, of sorts. Today, it is common to hear talk about an "environmental crisis," or a "climate crisis," a "political crisis" or a "constitutional crisis." To more recent ones, such as "COVID-19 crisis," "housing crisis," "adjunct labor crisis," and all other crises. What links them all, one to another? For one thing it is the noun "crisis" to which can be appended any sort of adjectival descriptor. All represent cross-roads that we have—for a variety of reasons—deemed significant, moments where we assume hard choices have to be made, but alas will probably not be made because of either the lethargy of the status quo or the vested interests of the powers that be. Crises, then, are places where we assume decisions have to be made. These are not just individual decisions, of course, but increasingly field-wide, country-wide, and, in the case of some, worldwide.

But calling something a "crisis" also protects certain interests just as it exposes others. A housing crisis, for example, is only a crisis if one does not have a house. An "adjunct labor crisis" is a crisis for those underemployed and under recompensed. In both cases the interests of the status quo, those in power, are protected. Potentially masked in calling something a crisis are the real structural problems that remain out of sight and hidden from view. I think it is important for us to draw attention to these structural issues instead of simply giving voice to them and repeating them as if they were a mantra.

I have tried to do this here—perhaps unconventionally—by looking at words, narratives, and genealogies. By looking at the etymology and genealogy of the term "crisis," for example, I have tried to expose something of the crisis in our own field. It is a crisis we point to, perhaps we name it, but often do nothing to correct, perhaps assuming it will autocorrect. Well, it never does. I have also suggested that our present crisis in the academic study of religion might well benefit from a glimpse at our collective past—a past we are often too quick to write off for a variety of reasons—in order to look to the future. I certainly do not mean by this that we ignore all the past's shortcomings—its woeful disregard to issues of race, gender, colonialism, and so on. Nor do I think we should become Orientalists—though I might add their language skills were first rate. Instead, I think we need to look at the past, see what happened, what went wrong, what went right, and, in the process try to move forward in a way that takes into consideration the past, but is not hamstrung by it. "The past has a voice," wrote Mordechai Kaplan, the founder of Reconstructionist Judaism, "but not a veto."

Will that solve our current crises, whatsoever they may be, be they real or imagined? I seriously doubt it, unfortunately. However, calling attention to them focuses our attention on such crises and such focus might well begin the process of change. After all, to quote someone who presence has played a large role in helping to shape the more critical wing of the academic study of religion in general—and the North American Association for the Study of Religion more particularly in general—quoting Ovid: "*Adde parvum parvo magnus acervus erit.*"

Aaron W. Hughes is the Dean's Professor of the Humanities and the Philip S. Bernstein Professor in the Department of Religion and Classics at the University of Rochester. His research and publications focus on both Jewish studies and Islamic Studies.

References

Hughes, Aaron W. and Russell T. McCutcheon. 2022a. *Religion in 50 Words: A Critical Vocabulary.* New York: Routledge.

Hughes, Aaron W. and Russell T. McCutcheon. 2022b. *Religion in 50 More Words: A Redescriptive Vocabulary*. New York: Routledge.
Jenkins, Philip. 2007. *God's Continent: Christianity, Islam, and Europe's Religious Crisis*. Oxford: Oxford University Press.
McLeod, Hugh. 2007. *The Religious Crisis of the 1960s*. Oxford: Oxford University Press.
Stroumsa, Guy G. 2021. *The Idea of Semitic Monotheism: The Rise and Fall of a Scholarly Myth*. Oxford: Oxford University Press.
Winslow, Octavius. 1868. *Practical Suggestions Appropriate to the Present Religious Crisis*. London: William Hunt and Company.
McCutcheon, Russell T. 2003. *The Discipline of Religion: Structure, Meaning, Rhetoric*. London: Routledge.

Chapter 2

The "Discipline" of Humanities
Rhetorics of Interiority, Discourses of Crisis, and Contemporary Nationalist Ideology

Lauren Horn Griffin

> No longer valuing personhood as something directed toward public life, contemporary nationalist ideology recognizes a public good only in a particularly constricted nation of simultaneously lived private worlds.
>
> (Berlant 1997, 5)

The humanities are in crisis. There is no shortage of articles and think pieces about this crisis, whether conceived as a lack of majors or a lack of funding, whether the central threat is capitalist modernity or the fetishization of the sciences. In the opening chapter of this volume, Aaron Hughes argues that, as a discipline, "the study of religion is always in crisis" (page 11). Similarly, this begs the question, if the humanities are always in crisis, are they ever in crisis? I searched JSTOR in an attempt to find the earliest references to "crisis in the humanities," and the exact phrase was used in 1922 (Waite 1922). Further, I found discussions of fears of the "old" humanities losing out to "new" scientific fields going back to the late nineteenth century, as professional programs were developing in public universities. As a speaker at a classical conference put it in 1898: "If the humanities are to continue to have the public recognition and support that their merit demands, the people must be made to appreciate their value not only as a means of culture but also as a foundation for the practical callings of the day" (Anonymous 1898, 429). In their book *Permanent Crisis: The Humanities in a Disenchanted Age*, historians Paul Reitter and Chad Wellmon argue that not only is this crisis as old as the modern university itself (nineteenth-century Germany, in their account), but that crisis is central to the self-understanding of the humanities. In fact, the humanities have been in crisis since at least 1621, when Robert Burton blamed their decline on melancholy: "In former times, kings, princes, emperors, were the only scholars, excellent in all faculties ... In those days, scholars were highly beloved, honored, esteemed ... scholars in our times complain of poverty, or crouch to a rich chuff for a meal's meat" (Burton et al. 1989, 367–368).

A quick survey of "crisis in the humanities" articles (in both academic journals and news media) in the twenty-first century reveals an overwhelming focus on the decline in humanities majors, a "crisis" manufactured, of course, by these very articles through claims that humanities majors do not get jobs. This claim, however, is not backed up by data. Humanities majors are employed at roughly the same rates as majors from other fields, and median income is similar as well. As a piece in *The Atlantic* put it, "the difference between humanities majors and science majors, in median income and employment, seems to be no more than the difference between residents of Virginia and North Carolina" (Schmidt 2018). In his chapter, Hughes explains: "Potentially masked in calling something a crisis are the real structural problems that remain out of sight and hidden from view. I think it is important for us to draw attention to these structural issues instead of simply giving voice to them and repeating them as if they were a mantra" (page 19). What if we move beyond the mantra—beyond the decades-old (centuries-old?) "crisis"—and focus instead on how the "crisis of the humanities" is a modern, tactical discourse that helps social actors and groups make strategic moves in the present? We can ask what is entailed in the contemporary classification of "crisis" as an extension of wider structures that make a particular vision of the world possible.

Russell McCutcheon's 2001 book *The Discipline of Religion* argued that the discipline of religious studies, by normalizing interiorizing discourses, legitimates the regulatory forces and institutions of social life. In other words, perpetuating the idea that humans naturally enjoy a private, interior life actually supports the creation of specific senses of freedom and zones of conduct, thereby managing and "disciplining" (in a Foucauldian sense) certain types of speech and dissent. Taking this argument beyond religion to focus on discussions about the value of "the humanities," we can ask how discourses of crisis in the humanities rely on the rhetoric so often applied to religion (i.e., the rhetoric of interior, personal matters) to privatize and silo humanistic inquiry. How has the classification of certain forms of inquiry as "humanities" in the contemporary university structured the relationship between individual and collective consciousness? How do articulations of "the humanities"—by positing a personal zone of belief, meaning, and value—function to discipline material viewed as divisive?

Taking Hughes's challenge seriously, rather than take at face value the "crisis" itself, we can instead unpack the management of rational/irrational, belief/practice, private/public in *discourses* of crisis. If we want to examine this particular moment in the ongoing crisis of the humanities, we must, as Hughes says, look at how we conceptualize it, and "pay attention to the social contexts against whose backdrops" we attempt to address this crisis (page 18). Religious studies as a discipline is particularly poised to talk about rhetorics of interiority, and this chapter highlights how discourses of crisis often lead to defenses that emphasize the personal fulfillment of studying culture, inadvertently making the "humanities" a private endeavor unworthy of public funding. Driven by a variety of (sometimes competing) interests, the use of such terms as "personal philosophy," "beliefs," and even "religion" has become the means by which some aspects of the world end up being set apart—sometimes privileged and sometimes denigrated, but generally cordoned off. What the current discourse of crisis are showing us, then, is that the survival of the humanities in the public university rests on the tension between what is considered the private zone of meaning and what is considered part of civil, social institutions.

Shifting from a Crisis of the Practical to a Crisis of the Personal

Humanities majors are marketable and practical, just as they have always been. Yet they are denigrated as unmarketable and impractical, just as they have always been. Humanists rush to show how marketable and practical their disciplines are, just as they have for at least a century and a half. So what is new? In a 2017 article in the journal *Raritan*, historian Andrew Hartman reflects on the culture wars of the 1980s and 1990s. He opens with a summary of a 1988 issue of *The Wall Street Journal* that covered a debate at Stanford over whether a course should teach John Locke or Frantz Fanon. Andrew Hartman concludes that the debates about the nature of humanities education have shifted:

> Such a debate would be nonsensical now. Instead, we are currently inundated with glowing features of the "problem-solving" technocratic mind at work. Now, Locke and Fanon find themselves on the same side-and it's looking more and more like the losing one. On the winning side? Books about leaders, entrepreneurs, innovators, disrupters, visionaries, game-changers. Sadly, even the almighty Western canon, whether in a traditional guise that includes Locke or in a revised form that embraces Fanon, seems feeble up against the cult of business. Defenders of the humanities are voices in the wilderness.
>
> (Hartman 2017, 128)

Reading this account years later, the technocratic version wherein many view the humanities as frivolous and not immediately practical still feels very familiar, but the idea that we have somehow moved out of a period of culture wars where the teaching of history, philosophy, and literature are no longer up for public debate is laughable. The "Western canon," historical narratives, and the literature that gets taught has been among the central debates of the 2020s (thanks in large part to the manufactured "critical race theory" crisis). As detailed below, politicians with national profiles have made the reification of "Western civilization" a central part of their education plans. If culture, as Hartman claims, found itself on the back burner in the first decade or so of the 2000s, it is back in full force.

Of course, as Hartman notes, discourses have long centered on the practicality question ("what are you gonna *do* with that degree?"). In fact, in *Permanent Crisis* (mentioned above), Reitter and Wellmon argue that the idea of the humanities was shaped from the beginning by an opposition to use value. The humanities have long been imagined as outsider disciplines in tension with the utilitarian principles of the universities that sustain them. For example, the cliché "underwater basket weaving," first appearing in print in the 1950s, has been used to deride a course or a degree as useless. However, the last several years have seen different clichés deployed, most notably "lesbian dance theory" (which, though years old, had a viral moment in 2022 when Colorado Congresswoman Lauren Boebert used it in a Fox News interview). This shift from underwater basket weaving to lesbian dance theory highlights that the crisis in the humanities it is not (or not only) about the ability to produce corporate cogs in a machine; in other words, the idea is not only that lesbian dance theory (like underwater basket weaving) is not immediately practical/profitable, but that lesbian is an "ideology"—something to be kept as personal opinion and out of publicly funded institutions.

Discourse of crisis in the humanities, in the framework of the culture wars, functions to separate certain aspects of the study of culture from public life. Discourses that frame the humanities as personal and ideological ("like a religion") thus work to deny them space in the public university. And the political effects of this privatization—the isolation of meaning—is the destruction of collective aims. William Arnal put it like this:

> The concept of religion is a way of demarcating a certain socio-political reality that is only problematized with the advent of modernity in which the state at least claims to eschew culture per se. Further, one of the current political effects of this separation—one of the political ends currently served by it—is the evisceration of substance, that is, collective aims, from the state. That is to say, the simple positing of religion is a covert justification for the modern tendency of the state to frame itself in increasingly negative terms: the secular state is the institutional apparatus by which the social body prevents the incursion by others into the personal and various other goals of individuals rather than being the means of achievement for common projects and the collective good.
>
> (Arnal 2000, 32)

Building on this, the following sections attempt to trace how, through discourses of crisis, "humanities" is becoming a rhetorical device for fabricating and managing a place in the individual human conscience; like "religion," it functions to cordon off a particular set of stuff from political life. In other words, perhaps the rhetorical kicker is not so much the idea that the humanities are not practical, but that they are personal.

Extending the Privatizing Power of "Religion"

If McCutcheon highlighted how "religion," with its presumption of an interior spiritual life, disciplined the messy past, we can extend that analysis here to see how recent discourses of crisis in the humanities are functioning in a similar way. As McCutcheon put it, "the presumption that an inner, spiritual life exists functions to discipline potentially unruly human material characterized by differing interests, creating of them a collective Whole, a nation of "civil" citizens comprised of governable selves" (261). When the material gets too unruly, or, as we might say today, too "divisive," we have to manage it. As the history of "religion" shows, privatization was a very effective way to do that. As Talal Asad explains:

> It was in the seventeenth century, following the fragmentation of the unity and authority of the Roman church and the consequent wars of religion, which tore European principalities apart, that the earliest systematic attempts at producing a universal definition of religion were made ... Herbert produced a substantive definition of what later came to be formulated as Natural Religion—in terms of beliefs (about a supreme power), practices (its ordered worship), and ethics (a code of conduct based on rewards and punishments after this life)—said to exist in all

societies. This emphasis on belief meant that henceforth religion could be conceived as a set of propositions to which believers gave assent, and which could therefore be judged and compared as between different religions and as against natural science.

(Asad 1993, 28)

In other words, the period after the Wars of Religion stressed the intellectual or cognitive definition of religion which, eventually, made the separation of the state from cultural institutions seem natural. In our own historical moment, we can see this privatized and cognitive character expanded to the political and the social through the language of "belief" (e.g., everyone has their own "political beliefs"), "ideology," and "religion" itself.

For example, at a 2021 public school board meeting in Hanover County, Virginia, one parent classifies everything from disabilities to social movements as "religion" in an attempt to cordon off them off from public life: "every sexual orientation, mental illness, marriage preference, minority group, social justice initiative and other *worldly religions* are raised up on this imaginary pedestal and just catered to." Even more explicitly, gender and sexuality were deemed "personal belief systems" in order to argue that allowing trans youth in public schools "would be equivalent to establishing a state religion" (see Johnson 2022). These school board meetings resulted in the publication of "Model Policies on Ensuring Privacy, Dignity, and Respect for All Students and Parents in Virginia's Public Schools" (2023), which explains: "The First Amendment forbids government actors to require individuals to adhere to or adopt any particular ideological beliefs. Practices such as compelling others to use preferred pronouns is premised on the ideological belief that gender is a matter of personal choice or subjective experience, not sex. Many Virginians reject this belief." Here, the First Amendment protecting religion is used to both protect and confine "ideological" and "personal beliefs." In other words, because upholding the status quo requires marginalizing opposition, the strategy is to deploy the private zone of belief to both confine and/or protect these "beliefs." Which you are free to think, of course, just not impose or enact. This is but one example of how terms (like belief) and categories (like religion) are deployed to cordon off certain elements from public life.

Applying Asad's analytical framework to the humanities more broadly, we can reexamine the current discourse of crisis that surrounds it. Proponents of the humanities often focus on the utility argument; that is, they read the opposing arguments for defunding the study of the humanities in public university as calls to articulate the skills they teach or to prove that their majors get good jobs. But a closer look at recent discourses of crisis reveal that the central point of contention has shifted from utility to interiority. Because of course, many of those who call for a defunding of public access to the humanities know both the value and the utility of studying culture, but the cordoning off of the humanities as private serves strategic functions: it confines humanistic inquiry to privately funded spaces, and it defends it as sacred and thus only accessible to people it deems worthy. Only the wealthy can pursue this type of education, and the poor will be trained only to work a particular job. If the cognitive understanding of religion normalized the aversion of the state's control over culture, disciplines (from religious studies to history to literature and media studies) that deal in culture can start to feel, to some, not secular *enough*.

Disciplining the Humanities through Discourses of Personal Enrichment

While Asad argues that definitions of religion after the "Wars of Religion" bolstered the separation of the state from cultural institutions, we can ask how the "culture wars" have functioned to further erode the public sphere. As detailed above, this rhetoric is easy to spot when it comes to humanities' defunders. But by addressing perceived crises of the humanities through terms like personal philosophy, beliefs, and ideology, humanists can perpetuate the idea of a preexisting, natural interior life outside of social and political life, which also contributes to the disciplining of cultural material. Often, when humanists try to explain their work to the world, they emphasize a private zone of meaning, and we can see increasing references to humanities disciplines as places for personal growth. For example, the staff writer on education for the *Washington Post* argued that the value of the humanities "in a STEM world" is that they "help us understand what goes on inside of us" (Strauss 2017). In a viral *New Yorker* article titled "The End of the English Major," the students interviewed referred to their humanities courses (or major) as a personal passion project (Heller 2023). In an *Atlantic* article titled "The Humanities are in Crisis," the author spends the majority of the piece bemoaning that students no longer want to craft a personal philosophy for their life, and thus they do not see value in the humanities. In that short article, the author, a history professor, refers to the importance of the humanities for developing one's "meaningful philosophy of life" four times (Schmidt 2018).

Most explicitly, though, in a 2022 *Washington Post* article an English professor argues that because the humanities are "ideological," they may not belong in the university (Hanlon 2022). Aaron Hanlon, in "The humanities are facing a credibility crisis," explains that humanities have always situated themselves in opposition to professionalized, utilitarian training (though he does not mention the glut of recent articles written to convince students and administrations of the utility and skills explicitly taught in humanities departments, nor does he address the development of "applied" and professionalized degrees being offered in humanities departments—none of which seem to be convincing those who wish to defund the humanities). Humanists, he suggests, have two choices: one, team up with the sciences, "not simply as critics or ethical watchdogs but as problem-solvers with knowledge and skills often lacking in other fields" (what this looks like in practice he does not say). Partnering with them will, presumably, allow us to borrow from their apparently non-ideological credibility. The argument is that studying "ideas" often looks and feels "political," which is "biased;" this is why, he explains, humanists either are not or do not appear to be objective, like a scientist. The implication is that evaluations of knowledge, ideas, or even politics and policy matters are not appropriate for public spaces—those are "personal beliefs" that are to be kept private, or at least "bracketed off" (to borrow from religious studies) while one remains agnostic on all things ideological. (He does, at some length, discuss how the sciences have plenty of political commitments and that their partnering with the humanities can help their own credibility as well, which is confusing because the entire piece is about how the humanities lost public credibility.) While the focus, in my chapter here, is on how "the crisis of credibility" is sown in the humanities specifically, no discipline is immune from this anti-intellectualist rhetoric. One might think science is safe, as it (as a discipline) is most often talked about in terms of hard, quantifiable data that produces "facts" (a claim that "the humanities" critically addresses, ironically). But reactions to the COVID pandemic have reminded us that no type of knowledge is immune from becoming "personal beliefs" and "ideology" at best, or "cults" or "conspiracies" at worst (see, for example, Fieldstadt 2021). From climate science to epidemiology, interiorizing rhetoric like belief-talk is a key discursive strategy for privatization and constraint.

So, if the humanities do not want to exist as the Ken to the sciences' Barbie, Hanlon offers a second option: leave the institutional university and go to private spaces (he suggests starting a podcast). That which we believe to be "ideology" must be privatized, and that which we believe to be "neutral" can remain. Of course, "the humanities" exist to critique this very claim; that is, to identify and explain how claims of neutrality and universality mask their participation in systems of power. But I digress. Hanlon concludes by explaining that "many humanities scholars and advocates believe the university is irreparably broken, but that doesn't mean a homeless humanities, just a different, more nurturing home." Thus, this humanist quite literally suggests the privatization of humanist inquiry, cordoned off to be protected (or "nurtured") as sacred, and confined to an appropriate space outside the publicly funded university.

Of course, like religion, the definition of "the humanities" is not bounded and consistent. Some trace the humanities to ancient Greece, others to the seven liberal arts of Roman empire, and still others to the Renaissance, when the humanities began to refer to the study of literature and history. Indeed, during the fourteenth and fifteenth centuries the humanities (resembling what we might now call classics) *contrasted* with divinity. In this division of humanity and divinity, brought into our own time and social context, the humanities would be the "secular" one, whereas now (I argue in this chapter) disciplines from women's and gender studies to media studies can be made to feel, to some, not secular enough. Humanities, like religion, is an object of the speaker using it, and comparison through taxonomy makes partners of some and draws boundaries with others (sometimes joined with "the arts," other times with "social sciences," for example). The fact that "humanities" is not a stable category provides flexibility in this bundling, allowing social actors to legitimize or delegitimize courses, departments, and scholarship according to their present concerns. Regardless of which disciplines become part of this bundle, by making the interiorizing move through rhetorics of belief, ideology and personal philosophy, "humanities" is feeling the effects of the modern disciplining concept of religion.

In sum, many humanities defunders know the importance of studying history and cultures, but the language of interiority functions exactly the way it did for religion—it both confines it but also defends it, protects it, sacralizes it. Why does this matter? Because the ways in which we respond to the "crisis of the humanities" takes the "crisis" of its value seriously. By continuing to point out its value for each individual (you'll explore your philosophy of life! It's enriching for you!), which tend to focus on personal fulfillment, we make it easier to cordon these disciplines off in the private sphere. In other words, our responses mirror the discourse and often focus on "moods and motivations" of the individual. Focusing not on the "crisis" but rather on the discourses of "crisis," as Hughes suggests, we might come up with more local, situated, and effective strategies to address crises that are manufactured and disingenuous.

Going Public?

In 1993, Asad argued that it might be a "happy accident" that intellectualist definitions of religion converged with the separation of culture from "spaces in which varieties of power and reason articulate our distinctively modern life." He notes how "this definition [of religion] is at once part of a strategy (for secular liberals) of the confinement, and (for liberal Christians) of the defense of religion" (Asad 1993, 28). The management of this tension between public and private may have been working well enough in 1993, but decades later we can see the previous contract beginning to crumble. Because the sun is beginning to set on the hegemonic cultural reign of white Protestant identity in the U.S., the same protection that was offered to minority groups now, to the (former?) default group, feels a lot more like confinement. One strategy, as I detailed above, to deal with this feeling of slippage is to expand "religion" (through terms like belief and ideology) in order to separate and confine more aspects of social and cultural life. Another strategy, though, is to claim cultural hegemony by supporting some idealized notion of public dominance (i.e., Make America Great Again). We see folks like Ron DeSantis of Florida attempt to maintain and/or create a particular white-Western-civilization narrative as default. These strategies, while seemingly contradictory, can function as two steps of the same plan.

In his book *Going Low: How Profane Politics Challenges American Democracy*, Finbarr Curtis analyses this extension of the secular beyond the separation what we colloquially call "religion" from the state:

> A distinction between religious rules and political rules has not existed in all societies in all times and places. The relatively arbitrary nature of these divisions makes for fraught contests over which rules govern everyone and which rules are private concerns that arise from voluntary commitments in a multi-religious society. Secular divisions can appear to marginalize the stuff called religion by restricting its public influence. But secular privacy can also help to invest the private sphere with an aura of sacrality in need of protection.
>
> (Curtis 2022, 9)

He goes on to describe what he means by illiberal secularism as "antigovernment rhetoric rather than the entirety of people's views about the good, the true, the beautiful" (ibid., 21). In other words, the Trump moment worked precisely because it did not offer an alternative set of beliefs, just disavowals of public goods. In this way, Curtis argues, the Trump moment was actually *more* secular in that it worked toward the privatization (whether in the name of protection or constraint) of everything. The illiberal secular strategy of profaning anything public worked because it had no ideological commitments—or rather, it flattened them by moving them to a private space—allowing for broader collaboration.

But perhaps the strategy of ceding control over public discourse in favor of protecting private spaces is no longer enough for the newly emboldened. If we pay attention, as Curtis does, to the *management* of rational/irrational, belief/practice, private/public in discourses of crisis in the humanities, we may well ask how some right-wing figures are actually working to reassert the state's control (through primary and secondary education) over culture.

At first blush, it may seem surprising to see people like Ron DeSantis or Jeremy Wayne Tate push the very disciplines that right-wing figures had wanted to defund. This defense might seem like a contradiction, or a turn from previous talking points that focus on practicality and utility. Of course, when convenient, DeSantis and others still echo that claim; for example, as part of his denigration of gender studies, DeSantis explained "we don't want students to go through, at taxpayer expense, a graduate with a degree in Zombie studies. If it was a private school, making those choices, that's fine, I mean, what are you going to do." In this 2023 speech, he goes on to advocate for "more practical subjects being taught." However, at the same time, DeSantis often advocates for more history and classics courses, and his education plan would mandate courses "Western" history and philosophy. He explains, "the core curriculum must be grounded in *actual* history, the *actual* philosophy that has shaped Western civilization" (Saul, Mazzei, and Trip 2023). DeSantis's plan also bans discussions about gender and race on the grounds that they compel "ideological conformity," begging the question, what becomes "ideology," and what is seen as neutral, or (in DeSantis's terms) "actual" knowledge? What is seen as "personal beliefs" and what is seen as "public good"? Religious Studies asks how groups and individuals mine divine timelessness from the stuff of human history and culture, and we can expand that framework here: how does the discourse of crisis in the humanities function to rhetorically create "knowledge" and separate it from "beliefs" and "ideology"? Here, rather than privatize everything, we see another rhetorical move to keep some histories and cultures "secular" (objective, normative, ideologically neutral) and therefore appropriate for public schools and universities.

Far from claiming that the study of history and culture is not valuable or useful, there has been a growing classical education movement among the political right. In Tennessee, Governor Bill Lee promoted a network of classical charter schools in partnership with Hillsdale, a conservative Christian college. Fox News ran an entire series in 2023 about the classical educational model. Jeremy Wayne Tate, founder of a company called The Classic Learning Test (meant to rival the College

Board's SAT), explained how the study of Western civilization and languages is central to a "good" education:

> Is the goal of education, fundamentally, to have worker bees in a factory, which in some ways I think is the origins of the compulsory education system we have right now? Or is the goal of education the formation of the whole human person to love what is good and to not love what is not good or what is evil? ... That is what education is. It's this passing down what is most important from one generation to the next and also about the shaping to pass down the values that the community holds most dear.
>
> (Garcia-Navaro 2023)

Now, Tate does not necessarily advocate that public dollars fund this type of education for all students (and we could unpack the classification of "good" and "evil," of course), but it is clear that the old "humanities are not practical" argument has given way to a culture war-centered discourse of crisis in the humanities. And someone like Jeremy Wayne Tate explicitly recognizes the collective value of, as he puts it, "reconnecting knowledge and virtue through meaningful assessments and connections to seekers of truth, goodness, and beauty." He goes on to explain that he emphasizes reconnection "because our understanding is that this unnatural separation of virtue, character education, and knowledge is new." His curriculum, in terms of Finbarr Curtis's framework described above, is not "secular" like Trump's. Here we see a rather explicit attempt to "reconnect" culture with the state (or, at the very least, with state funding). Using a vague but articulated idea of "Western civilization" and "classical education," Tate and others explicitly attempt to reinsert particular culture, substance, and collective aims into public education.

This is not to say that Tate, DeSantis or others pushing classical education are always on the same side of the public/private binary, nor that they are internally consistent—the discursive management of the intersection of public/private is strategic and dependent on the context. Take this example from an article written about a classical education charter school. A classical school, Great Hearts, opened near my home in Louisiana. In an article discussing this growing charter network and its goals, the author interviews several Great Hearts students and concludes that they "seem refreshingly disconnected from contemporary political ideology" (Eden 2019). The author notes that "for many of today's students, 'justice' may be defined as whatever political opinion is trending on Twitter." But not these students—while others toil under social constraints, he seems to say, these students are cultivating their own ideas about virtue and justice that are objective, true, apolitical and ahistorical. Here, we see a very clear example of the positing of a natural interior life outside of social and political life (though, of course, it is quite easy to see how the rise of classical schools is very much part of a contemporary political conversation). Throughout the article, the author dances with the slippery private/public binary, sometimes claiming humanistic inquiry as a public good and sometimes perpetuating the private zone of individual belief. For example, one teacher explains that Great Hearts students emerge "as people with very strong character," and she explains that if she taught at a regular public school, she would be forced "to teach in a way that wasn't oriented toward character formation," and she would "have a moral struggle not teaching that way" (Eden 2019). Great Hearts is very clear that they are *not* a religious school and not teaching adherence to any religion (they are a public charter after all), so we might ask why this teacher presents "character formation" as forbidden in public education. One quick glance at the prominence of antibullying campaigns in public elementary schools shows that character formation is built into both the culture and the required curriculum of public schools. Yet this teacher deploys interiorizing rhetoric to "character" in order to privatize something that most people assume is a public good. Whether making claims about the neutrality of "real history" that mask their participation in systems of power, or cordoning off as sacred something that most people saw as secular, these all function as rhetorical strategies for controlling (whether expanding or limiting) particular forms of expression.

Particular groups and individuals have created private schools and media spaces to carve out a space to exist, but after the rise of Trump and resulting feelings of empowerment, many have deployed similar strategies to exert power in the public square. Of course, there are some who do simply want to privatize everything, and there are others who are very explicit about wanting to align the state with a certain narrative. These two different strategies may seem contradictory—one, privatize everything to preserve your own minority group, and two, enter the public square in support of some nostalgic notion of once-public dominance, but we can read them as two sides of the same strategic coin. Furthermore, Hughes also points out that a crisis is not a crisis for everyone (page 15). Some people profit (in both cultural capital and actual capital) well from the crisis in the humanities, and Tate's Classical Learning Test and the charter school industry are but two examples.

Conclusion

Moving beyond any perceived crisis (practicality, jobs, finances) toward a focus on the contemporary discourse of crisis, we can see how financial (Corrigan 2023) and cultural (Weingarten and Edelman 2022) crises are rhetorically manufactured for the stated goal of eroding trust in public institutions. This is true of conversations surrounding both K-12 public education and of public universities. Many humanities defunders know that the humanities are valuable, effective, and useful, and they know that humanities courses actually make the university money (Fea 2014). The crisis, then, is not the humanities' utility or value, but rather who gets access to it. While we can see attempts in some right-wing figures, like DeSantis, to recapture the public sphere in the name of some idealized version of white Western civilization, the overwhelming move is toward the privatization of everything, leaving the public university as a space to train workers for specific jobs. In other words, an analysis of the discourse instead of the "crisis" itself shows that the humanities are not *undervalued* by its defunders—they are simply being situated in opposition to liberal democratic institutions. Thus, our attempts to take these "crises" seriously (whether in terms of practical skills or funding) will likely prove futile. Calling it a crisis, as Hughes puts it, makes us "assume decisions have to be made" (page 19). So we try. We try to argue that students will be fulfilled, or that they will gain practical skills. I am not arguing that showcasing the vital skills of humanities education is a bad move, or that including other relevant skill sets as part of our course offerings is a misstep, but before we bend over backward to create more professionalized or applied courses and degrees in our units, perhaps we could pause to ask why we are taking these "crises" seriously. Sites of public discourse—spaces in universities where concepts like politics, ethics, and religion are critically analyzed and evaluated—cannot exist if one envisions a society with virtually no public at all.

On the other hand, in examining "crisis" instead of crisis, we may well ask how some right-wing figures are actually working to reassert the state's control (through primary and secondary education) over culture, while the rhetoric of humanists like ourselves often works to constrain it in order to manage dissent. Rather than seeing enemies of humanities education on one side of the private/public binary and champions of it on the other, both groups rely on the disciplining rhetoric of interiority (so common to "religion") in order to protect or to constrain.

It is worth asking, then, how discourses of crisis in the humanities contribute to the culture war on public goods. Perhaps in addition to arguing the technocratic usefulness and personal fulfillment potential of humanistic endeavors, we should start by recognizing how personal fulfillment rhetoric can function to isolate. By creating atomized individuals who curate their own personal "meaning" from the stuff of history and cultures, discourses of crisis compel us humanists to participate in the type of content management that, in our attempt to protect, also curtails and constrains.

In his chapter, quoted above, on the definition of religion and its functions, Arnal concludes, "this very definition of the modern democratic state in fact creates religion as its alter-ego: religion, as such, is the space in which and by which any substantive collective goals are individualized and made into a question of personal commitment or morality" (Arnal 2000, 32). Manufactured "crises" in the humanities highlight how the previous agreement was functioning in the first place: managing dissent and constricting public life. We know that "the humanities" have not always been seen as the realm of the private interior beliefs, and watching culture war-style discourses of crisis in the humanities work to cordon off humanistic inquiry makes visible these undisclosed ground rules that have long existed. In McCutcheon's words, "all critique may well turn out to be premised on the ways we manage that slippery point at which the discursive moments of public/private intersect" (McCutcheon 2001, 261). We happen to have found ourselves in a moment of slippage, and we can feel it.

Lauren Horn Griffin is assistant professor in the Department of Religious Studies at Louisiana State University. She is the author of *Fabricating Founders in Early Modern England* (Brill 2023). Her research and teaching focus on religion, politics, media, and technology.

References

Anonymous. 1898. "Proceedings of the Classical Conference Held at Ann Arbor, Michigan, March 31 and April 1, 1898." *The School Review*, 6(6): 424–481.

Arnal, William E. 2000. "Definition." In Willi Braun and Russell McCutcheon (eds.), *Guide to the Study of Religion*, 21–34. London: Continuum.

Asad, Talal. 1993. *Genealogies of Religion: Discipline and Reasons of Power in Christianity and Islam*. Baltimore, MD: Johns Hopkins University Press.

Berlant, Lauren. 1997. *The Queen of America Goes to Washington City: Essays on Sex and Citizenship*. Durham, NC: Duke University Press.

Burton, Robert, Thomas C. Faulkner, Nicolas K. Kiessling, and Rhonda L. Blair. 1989. *The Anatomy of Melancholy*. Oxford: Clarendon Press.

Corrigan, Lisa. 2023. "The Evisceration of a Public University." *The Nation*, August 16. Retrieved from www.thenation.com/article/society/wvu-cuts-higher-education/

Curtis, Finbarr. 2022. *Going Low: How Profane Politics Challenges American Democracy*. New York: Columbia University Press.

Eden, Max. 2019. "Great Hearts, Great Minds." *City Journal*, September 8. Retrieved from www.city-journal.org/article/great-hearts-great-minds

Fea, John. 2014. "The Humanities Make Money for Colleges and Universities." *Current*, March 21. Retrieved from https://currentpub.com/2014/03/21/the-humanities-make-money-for-colleges-and-universities/

Fieldstadt, Elisha. 2021. "Kentucky Lawmaker Tweets Meme Comparing Anthony Fauci to Cult Leader Jim Jones." July 21. Retrieved from www.nbcnews.com/news/us-news/kentucky-lawmaker-tweets-meme-comparing-anthony-fauci-cult-leader-jim-n1274623

Foucault, Michel. 1988. *Technologies of the Self: A Seminar with Michel Foucault*. Luther H. Martin, Huck Gutman, and Patrick H. Hutton (eds.). Amherst, MA: Massachusetts University Press.

Garcia-Navaro, Lulu (Host). 2023. "Why Conservatives Can't Stop Talking About Aristotle." First Person podcast, May 24. Retrieved from www.nytimes.com/2023/05/04/opinion/classical-education-conservative-movement.html?

Hanlon, Aaron. 2022. "The Humanities Are Facing a Credibility Crisis." *The Washington Post*, April 15. Retrieved from www.washingtonpost.com/outlook/2022/04/15/humanities-sciences-credibility-crisis-public-trust/

Hartman, Andrew. 2017. *Raritan*, 36(4): 128–140.

Heller, Nathan. 2023. "The End of the English Major." *The New Yorker*, February 27. Retrieved from www.newyorker.com/magazine/2023/03/06/the-end-of-the-english-major

Johnson, Jessica. 2022. "Christian Nationalism Is a Threat to Some Virginia Schools." *Washington Post*, October 10. Retrieved from www.washingtonpost.com/opinions/2022/10/10/virginia-schools-threatened-trans-white-nationalism/

McCutcheon, Russell. 2001. *The Discipline of Religion*. London: Routledge.

Reitter, Paul, and Chad Wellmon. 2021. *Permanent Crisis: The Humanities in a Disenchanted Age*. Chicago, IL: University of Chicago Press.

Saul, Stephanie, Patricia Mazzei, and Gabriel Trip. 2023. "DeSantis Takes on the Education Establishment, and Builds His Brand." *The New York Times*, January 31. Retrieved from www.nytimes.com/2023/01/31/us/governor-desantis-higher-education-chris-rufo.html

Schmidt, Benjamin. 2018. "The Humanities Are in Crisis." *The Atlantic*, August 23. Retrieved from www.theatlantic.com/ideas/archive/2018/08/the-humanities-face-a-crisisof-confidence/567565/

Strauss, Valerie. 2017. "Why We Still Need to Study the Humanities in a STEM World." *The Washington Post*, October 18. Retrieved from www.washingtonpost.com/news/answer-sheet/wp/2017/10/18/why-we-still-need-to-study-the-humanities-in-a-stem-world/

Waite, Mary L. 1922 "Notes and News on International Educational Affairs." *The Journal of International Relations*, 12(4): 558–569. https://doi.org/10.2307/29738518.

Weingarten, Randi, and Jonah Edelman. 2022. "Extremists Are Using Lies to Undermine America's Public Schools." *Time*, April 29. Retrieved from https://time.com/6172216/public-schools-extremists/

Chapter 3

"I Went to the Crossroads, Fell Down on my Knees"
On the Rhetoric of Crisis and Academic Labor

James Dennis LoRusso

In June of 1968, the British rock 'n' roll band Cream, fronted by lead guitarist and vocalist Eric Clapton, released its third album, *Wheels of Fire*, a double album recorded over the course of many months, which included several live tracks from recent performances. The album featured a live version of "Crossroads," a song that would acquire iconic status. Undoubtedly, the song's main appeal to its young, primarily white listeners was its driving backbeat and Clapton's heavy-hitting guitar. Yet largely unknown its audience was the fact that "Crossroads" was not, in fact, an original work of the band but rather an arrangement of a much older song named "Cross Road Blues" written and recorded by Mississippi delta blues performer Robert Johnson.

In the wake of Cream's live version, the relatively obscure Johnson would become a central character in the folk mythology of rock 'n' roll's origins, which in the popular imagination had sprung organically from poor, itinerant African-American bards of the American South during the early twentieth century. His work would be taken up by other legendary acts like Led Zeppelin, the Rolling Stones, and the Red Hot Chili Peppers. In *The Blues Brothers* (1980) Dan Aykroyd and John Belushi would perform Johnson's "Sweet Home Chicago" during the film's climactic scene. These appropriations of Robert Johnson's work by white artists and for white audiences exoticized even as they celebrated African-American cultural forms. As Amanda Lucia argues, such "exoticism is a constructed representation of the other in service of the production of the self" (Lucia 2020, 8), and Cream's cover of "Crossroads" helped to craft rock 'n' roll's sense of itself; it served as a marker of Clapton's authenticity, as a way of locating him in a lineage extending back to a mystified past of Southern black America. This chapter will not be an extended discussion on the ethics of *cultural appropriation*, but it is crucial to highlight an awareness that my own "appropriation," as the act of a white, educated elite, of Johnson's composition takes part in these broader patterns.

A discussion of mythology surrounding "Cross Road Blues" and the figure of Robert Johnson, however, does provide an illustrative example for thinking through Aaron Hughes's remarks about the discursive quality of "crisis" delivered at the 2021 annual meeting of the North American Association for the

Study of Religion. I use the case of Johnson's story to echo Hughes's assertion that crisis represents a tool of classification rather than a distinct phenomenon. Nonetheless, people enlist the rhetoric of crisis in the service of or in resistance to particular interests, and, thus, I argue that it does affect the social worlds that people inhabit in material ways. Next, I extend this analysis to the so called "crisis of the American Worker" that captured public discourse during the early 1970s to show how this perceived "crisis" eased the transition to the emergent neoliberal economic order that defined the late twentieth century by entrenching the neoliberal discourses of work that prevail still. Finally, I turn to the perceived crisis in academic labor amid the global pandemic and explore the ways that the rhetoric of crisis reinforces the acute material inequalities that structure the academy today.

I Sold My Soul for Rock 'n' Roll

Robert Johnson himself remains an elusive figure, making him a prime candidate on which to anchor rock 'n' roll's origin story. The only surviving evidence of his actual work, including "Cross Road Blues," is a series of recordings that he made over three days in November 1936 and at another recording session in 1937 (LaVere 1990, 46–47). The lyrics of the song express the foreboding facing a man standing at a rural crossroads as dusk falls. Unable to "flag a ride," he laments the prospect of being stranded alone, as a black man in the Jim Crow south, yearning for the comfort of a woman ("rider") and companionship of a friend ("Willie Brown"). Unlike the upbeat tempo and overdriven guitar licks found in Cream's version, Johnson serves up a mix of lumbering rhythm, intermittent slide runs, and a vocal intensity conveying the desperate circumstances of a man in a state of crisis.

Indeed, as Aaron Hughes suggests, the image of the crossroads is bound up with the genealogy of "crisis." Crisis, he notes, implies a turning point, a liminal space of both threat and opportunity, the experience of which elevates, at once, anxieties of what is to come and utopian longings. In this vein, the lyrics of "Cross Road Blues" oscillate between fears of being caught out after dark under Jim Crow and the solace of intimacy. Similarly, when we imagine higher education generally or the academic study of religion specifically as "in crisis," we situate ourselves at a crossroads, a turning point that brings into focus our worst fears and clarifies our ideals.

Hughes also notes that crisis is ultimately a rhetorical act, as a way of imagining circumstances as having deviated from the norm. To label something as a crisis is to perform an act of compression. It takes complexity and renders it simple. It condenses a range of overlapping, mutually informing set of conditions into a single classificatory scheme. In short, the rhetoric of crisis is reductionist. There is little simplicity in the life of a black man under the weight of racial oppression in 1930s Mississippi, and the factors contributing to academy's uncertain future remain myriad. Indeed, for the study of religion, Hughes rightly points out that "crisis" is perhaps a necessary pretext for its very existence. It is the ongoing threat posed or opportunity presented by the perennial aspiration to separate the "academic" study of religion from theology that has informed the inflection points of the field. Moreover, for him, the stubborn persistence of this crisis, while manufactured, nonetheless sharpens the field's sense of purpose and consequently illuminates the trajectory that ought to be pursued. Crisis nourishes in scholars of religion the perpetual recommitment to critical, non-confessional study. Were the field to lose this sense of crisis, it risks slipping from this foundational mission.

I largely agree with Hughes's contention that crisis is an act of classification rather than an observable set of conditions in the world. It is a rhetorical construction, however not devoid of real-world effects. Calling something a crisis sets things in motion; declaring a state of emergency establishes the possibility of mobilizing certain resources and of pursuing otherwise unavailable strategies. To classify the spread of COVID-19 as a pandemic focuses attention to the fact that a real threat is present. Robert Johnson laments standing at the crossroads because real people suffered physical violence at the hands of white supremacy. Real lives are affected in material ways through acts of classification.

The practice of invoking crisis, then, remains bound to the material conditions of society. It not only illuminates those circumstances but also, as Hughes explains, conceals certain interests, structures, and social relations. The COVID-19 pandemic may have shed light on the ill-preparedness of the public health architecture to address the outbreak, but it simultaneously obscures the fact that, for much of the world's population, including for the poor in affluent nations, public health measures have been anemic at best and inaccessible at worst for a long time. Contagion only becomes crisis because it threatens to, and finally does breech the established mechanisms designed to force all suffering downward to the poor, the exploited, and the marginalized. The rhetoric of crisis expresses a desire to return to acceptable levels of human suffering, which, of course, is only acceptable to the privileged minority who depend on it to ensure their privilege in perpetuity.

The popular mythology that surrounds Robert Johnson's "Cross Road Blues" illustrates how crisis enables exploitative social relations. Johnson's persona has become the stuff of legend because the verifiable details of his life remain unavailable. According to popular lore, Johnson was not a particularly gifted guitar player as a young man, but after a three-year disappearance, he suddenly emerges as master of his instrument. As the National Blues Museum (2022) recounts, stories circulated that "he sold his soul to Devil at the crossroads of Highways 49 and 61" in a Faustian bargain to acquire his newfound virtuosity. In the end, his time as a performer would be short, however, as Johnson passed away at the young age of twenty-seven, again, under somewhat mysterious circumstances.

Perhaps owing to the brevity of and dearth of information about his life, these tales facilitated the evolution of the historical Robert Johnson into the quasi-mythic blues master at the heart of rock 'n' roll's prenatal phase. Even though we know that such tales of a tortured soul in crisis, sold and reaped, have been repeatedly debunked, they remain appealing because they mystify the more complicated story of rock 'n' roll's genesis. While rock music did arise in the context of shifting attitudes about race and civil rights, it equally must be understood as product of the deliberate efforts of the culture industry to retool "race music" to sell to young white Americans. The pursuit of profit mutes the racial terror manifest in Johnson's "Cross Road Blues" and is used by Clapton to construct an image of a legitimate rock musician with real "soul," despite his own racist statements. The commodification of Johnson's "crisis-at-the-crossroads" mythology calls attention to the broader way that crises not only conceal existing uneven power distributions but may be actively enlisted in sustaining those very inequalities.

All in all, the examples of "Cross Road Blues" and COVID-19 elucidate three dimensions of crisis. First, as Hughes points out, crisis is a discursive construction and second, the rhetoric of crisis is implicated in material conditions. Third, crisis establishes a turning point at which interests are established, advanced, or challenged. Crisis stands at the crossroads of threat and opportunity. The next section of this chapter explores how these elements operated during another moment of perceived crisis—the "crisis of the American worker" that drew the attention of government and business elites in the early 1970s. The dynamics of this so-called crisis, I will ultimately argue in the third and final section, set the stage for making sense of the perceived crisis of academic labor in the twenty-first century.

"The Crisis of the American Worker"

Like "crisis," "work" is a term rife with rhetorical potential, but while critically oriented scholars have devoted noteworthy attention to the constructed quality of term like "religion" or "gender," "work," as management scholar Peter Fleming observes, "strangely remained one of the few concepts that retained a sense of preordained immutableness" (Fleming 2015, 1). Indeed, this sense of inevitability, of universality is what drove me to position my early scholarship at "the intersection of religion and work."

I preferred "work" over other terms, specifically "labor," because it seemed to transcend class boundaries and even history. "Labor" conjures images of class struggle, capitalism, and general strikes. "Work," on the other hand appears almost benign, presenting as an ahistorical and apolitical social fact, as a part of the natural landscapes upon which human beings tread. Work is at once many things and nothing. It is a place when we "go to work" but also refers to anything we are "working on." To stay fit, we "work out," and when something is good and right, we might say "it's working." Potentially, the term "work" could characterize any human act.

Yet, in my own research, "work" typically referred to jobs, careers, or how one "makes a living." It is certainly a product of the history of political economy, but the term "work" reduces capitalist social relations to a collection of free individual economic actors. "Work" renders the uneven distribution of class power by rendering the accumulations of capital as categorically identical to wage labor. Rich and poor, employee and investor are all engaged in work to improve our lives. "What we call work," Fleming asserts, "is the social embodiment and ritualistic calculus of" the class exploitation that lies at the heart of capitalism (Fleming 2015, 3).

The ideology of "work" essentially operates as a lubricant for the engine of the marketplace, and at various points in time, the rhetoric of crisis gets deployed when capitalism needs an oil change. In this section, I will explore how a so called "crisis of the American worker" carried American capitalism through the tumultuous period of the late 1960s and early 1970s, setting the stage for the rise of the neoliberal economic order of the last several decades.

Even today, Americans remember the transition from the 1960s to the 1970s as a pivotal moment. It was a time of civil rights, sexual revolution, and moon landings, but it also saw strife, riots, violent protest, and Kent State. It was an ambivalent time, when the promise of progress was tempered by a perceived threat of social disintegration. For many, this was a time of crisis and for rethinking the role of fundamental institutions like family, religion, politics, and work.

A perceived crisis of work garnered the particular attention of political and economic elites. In 1968, for instance, famed management guru Peter Drucker published *The Age of Discontinuity*, a book that signaled a radical departure in his thinking. As I have argued elsewhere, Drucker had spent his career promoting effective leadership practices and casting management as a moral enterprise that promised to solve society's ills (see LoRusso 2017, ch. 1). In *The Age of Discontinuity*, however, he identified four "discontinuities" upending the conventional social order: (1) rapid technological change; (2) globalization; (3) disenchantment with large institutions; and (4) the emerging knowledge economy (Drucker 2008, xxvii–xxix). These trends, he argued, necessitated a revolution in the focus of business management from bureaucratic administration to entrepreneurialism. "The businessman will have to acquire a number of new abilities, all of them entrepreneurial in nature, but all of them to be exercised in and through a managerial, and usually a fairly large and complex, organization" (ibid., 43). Moreover, in the emerging post-industrial landscape, the impetus to work would have to change. "Motivation for knowledge work," he predicted, "must come from within the worker himself. The traditional motivation, that is, external rewards—pay, for instance—do not motivate him" (ibid., 288).

Others echoed this need to reorient the work ethic amid the perceived crisis of work. In his 1971 Labor Day address to the nation, President Nixon lamented that "recently we have seen that work ethic come under attack" and but reassured his audience that it was not "going out of style." He continued:

> let us also recognize that the work ethic in America is undergoing some changes ... We must give the individual worker more responsibility, more of the feeling that his opinion counts ... Productivity means getting more out of your work ... job satisfaction is the key to productivity.
>
> (Nixon 1971)

Like Drucker, Nixon found the solution to crisis in a renewed work ethic focused on making work a desirable end rather than a means to material reward.

The President's call for renewal sparked a multi-year investigation by the U.S. Department of Health, Education, and Welfare, which ultimately produced its findings in the 1974 *Work in America* report. The report observed that American workers were stifled in "dull, repetitive, seeming meaningless tasks, offering little challenge or autonomy...causing discontent among workers at all occupational levels" (O'Toole et al. 1974, xv). This "new need for job satisfaction is the key to quality of work," the report suggested (ibid., viii). *Work in America* consulted an eclectic mix of experts, including Peter Drucker, transpersonal psychologist Abraham Maslow, and Stanford futures researcher Willis Harman. A former engineer, Harman turned to futures research at the Stanford Research Institute in the late 1960s and advocated for what he called "Humanistic Capitalism" (see Harman 1974). He argued that "in a technologically advanced society where production of sufficient goods and services can be handled with ease, employment exists primarily for self-development, and is only secondarily concerned with the production of goods and services" (Harman 1979, 59). In predicting the end of scarcity, Harman declared the coming of a *transindustrial* society in which "concern would shift to the inner frontiers of mind and spirit" (ibid., 3). Once again, the solution to the crisis of work is to be found in highlighting its immaterial rewards.

Yet, the benefit of hindsight such optimistic forecasts as absurd. Material inequality would not diminish but would widen in the coming decades. In fact, the time of "crisis"—the early 1970s—was precisely the period when inequality, which had diminished drastically since the end of the Second World War, would reverse course and begin its march to the acute level seen in the twenty-first century. The call to attend to the immaterial elements of work—meaning, quality, and purpose—therefore must be seen in relation to the underlying material transformation that was taking place at the time. The so-called crisis of the American worker coincided with other, more pernicious systemic changes in the postwar economic order. As David Harvey points out, Keynesian liberalism, the established macroeconomic orthodoxy, no longer insured sustained economic growth. This "crisis of capital accumulation," he asserts, led to a break down in the economic consensus, defined by robust public investment, strict regulation of markets, and concord between capital and labor (Harvey 2005, 13). Subsequently, economic elites embarked on "a *political* project to re-establish the conditions of capital accumulation," specifically by eroding the power of the regulatory power of the state and prowess of organized labor (ibid., 19). The perceived "crisis of the American work" therefore must be seen in the context of burgeoning neoliberalization. I would argue that this rhetoric of crisis advanced the material goal of capital accumulation precisely by redescribing work as an immaterial good whose primary value lies in its capacity for self-improvement rather than its material rewards. Under neoliberalism, the axiom that "work should be more than a paycheck" has justified flattened wages, an increasingly anemic working class, and unprecedented concentrations of wealth and power in the hands of the bourgeoisie. Here, then, crisis misdirects our attention inward while outward conditions become increasingly exploitative. If the crisis of the American Worker is fundamentally a neoliberal discourse, then what should we say about the numerous voices decrying a "crisis" in academic labor? Is this too simply more complicit rhetoric?

The Crisis of Academic Labor

Since 2020, a litany of publications have employed the rhetoric of crisis to discuss the impact of COVID-19 on academic labor. Titles like "Care in times of the pandemic: Rethinking meanings of work in the university" (Altan-Olcay and Bergeron 2022) or "The 'new normal' of academia in pandemic times: Resisting toxicity through care" (Plotnikof and Utoft 2021) characterize the pandemic as a turning point, as a time for "rethinking" and "new" normal. Moreover, their focus on "care" mirrors the neoliberal discourse on work in which the solution to suffering lies in the psychological and immaterial rather than structural reform. Such examples exhibit more continuity, rather than a break with established crisis discourse, and therefore they reveal little about how the pandemic is a crisis for academic labor. Each of these articles advocates individualized solutions to systemic global phenomenon, citing experiential impacts with minimal empirical support causally linking the pandemic to the specific problems with which they are concerned.

While empirical data of the pandemic's effect on academic labor remains scant, the American Association of University Professors (AAUP) does offer some insights. According to survey results released in 2021, "more than half (54.7 percent) of responding institutions froze or reduced salaries and more than a quarter (27.7 percent) eliminated or reduced fringe benefits for full-time faculty members in response to the COVID-19 pandemic." Furthermore, one in ten institutions furloughed faculty while others (40 percent) altered their tenure-clock standards (AAUP 2021b). Some of these measures were temporary and have already been reversed, but others, like benefits reductions and efforts to modify tenure, could prove to be lasting, more concerning developments for academic laborers. Perhaps the most troubling element observed in these AAUP reports is the decline in real wages for faculty. For the first time since the Great Recession (2008), wages (adjusted for inflation) failed to increase but instead decreased 0.4 percent in 2020–2021. Even more shocking, wages fell a full five percent in 2021–2022, which was the largest annual drop since the AAUP began tracking salaries in 1972 (AAUP 2021–22).

So, what can be said about this information? First, the data indicate that the pandemic did have a measurable impact on faculty income, reversing a decades-long trend of moderately increasing pay. Second, draconian, even if temporary, measures like hiring freezes and furloughs certainly disrupted the status quo. However, it is important to note that these numbers deal exclusively with full-time faculty. According to the AAUP, most academic laborers (61.5 percent) hold contingent appointments, with some forty-two percent working just part-time. In fact, the AAUP provides only provides minimal data for the 2019–2020 academic year—prior to the pandemic—because it did not gather information on part-time faculty for the subsequent two years at all. However, for 2019–2020, it does report that part-time appointments declined by as much as 10.6 percent, and therefore one could reasonably predict that the impact on part-time or adjunct labor during the pandemic was catastrophic.

The AAUP, like the rest of us in the academic world, express extreme dismay at the appalling conditions facing contingent academics, particularly for those at the part-time rank. Yet, the fact that they devote most of their energy to the concerns of the privileged minority who comprise the tenured professoriate makes their sentiments seem to be little more than "thoughts and prayers." For instance, while matters related to contingency are acknowledged briefly in the association's *Annual Report on the Economic Status of the Profession*, the lion's share of its investigations addresses ongoing threats to academic freedom, the weakening of tenure and ongoing representational disparities among the top ranks. To be sure, these paramount concerns deserve attention, but the failure to prioritize the exploitative conditions under which the majority of academic laborers work bears witness to the way in which AAUP aligns with the power structure rather than the demographics of the academy.

To suggest that there is now, in the wake of the pandemic, a crisis in academic labor is to make light of the fact that the exploitation of contingent faculty is neither exceptional nor particularly new. In fact, what has changed, as borne out by AAUP's priorities, is administrators and state-level governing bodies have seized on the pandemic to further erode the power of the tenured professoriate. The Board of Regents in the state of Georgia moved in September 2020 to explore changes to post-tenure review, and on September 9 of the following year, it formally approved new policies that, according to an AAUP report, would eliminate due-process procedures for the revocation of tenure (AAUP 2021a). This, along with other moves by institutions and states across the U.S., illustrates how the pandemic has placed privileged academics in precarity, which for the tenured professoriate is a deviation from the norm. However, for contingents, like myself, life did get worse, but little was novel. Precarity for part-time faculty simply intensified, because precarity for the majority of academic laborers has become an acceptable and, indeed, necessary condition of American higher education. The privileges accorded to the tenured and to university administrations persist only because gig workers essentially carry out much of the actual teaching in the classroom.

So, at the end of the day, what can we say about the perceived crisis in higher education? As in the early 1970s, destabilized conditions facilitate the deployment of crisis discourse that authorize exceptional actions. The pandemic shuts down classrooms and relegates teaching to online environments. Schools suspend hiring, furlough faculty, and, in some cases, delay or renege on existing tenure-track appointments. College administrations and state boards of education exploit this moment to bolster their own power over the tenured professoriate. To paraphrase Robert Johnson's "Cross Road Blues," we stand at the crossroads, trying to flag a ride, thinking about better times. Yet, better times for whom? For the adjunct whose "old normal" was already defined by obscene precarity? Certainly not. Crisis threatens academic elites, who have seen their workloads increase, their job security shorn away, and privileges revoked. On the other hand, for management, times are better, as the neoliberalization of higher education accelerates. The crisis presents as both threat and opportunity, provoking uncertainty about the future and a reassessment of the status quo.

Moreover, crisis conceals existing structures, systems, and interests by obscuring how pre-pandemic conditions were already untenable for most academic laborers. Contingent faculty are not in crisis; their very existence implies the presence of exploitation. They do not stand at a crossroads but instead live under the constant threat of professional crucifixion. Threat is systemic. However, just as crisis conceals, it can also reveal. If academic elites have entered liminality, perhaps they might be able to see that new ways for organizing academic labor are possible. Perhaps they will see that their fate is bound up with their colleagues from whose labor their begrudgingly benefit. Perhaps the whiff of precarity will awaken their sense of injustice in their own backyard even as they devote their energies to understanding and, at times, even advocating against it elsewhere. Then again, maybe this crisis will eventually pass.

James Dennis LoRusso is Instructor of Religious Studies at the University of North Florida. He is a former associate research scholar in the Center for the Study of Religion at Princeton University, and is the author of *Spirituality, Corporate Culture, and American Business: The Neoliberal Ethic and the Spirit of Global Capital* (Bloomsbury, 2017).

References

AAUP. 2021a. "Academic Freedom and Tenure: University System of Georgia." Retrieved from www.aaup.org/report/academic-freedom-and-tenure-university-system-georgia (accessed October 1, 2022).

AAUP. 2021b. "Annual Report on the Economic Status of the Profession, 2020–2021." Retrieved from www.aaup.org/report/annual-report-economic-status-profession-2020-21 (accessed August 29, 2022).

AAUP. 2022. "Annual Report on the Economic Status of the Profession, 2021–2022." Retrieved from www.aaup.org/report/annual-report-economic-status-profession-2021-22 (accessed August 29, 2022).

Altan-Olcay, Özlem, and Suzanne Bergeron. 2022. "Care in Times of the Pandemic: Rethinking Meanings of Work in the University." *Gender, Work & Organization*, 31(4): 1544–1559.

Drucker, Peter. 2008. *The Age of Discontinuity: Guidelines to Our Changing Society*. New Brunswick, NJ: Transaction Publishers.

Fleming, Peter. 2015. *The Mythology of Work: How Capitalism Persists Despite Itself*. London: Pluto Press.

Harman, Willis W. 1974. "Humanistic Capitalism: An Alternative." *Journal of Humanistic Psychology*, 14(5), 5–32.

Harman, Willis W. 1979. *An Incomplete Guide to the Future*. New York: W. W. Norton.

Harvey, David. 2005. *A Brief History of Neoliberalism*. New York: Oxford University Press.

LaVere, Stephen. 1990. *Robert Johnson: The Complete Recordings* [box set booklet]. New York: Columbia Records.

LoRusso, James Dennis. 2017. *Spirituality, Corporate Culture, and American Business: The Neoliberal Ethic and the Spirit of Global Capital*. New York: Bloomsbury Academic.

Lucia, Amanda. 2020. *White Utopias: The Religious Exoticism of Transformational Festivals.* Oakland: University of California Press.

National Blues Museum. 2022. "Stories of the Crossroads: Blues Myths." Retrieved from https://nationalbluesmuseum.org/stories-of-the-crossroads-blues-myths-did-robert-johnson-really-sell-his-soul-to-the-devil (accessed September 24, 2022).

Nixon, Richard M. 1971. "Address to the Nation on Labor Day." September 6. Retrieved from www.presidency.ucsb.edu/documents/address-the-nation-labor-day (accessed September 19, 2022).

O'Toole, James, et al. 1974. *Work In America: Report of a Special Task Force to the Secretary of Health, Education, and Welfare.* Cambridge, MA: MIT Press.

Plotnikof, Mie, and Ea Hog Utoft. 2021. "The 'New Normal' of Academia in Pandemic Times: Resisting Toxicity through Care." *Gender, Work & Organization,* 29(4).

Chapter 4

Theology and Religious Studies
A Relationship in Crisis?

Suzanne Owen

In the U.K., religious studies is often housed within theology or divinity departments, with many of these offering a single-honors degree in theology and religious studies (TRS), and for both programs there exists a single set of benchmarks for taught degrees in TRS. It is worth noting as an aside that the 2021 benchmarking exercise for TRS, it has emerged, had been vetted by the Council of Anglican Bishops. Together theology and religious studies also form a single unit of assessment in the Research Excellence Framework (REF), which assesses the quality of research in higher education. In this chapter, I examine this relationship as it has developed, particularly at the University of Edinburgh where I studied, and argue that religious studies has often suffered unfairly due to concerns about the viability of Theology in the modern university in the U.K. Therefore, my question is: Whose crisis is it anyway?

I completed my MA (Honors) undergraduate degree in religious studies at the University of Edinburgh in the Faculty (now School) of Divinity in 1997. As a mature student, and with no religious background or affiliation, I was aware that theology was the main concern in the faculty, which was located in New College, an imposing sandstone building blackened by soot close to Edinburgh Castle, and that it was largely focused on training candidates for ministry, primarily in the Church of Scotland. Originally founded as the Free Church College, the library still retains its stained-glass windows and Martin Hall, one of the rooms used for teaching and seminars, has a large cross on the wall.

In my program, alongside the core courses in religious studies, students had to choose two options, so I opted for South Asian studies (my main interest) and biblical studies because I knew nothing about biblical texts and was planning at that time to go on to train as a religious education teacher in schools. While biblical studies was taught at New College, the other subjects were located at a different part of the university to cater to students taking religious studies as an outside option, but also because several of the lecturers were from area studies departments, such as South Asian studies. Being split between the divinity and arts faculties provided me with a comparative view of different departmental expectations and cultures.

I began my MSc by research (we had to opt for MSc otherwise it would have automatically been called an MTh) in September 2001. As this was in the weeks after 9/11, the head of the School of Divinity welcomed us new starters saying that the study of religion was more important than ever, leading to positive expectations for an academic career, not least because I'd been informed that several lecturer positions would open in religious studies across the U.K. as there would soon be a raft of retirements from the 1960s and 1970s generation of RS scholars. In addition, my supervisor James L. Cox was proactively forging the study of indigenous religions within religious studies, though I tried to aid my chances by developing my methodological and area study interests. By the time I'd finished the PhD in 2007, positions were few (except in the study of Islam), retired professors weren't being replaced, the world religions paradigm still dominated, and institutional interest in the academic study of indigenous cultures had, if anything, decreased.

I think many of us who had chosen to pursue a PhD in religious studies have found this situation perplexing, and much of it seems outwith our control. In the U.K., religious studies as a distinct subject began in the 1960s and had been growing until around 2010, when several factors led to a sharp decrease in undergraduate recruitment (and across some humanities subjects more generally), in part due to an increase in tuition fees for undergraduate study, jumping up to £9000 per year in 2012 in England, as well as the end of student maintenance grants from 2016. In the 1960s, religious studies had emerged to address several specific crises. Religious education as Christian instruction in schools was being questioned as government-led multiculturalist policies came in, and so phenomenology of religion (as spear-headed by Ninian Smart) came in to push for greater inclusivity under the banner of "world religions." Also, undergraduate numbers in theology were low in comparison to their postgraduate numbers (although the latter were highly profitable due to a steady stream of North American students drawn to the birthplace of the Scottish Reformation), and at Edinburgh, in order to justify remaining in the New College building, the School of Divinity took over the subject area of religious studies from the Arts and Humanities Faculty. In other words, a crisis in theology in higher education, and Christian-based religious education in schools, was stalled by the emergence of religious studies.

Religious studies was welcomed at New College, though not always warmly. In his retirement speech in the mid-1990s, one biblical studies professor reminisced about when there were only male students—and I expect mostly candidates for church ministry, who could read Greek, Latin and Hebrew—implying that standards had fallen in the School of Divinity with the increase of women students and perhaps the inclusion of religious studies. He retired a year or two before the theologian Ruth Page became principal of New College (while I was an undergraduate), and the first female professor in the School of Divinity to get her own portrait hung in the Senate Room, a wood-paneled seminar room surrounded by otherwise older white men largely if not wholly connected to church ministry. Perhaps also the biblical studies professor was uncomfortable with the rise of religious studies, though as an undergrad I was aware that even my religious studies lecturers were all ordained ministers in various Christian denominations. As religious studies dominated the undergraduate student body in New College, the daily prayers ended, such as the one which began the first lecture of the day (in New Testament) and the one spoken in the dining hall at the start of lunch.

By the time I'd returned for my postgraduate studies in 2001, much had changed. Very few candidates for the Church of Scotland were coming through New College anymore, which I'd heard was because it was deemed too "liberal," also that an age cap had been proposed, which may have discouraged mature students. For myself, I persisted in studying an indigenous culture for my PhD despite the warning that no one would hire me. Taking this on board, I tutored in Canadian studies and social anthropology to increase my options. However, while religious studies departments would hire anthropologists, I discovered that this was not reciprocal.

Jobs had dried up in religious studies and I was lucky to get a position at all. I nearly didn't apply to the position of lecturer in world religions at Leeds Trinity, especially as it included teaching on the Catholic Certificate in Religious Studies course for those interested in teaching in Catholic schools. However, I had hoped there would be room for the study indigenous religions within a Catholic model of higher education, and to some extent that was realized. At the interview, I'd asked why they were starting a degree in religious studies, which began in 2008, the year I was hired, and I was told it was because of student interest. Well, I saw why once I'd arrived—there were only four theology students progressing into second year and I expect they thought religious studies would save theology by bringing in more students, who would be taking most of the theology modules as well. However, I was not exactly the person they'd hoped for, which is to say someone more oriented toward interfaith. Over time, as student recruitment dropped and the theologians found pastures new, we withdrew the theology and religious studies program altogether. As a Catholic foundation university, Leeds Trinity is keen to keep some sort of religion program going. As it stands currently, the program is called philosophy, ethics and religion, without any theological component remaining as those staff members had not been replaced. Nevertheless, there is still an assumption (for better or worse) that the study of religion is "theology," and not only within institutions.

In 2018, the British Academy published a report on theology and religious studies teaching in U.K. universities. As well as using theological language to talk about both religious studies and theology, it portrayed the subject negatively as having student numbers in terminal decline and being dominated by older white male staff. The British Association for the Study of Religions (BASR) produced a data-driven response, where David G. Robertson, aided by Jonathan Tuckett, unpicked the data to show that religious studies, in various guises, was holding up much better than theology (this report is available on the BASR website). Though the picture was far from rosy, religious studies was (as suspected) doing better overall in staff diversity and for recruitment, especially in combined studies and as part of philosophy, ethics and religion (though the latter has a philosophy code and was therefore not picked up by the BA report). Since the early 2000s, there was a consensus among scholars of religion broadly that a "united front" was needed to shore up religious studies departments as well as theology departments. Indeed, this was one rationale behind the renaming of AUDTRS (Association of University Departments of Theology and Religious Studies), founded in 1990, to TRS-UK in 2013, also in recognition that in some cases theology and/or religious studies were no longer departments but had been merged into larger conglomerations. In any case, TRS-UK has been dominated by staff from the Russell Group universities, who all had theology departments for centuries without religious studies and, arguably, retain theology as a primary concern. The TRS section of the British Academy includes perhaps only a dozen scholars *not* from theological or biblical studies. In BASR discussions with the BA, following our response to their report, they acknowledged the need to change to reflect the student body, but as a single member is elected each year, selected by the existing members, and with the need to also improve their representation of gender and ethnicity, change will be a long time coming. In the meantime, the lack of state research funding is made up for by private funding bodies with a theological agenda, such as the John Templeton Foundation.

Many of us at the BASR have since concluded that we should move away from our role as a prop to theology and encourage other partnerships, though as always there is the problem of hiring only one or two religious studies specialists whether the subject is paired with Theology or something else, such as politics and/or philosophy (as is the case now at Lancaster). However, with theology's numbers in freefall at undergraduate level, it may yet take religious studies down with it. As an interdisciplinary field, we have the skills and flexibility to work alongside most other subjects who often assume, as a result of the institutional dominance of theologians and the choice to promote the TRS brand, that we are all "theology."

A separate threat to religious studies in the U.K. is sociology of religion, which has taken much of that space regarded as the secular study of religion and yet often works on behalf of churches and government interests in statistics and the alleged role of "faith" in providing social cohesion (most obviously in the collaboration between Linda Woodhead, who is a senior figure in the Inclusive Church, and the Tony Blair Foundation). There are many excellent scholars in sociology of religion, and rather than fight them for that space, we can go where sociologists might not tread as an inter- and multi-disciplinary subject area. While good scholarship has thrived under the TRS banner, there are other bridges we can build within the university, as there's little tolerance, from an administrative perspective, for small subject areas to exist on their own. On the other hand, there is evidence to suggest that RS scholars can thrive in these situations, offering institutions good value for interdisciplinary research and teaching collaboration, something which does not seem to always be the case for theology.

If we look to the origin of the crisis in the academic study of religion in the U.K., notwithstanding the general crisis in humanities (which is another concern), I suggest it is more a crisis in theology as an academic subject that is pulling religious studies down with it. To some degree, this is because of choices that we have made in the past. However, if we examine what is in crisis, and who is saying it, we can take further steps to distance the subject from theology.

Suzanne Owen is an associate professor in religious studies at Leeds Trinity University, U.K. She obtained her PhD from the University of Edinburgh and researches contemporary indigenous and pagan religions.

Chapter 5

Scholars Are People Too
The (Sometimes) Difficult Shift to the Discourse of Crisis

Russell T. McCutcheon

During the Q&A that followed NAASR's 2021 plenary address by Aaron Hughes I could not help but think of a March 29, 2005, episode (season 1, episode 2, entitled "Diversity Day") of the U.S. adaptation of the (originally British) television series, *The Office*—an episode that has stuck with me, perhaps because of what I take to be the subtle but nonetheless sophisticated theoretical point that it makes (and maybe also because of the series's endless re-runs on U.S. television throughout the pandemic).[1] In the episode's subplot, Jim Halpert—the likable paper salesman who is secretly in love with Pam Beesly, the receptionist (and she with him as well)—has an absolutely terrible day in which he is repeatedly interrupted while trying to finalize an annual sales call that, in the past, has dependably resulted in a quarter of his year's commissions. (He even has a small bottle of champagne, in his office desk drawer, in anticipation of celebrating the sale.) And then, when he finally gets through to the client, after repeated delays and frustrations from his workmates as well as from his less than accommodating boss, it turns out that his arch nemesis in the office, Dwight Schrute, has already made the call, has already made the sale—and has already made the commission. Although it may go without saying, it's a bad day for Jim. In fact, we might even go so far as to call it a "financial crisis," what with the amount of annual salary that was on the line from this one sales call.

But those who are familiar with this episode know that at the end of the work day, after participating in what turns out to be an inane and, by some contemporary standards, an outrightly offensive diversity training session at work (in fact, the episode's main plot is so problematic by the standards of many contemporary viewers that it's now being reported that streaming services may skip over it entirely when playing the series), Pam, who happens to have been seated next to Jim in the conference room, has fallen asleep with her head resting on his shoulder.

The meeting ends.
The room empties.

---

1. The description of this episode is adapted from my own Afterword, "Origins Today," to *Fabricating Origins* (McCutcheon 2015, 77–92).

Alone, the two of them remain seated in the room, Pam still asleep.
Jim looks at the camera, aware he's being filmed of course, unsure what to do.
He softly wakes her.
She rises, self-conscious and a little chagrined, fixing her hair.
She leaves the room.
He remains, alone in the chair.

From there we cut to the confessional-shot, where the actor, seated alone in a spare office, sometimes speaks directly to the filmmakers, in character, debriefing on the day's events—don't forget, the staff of this office all know that they're being filmed for a public television documentary. And now viewers learn that what had been Jim's terrible, horrible, no good, very bad day has suddenly been utterly transformed, in a way that he could never have imagined, even just moments before. "Umm ... not a bad day ...," he says to the film crew, with a small but self-satisfied grin.

And, just like that, his day has utterly changed, right before our very eyes; there's no longer a financial crisis—though, sure, he's still lost considerable salary. But his focus, his priorities, and thus the way that he sorts through the day's many events when making sense of it all has been recalibrated, completely; he's created a whole new narrative basis for an answer to the perennial question: "How was your day?"

I draw on this example from recent popular culture as a place where Hughes's paper helps us considerably to see what is going on; for, as he argued (but now in my words), crises exist at the level of discourse, among a group whose members share affinities, share narratives, and share goals—and thus share the identities that then result. Change any of those elements and, suddenly, it's either not such a bad day or it's a date that—to borrow then U.S. President Franklin D. Roosevelt, from his still well-known December 8, 1941, address to Congress, asking it to declare war on Japan—"will live in infamy."

But in response to the critical tools that Hughes offered to his listeners, to examine how such things as rhetorics of crisis (not to mention rhetorics of infamy) work—*when* they're invoked, *why* they're invoked, *who* gets to invoke them, and *what* might be accomplished by making such claims—we instead learned from some in attendance, at a variety of points during the Q&A, about the various *actual* crises that seem to preoccupy them: from the crisis of the scientific study of religion to various crises of the contemporary corporatized university and, yes, even the crisis of Donald Trump's place in current American politics, not to mention some ill-defined things said to be "existential crises." So, instead of following Hughes and examining *why* and for *whom* such issues or events count *as* crises, and what might be accomplished by describing them as such—critical questions that, in my hearing, his paper encouraged us to ask—some in the audience struck me as being a little dumbfounded that someone would apparently deny that each of these were in fact *real* crises, and thus moments of such *undebatable* consequence that to label them in any other way, or to overlook them altogether, was somehow to diminish not just these set-apart moments or the situations themselves but, more importantly perhaps, also those who are so deeply concerned about them.

And that, in my estimation, was where the conference's opening session ended—with both the virtual Q&A and the chat active with a variety of participants affirming each other via their judgements that this or that was indeed an *actual* crisis and with Hughes, at least in my reading, somehow taking the fall for the sort of critical analysis that he had placed before us and expected us to use. What's more, judging by some of the panels and paper titles that, at least at that point in the conference, were yet to come that weekend, it seemed entirely likely to me that the divide that was so obvious during that opening sessions—between those interested in studying the *discourse* on crisis, on the one hand, and those simply making claims about *actual* crises, on the other—would likely continue. And, when revising this response some time after the conference ended, that prediction proved entirely correct; for while a number of contributions to the weekend's program attempted to keep our eyes firmly on what is at stake in either framing (or denying to frame) something *as* a crisis (to draw on Lauren Horn Griffin's apt phrasing of the issue from her response to the opening paper), yet others skipped over this critical step entirely and went straight to making claims about various crises, with an interest in how they should properly be addressed or assessing how others have responded to them.

I find this divergence, especially in a NAASR meeting of all places, rather problematic and worth thinking about; for Hughes's paper struck me as entirely in keeping with the organizer's call for papers for this year's program. As posted on the NAASR website, it asked the following two questions: "[W]hat happens when we classify something as a 'crisis'? ... How does this designation illuminate or obscure certain political or ideological dynamics?"

Judging by such a call it therefore seemed to me that this year's meeting would be about the *discourse* on crisis, a theme that prompted me to agree to the kind invitation to join the opening panel. Case in point: instead of claiming that former U.S. President Donald Trump signifies a crisis of American democracy, a scholar in the tradition presumed in the call could instead ask for *whom* is Trump's continued involvement in U.S. politics a crisis? After all, for roughly half the country it currently seems that this is not the case whatsoever; as reported in a Quinnipiac poll on October 19, 2021, 78 percent of registered Republicans favor Trump running for President again in 2024 and 41 percent of Americans surveyed respond that he has had what they characterize as a mainly positive effect on U.S. politics (Quinnipiac University 2021). (Perhaps it was the ambivalence of the electorate, or maybe a concern for what the designation of something as a crisis would entail for the American body politic, that kept pundits from ever declaring that a "constitutional crisis" was taking place in Trump's first four years in office—despite what many agree to have been his flouting of longstanding norms and possibly even federal laws.) Moreover, I'm not even sure what those in the session who were not American (after all, NAASR attracts a wide array of participants, especially given the ease of joining this year's virtual sessions let alone the "North American" in its title) even made of the ease with which specifically U.S. politics was, once again, self-evidently of importance to us—that is, just which "us" is necessary for all of this crisis rhetoric to be invoked and to work? For, as Hughes so rightly pointed out, for an extremely small segment of international society the global COVID-19 pandemic of the past two years has been a financial windfall and thus anything but a crisis; for, just as in times a war, certain sectors of the economy do exceedingly well at times such as these. (Consider that in an article from April 30, 2021, Forbes reported that Jeff Bezos's wealth had by then increased by $86 billion since January 2020—due in large part to the mass move to online shopping throughout the pandemic; see Peterson-Withorn 2021.) So theorizing efforts to designate either Trump's presidency or the pandemic, let alone anything else, as "a crisis," and thereby trying to determine what's entailed in this act, and thus what it triggers or prompts when it is or is not used, is what I heard Hughes to be inviting the scholars in attendance to consider. So the fact that his paper had such an uphill climb during parts of the Q&A—when, to my ears at least, some of the participants in that evening's session seemed to be personally affronted that someone might suggest that, for instance, the pandemic was not an obvious example of a real crisis, what with how, at the minimum, it had turned many of our lives upside down (notably those of academic parents), is therefore something to mull over in earnest as we continue to examine what's happening at this particular moment in our scholarly organization, our universities, and even our society writ large.[2]

And mulling over this is something that I would like to do now, just a little, to try to make sense of the response that Hughes's paper evoked on the part of at least some of those who joined that first evening's session—a response that was significant enough that it continued to be discussed throughout not only the rest of the panel that comprised replies to his plenary but also during the remainder of the meeting's weekend. What I hope becomes evident in the foregoing is that I have no interest in judging my colleagues or assigning blame; instead, I am quite interested in how this discrete and, for some, possibly forgettable moment might tell us something about the situation in which our profession now finds itself—an insight gained by applying a dose of self-reflexive social theory, since, as a colleague recently phrased it to me, scholars are people too.

What made the reaction to Hughes's paper stand out for me was that it seemed curiously similar to how many people once responded (and still respond) to so-called reductionists when they dared to study the claims, actions, and organizations of those who were identified (sometimes, though not always, self-identified) *as* religious, but doing so in ways that were not already offered or sanctioned by these people themselves. As anyone familiar with our field's mid-twentieth-century history will know, such scholars were met with harsh criticism given that their methods were said to demean the religious people under study by failing to, as the old saying went, "take religion seriously" (on this particular claim, Elizabeth Pritchard argues: "'Taking seriously' is a controlled experiment in which

---

2. That Hughes signaled early on that evening that the pandemic had had a significant impact on scholars, and that he is himself a parent of two with who knows what parenting challenges of his own over the past eighteen months, seems not to have been something those who reacted negatively necessarily knew or dwelled upon.

risks are alluded to but ultimately avoided" [Pritchard 2010, 1089].) In fact, I have had this very complaint levelled at my own work throughout my career, such as Robert Orsi's (2004) onetime criticism of my use of the supposedly dehumanizing word "data" when discussing the human moments or situations that a scholar of religion might study (in response to his claim see McCutcheon 2006).[3] What was of note, then, was that what struck me as Hughes's rather less than controversial effort to persuade us to stand back and examine when and how the rhetoric of crisis is used was, apparently, likewise seen by some as a threat to those in attendance who were presumably using occasions *designated as* crises in their own socially formative acts of self-identification—i.e., it was a threat to what they either presumed or wished to be seen as an unquestioned social consensus that such-and-such a circumstance was intolerable, a dire threat, a defining moment, or a unique challenge. And, in response, those sharing this presumption, and thus those wishing to signal a set of shared affinities, quickly rallied to support one another against the perceived threat of, well, scholarly analysis, doing so either vocally or in the virtual meeting's chat.

What I assume was threatening about the method that Hughes proposed—a form of scholarship, I should add, that's surely commonplace in the work of virtually all NAASR members, *at least when they are studying "them" (whether ancient or contemporary) and "their" normative claims, modes of authority, social organizations, etc.*—was that it linked the claim that something, such as the pandemic, was a crisis to contingent, contextual circumstances and social interests, notably of those who were making such a claim and thus strategically using such a designation. For this approach relativizes a claim (in that crises are now seen as being relative to the interests of those naming things or moments as such)—claims that, when such rhetorics are working properly among like-interested speakers and listeners, do quite the opposite: they effectively mark an occasion or an issue *as* anything but relative, i.e., a moment or situation is instead represented as unique, enduring, and especially dire, representing it as a circumstance that must be met not just with consequential but also coordinated action (e.g., from responses to the climate crisis and the pandemic's ongoing supply-chain crisis to the border crisis and even the crisis of the humanities job market in academia). Hughes's proposed methodological shift, however, required a degree of self-reflexivity that, though now assumed by many to be widely adopted across much of academia, turned out to be a little too challenging (because too close to home) for some; for inquiring into the interests of those making such claims, looking at the classifier rather than that which carries the label, and asking what might be gained or at least accomplished by such a designation, prevents the otherwise

---

3. As I have written on previous occasions, the word is important in my work because it keeps ever present the important realization that the scholar's curiosities, assumptions, and methods produce the items on which we work and thus that they are not naturally occurring or self-evidently interesting items. My concern is that those who fail to use this term often fail to recognize that there is nothing authentic or necessarily important about that which happens to be the focus of the scholar's attention.

smooth workings of this rhetoric and thereby calls into question the seemingly self-evident affinities and identities that it helps to shape. And this—not unlike studying what others see as their unique and deeply meaningful religious claims as if they are nothing more or less than ordinary social or political claims—is understandably perceived as a threat to those invested in making such claims, sharing such affinities, and reproducing such identities.

Simply put, the response of some to the plenary address was an occasion when we saw the usually undisclosed limits of what are for many the otherwise unproblematic (or what, by now, some colleagues may even see as somewhat pedestrian) theses on method once offered by Bruce Lincoln; but, as it turns out, they're not pedestrian at all, for on this occasion there was a pronounced failure (to adapt the language of his thirteenth and final thesis) to distinguish between asserting the existence of "a crisis," on the one hand, and adopting the stance of scholars who study how both "crisis-claims" and "regimes of crisis" function to make happenings into crises. It therefore occurred to me as a moment when, as Lincoln notes, "one has ceased to function as historian or scholar."

What makes this failure even more interesting to me is that, as already suggested, this shift in scholarship (i.e., from studying truth to truth claims and, most broadly, regimes of truth, as Lincoln put it) is usually rather uncontroversial for the so-called critical scholars of religion who often comprise NAASR's membership—but now we see that this turns out to depend upon what or whom one might be studying. Consider the ease with which a critical scholar would probably understand not just the perhaps inconsequential e.g. of Jim Halpert's day but, for instance, a more impactful designation such as, say, calling something "a coup," aiming to see it too as being far from an innocently descriptive term that's somehow directly linked to a so-called actual fact on the ground (i.e., an actual coup). To press this point, consider the international news stories not just about what went on in Egypt in early July 2013 (see Kirkpatrick 2013) but, more specifically, about the U.S. reaction to what went on. With around $1.5 billion in annual U.S. foreign aid on the line at that time (second then only to its aide to Israel), the Obama administration's reaction was curiously (or predictably?—now *that's* the question Hughes helps us to answer) focused on what to classify—and thereby how to understand and react to—what just happened. Sure, an Egyptian general had stepped in front of a television camera to make an unanticipated speech, the duly elected (though then widely unpopular) President had been deposed and detained by the military, a number of his party's senior leadership were also detained, the Constitution was suspended, and military officers swore in its own pick as interim President. Accordingly, it looked an awful lot like a coup and it sure smelled like a coup, yes—but was it a coup? Or, to be more specific in our question, why was the U.S. government at the time so careful *not* to designate these events *as* a coup?

To answer this we would be wise to heed Hughes's advice and ask some questions about the context of such a classificatory judgment, including the implications for social actors who do or do not make such a call. We could then inquire into the legal context (making the discourse on coups just as relative as the discourse on crises): the U.S.'s Foreign Assistance Act of 1961 (22 USC)—specifically, chapter 91, subchapter II, section 8422 (Authorization of Assistance) reads as follows (the emphasis is added):

> (3) Additional authority
> Except as provided in sections 2753 and 2799aa–1 of this title, the second section 620J [1] of the Foreign Assistance Act of 1961 (as added by Public Law 110–161) [22 U.S.C. 2378d], and any provision of an Act making appropriations for the Department of State, foreign operations, and related programs that *restricts assistance to the government of any country whose duly elected head of government is deposed by military coup or decree*, and except as otherwise provided in this subchapter, amounts authorized to be made available to carry out paragraph (2) for fiscal years 2010 and 2011 are authorized to be made available notwithstanding any other provision of law.[4]

"Military intervention,"[5] "national reconciliation," or "popular uprising," therefore sounded to some like pretty good choices when the alternative of classifying it as a coup entailed criminalizing what had just happened with this very strategic U.S. ally in the Middle East.

Though, to be honest, I'm not entirely sure why reporters were so focused on the rhetorical contortions among government spokespeople at the time, working to avoid the "c" word—or why all the contortions to begin with—since section 2753 of the law states the following as being among its four conditions for exemption:

> (a) Prerequisites for consent by President; report to Congress
> No defense article or defense service shall be sold or leased by the United States Government under this chapter to any country or international organization, and no agreement shall be entered into for a cooperative project (as defined in section 2767 of this title), unless—
>   (1) the President finds that the furnishing of defense articles and defense services to such country or international organization will strengthen the security of the United States and promote world peace ...

Thus, it turns out that all it takes is for the U.S. president to determine that such international developments are in the U.S.'s interest to support the action and, voila, what at first blush seemed like a coup that would end U.S. funding is now a populist uprising that the U.S. supports (McCutcheon 2013).

Now, I assume that many will find this brief example, perhaps not unlike my pop culture e.g., unhelpful because it is so obviously the case that, as scholars interested in how classification systems work might say, coups exist in discourse—discourses that certainly have practical effects. But shift to another c-word (i.e., crisis) and we quickly learn that this move is apparently a little more difficult for some to make. For even if unwilling to follow Hughes and his focus on

---

4. Find the law at www.law.cornell.edu/uscode/text/22/8422 (accessed November 25, 2021).
5. This was *The Guardian*'s choice for its headline; see Black (2013).

the rhetoric of crisis, there's surely agreement on the part of many that there's much we can learn from the discourse around classifying something *as* a coup in U.S. law, not unlike what we might glean from the recent tendency to label (and thereby delegitimize) governments with which our own disagrees as "regimes" or, as we saw with President George W. Bush's administration, deploying the term "enhanced interrogation techniques" to avoid the implications of such actions being designated as internationally outlawed "torture"—not to mention the practical implications of naming something *as* a religion (as opposed to politics), *as* a myth (as opposed to history), *as* a ritual (as opposed to a habit), *as* sacred (as opposed to secular), etc. For in each of these cases we likely all agree that, upon closer inspection, the seemingly stable, descriptive term turns out to be a socially formative category used for strategic purposes and tactical effects, by situated and therefore invested social actors. The challenge for scholars, however, is to see this happening no less when, for instance, "the crisis of academic labor" is discussed, despite many of our own affinities with those who represent the recent and current Humanities job market as such. After all, our own investments should not cloud our ability to make critical judgments about our own circumstances. This is what I take self-reflexivity to mean at its best.

But as troublesome as I thought some of my colleagues' failure on this point was—what with how it demonstrated the limits of so-called critical thinking when self-interest and self-identity are on the line—I must repeat that I do not wish my comments on that evening's Q&A to be read as a criticism of those who seemed to have been so bothered by Hughes's comment on how even the so-called crisis of the pandemic will pass and is therefore relative to the changeable interests of specific social actors who name it as such;[6] instead, as someone interested in the history of our field and the contemporary conditions in which the study of religion takes shape, I'd like to propose that we further theorize this situation to better understand the moment in which academics (or the smaller sample size of those scholars of religion joining that session) now find themselves. To rephrase: what wider factors (not unlike that U.S. law inspiring rather artful uses of the word "coup" a few years ago) contributed to that situation being read as what I've characterized as an offense to some in that virtual room; it's a question in need of asking given that Hughes's paper struck yet others, as I've already noted, as making a rather basic, though nonetheless important, point.

I'd therefore like to close this brief ethnography of a plenary session by suggesting that the last nearly two years of teaching in what many scholars have found to be rather trying circumstances, while juggling commitments outside their profession's usual tasks that now impinge on their work in ways that they previously had not (e.g., the lack of in-person elementary schools and child care due to COVID-19 protocols in those institutions) has created a set of conditions in which

---

6. Watching news coverage of the mid-December 2021 tornadoes that devastated parts of the U.S. (from Arkansas to Illinois), and hearing various governors say, in response, such things as "we shall rebuild, we shall overcome this," I could not help but think of Hughes's effort to relativize crisis rhetorics.

academics (or, more properly, certain sub-sets of scholars, particularly those in the U.S.), already long feeling pressure from declining government budgets and increased work expectations, have reached what they consider to be a breaking point—evidenced in the speed with which Hughes's approach, often unproblematically adopted by many in the room when studying others, was heard by some as a threat requiring a coordinated response.

In making this claim one cannot help but acknowledge the privilege of academics during the past two years; for unlike so-called frontline workers (nurses, doctors, fire fighters, delivery people, postal workers, etc.), academics in full-time positions were in large part able to adapt to the remote environment—though part-time and non-tenure track instructors often paid the high price of universities unsure of their COVID-era enrollments and budgets by failing to have their employment continued. Thus, we must consider a surprisingly wide continuum of what the "pandemic crisis" was for a variety of different actors here in the U.S.—and that includes academia And it is an even wider continuum if we do just a little cross-cultural work and include the many other national settings in our analysis (a breadth made all the greater when we study its impact on those outside North America and western Europe). But, as we all likely know, privilege, like the rhetorics examined herein, is a relative thing, and thus those in tenured positions who were academic parents working at home no doubt felt considerable daily stress juggling work and family life (likely in constant fear for their own children's health, let alone their need for schooling and social interaction while carrying out their work from their livings rooms and kitchens). And it seems that this was among the sub-sets in attendance during Hughes's session who evidently did not feel that their concerns and additional labor was being acknowledged by means of the relativizing analysis that others were adopting toward the "pandemic crisis."

My sense is that their concerns were also heightened because, in many cases, it seems that their employers (a university's higher administration) had not taken the threats of COVID-19 seriously enough, at least in some faculty members' estimation. In the U.S. at least, where even public colleges' funding models often have them competing with each other for the tuition revenue associated with incoming first year students, practical and sometimes extensive COVID-19 precautions on campus (everything from plexiglass installed in classrooms to testing, contact tracing, and vaccination programs) were sometimes seen by faculty to conflict with some schools' "business as usual" messages that were being sent to parents and students. The potential contradiction between these two approaches—one designed to limit the health risk of exposure on campus while the other intended to limit the financial risk of students sitting out the year and thereby jeopardizing a school's operating budget—seems to have put many faculty members in the difficult (if sometimes untenable) position of caring for their own safety (and thus their family's as well) while meeting what faculty saw as the unrealistic expectations of at least a sub-set of administrators and even students (such as those wishing to attend classes in-person and even do so unmasked, with no disclosure concerning vaccine status). Add to this some faculty members' presence in regions of the country where state governments had banned more proactive avoidance measures on the part of employers (such as hastily enacted laws against mandating either masks or vaccinations) and one arrives at a nearly two-year period of compounding daily anxiety for many faculty members. Taking into account the hierarchical nature of authority on a university campus, and (in some cases, at least) the lack of effective faculty governance and thus participation in administrative decision making (i.e., weak and merely symbolic faculty senates), and I believe that we arrive at a point where the perceived lack of affirmation or recognition in a venue where many in attendance are assumed to be professional peers (i.e., a scholarly conference) leads to a moment when the usually operating compartmentalization and self-censorship of professional life was abandoned.

Should my analysis be persuasive then the conclusion that I reach is that the response during that evening's Q&A had little, if anything, to do with Hughes's comments or approach—one with which it should be clear that I, and undoubtedly many others, fully agree and therefore see as utterly uncontroversial. Instead, the evening session provided an opportunity for some participants to focus on, whether intentionally or not, a longstanding (and, in my opinion, quite legitimate) anxiety, responding in the more egalitarian setting of a group of generally like-minded scholars by saying things that, for purposes of maintaining their professional status at work, they likely are not able to say (at least publicly) in their workplaces or to their superiors—be that person a Department Chair, an Associate Dean, a Dean, a Provost, etc. Unbeknownst to the NAASR organizers, the conference—the second consecutive of its annual meetings to be virtual due to what many members see to be health threats associated with travel—along with its theme and Hughes's plenary, thus provided a safe place for alienated faculty from across the ranks to vent—more than likely a much-needed opportunity.

The moral of the story is that scholars are themselves no different from the people whom we study; for we deploy the usual set of techniques to establish group identity and to nurture what we take to be shared affinities and common alienations. Our critical intelligence, as useful as it is when engaging in the study of distant peoples and places—whether chronologically or geographically—can sometimes be of surprisingly little assistance when those things that we ourselves value feel under threat, even if that threat comes from the critical gaze of a colleague. While I would encourage scholars of religion to be rather more bold and uncompromising in the application of such critical, self-reflexive scholarship—even when it is felt to be applied uncomfortably close to home—we can take away something from this episode to help us understand the push-back that our work often receives either from the people being studied or, as is more likely, from those of our colleagues who hold them dear.

Acknowledgements

My thanks to Richard Newton, Vaia Touna, and Merinda Simmons for comments on an earlier draft of this chapter.

Russell T. McCutcheon is university research professor and, for 18 years, was the chair of the Department of Religious Studies at the University of Alabama. He has written on problems in the academic labor market throughout his 30-year career and helped to design and run Alabama's skills-based MA in religion in culture. Among his recent work is the edited resource for instructors, *Teaching in Religious Studies and Beyond* (Bloomsbury 2024).

References

Black, Ian. 2013. "Egypt's Revolution and Diplomacy: When a Coup is a 'Military Intervention'." *The Guardian*, July 4. Retrieved from www.theguardian.com/world/2013/jul/04/egypt-revolution-coup-military-intervention-analysis (accessed November 25, 2021).

Kirkpatrick, David D. 2013. "Army Ousts Egypt's President; Morsi Is Taken into Military Custody." *The New York Times*, July 3. Retrieved from www.nytimes.com/2013/07/04/world/middleeast/egypt.html (accessed November 29, 2021).

Lincoln, Bruce. 1996. "Theses on Method." *Method & Theory in the Study of Religion*, 8(3): 225–227.

McCutcheon, Russell T. 2006. "'It's a Lie. There's No Truth in It! It's a Sin!': On the Limits of the Humanistic Study of Religion and the Costs of Saving Others from Themselves." *Journal of the American Academy of Religion*, 74(3): 720–750.

McCutcheon, Russell T. 2013. "The C-Word." Retrieved from https://edge.ua.edu/russell-mccutcheon/the-c-word/ (accessed November 25, 2021).

McCutcheon, Russell T. 2015. *Fabricating Origins*. Sheffield: Equinox.

Orsi, Robert. 2004. "Fair Game." *Bulletin of the Council of Societies for the Study of Religion*, 33(3–4): 87–89.

Peterson-Withorn, Chase. 2021. "How Much Money America's Billionaires Have Made during the Covid-19 Pandemic." Retrieved from www.forbes.com/sites/chasewithorn/2021/04/30/american-billionaires-have-gotten-12-trillion-richer-during-the-pandemic/ (accessed November 20, 2021).

Pritchard, Elizabeth A. 2010. "Seriously, What Does 'Taking Religion Seriously' Mean?" *Journal of the American Academy of Religion*, 78(4): 1087–1111.

Quinnipiac University. 2021. "78% Of Republicans Want to See Trump Run for President in 2024, Quinnipiac University National Poll Finds; Americans Now Split on Border Wall as Opposition Softens." Retrieved from https://poll.qu.edu/poll-release?releaseid=3825 (accessed November 20, 2021).

Part II

Language

Crisis as a Turning Point

Chapter 6

Profit and Loss

The New Time of Crisis

Zoe Anthony

In this chapter, I focus on the deployment of the term "unprecedented" within the context of the COVID-19 crisis by interpreting the idea that "crisis" is a point of radical decision. I define the "unprecedented" simply: an event without precedent; that is, one never having occurred in time up until this point, without any prior event to yield to what is new. Determining *what* precisely is unprecedented about the COVID-19 crisis is secondary for this chapter. Instead, what I am interested in are the rhetorical moves that attend to the claim of the unprecedented: that never before within history have we seen something like this. One might ask immediately: what is understood by "this" crisis—what is it in this context that is understood to be unprecedented—and who is it who either has or has not experienced something like it? What makes something unprecedented is not only that it has never occurred before, but that there is no *history* for what is happening. There is no precedent for this context, nothing, as in the Latin verb, *praecedere*, that has gone before, and thus no relevant background knowledge exists to apply in this radically unfamiliar situation. The unprecedented, therefore, is a claim about practice as much as it is a claim about history, because there is, it is claimed, no prior example from which to draw conclusions about what to do, now.

The claim that the COVID-19 crisis is unprecedented can be fruitfully addressed by a comparison of the work of Walter Benjamin and Reinhart Koselleck. The former explores a messianism that relies on the ideas about the unexpected, ever-anticipated eruption into history that would end all history, the latter whose focus is on the historical development of the category of "crisis" as a temporal classification that yields continually new pictures of time.[1] I use the conceptual tools of Benjamin and of Koselleck to attempt to offer a clearer picture of what is theoretically noteworthy within this moment in time, vis-à-vis the rhetorical gesture of the unprecedented event of the COVID-19 crisis. There is an important tension in the description of crisis between these two figures in terms of the idea of crisis—both are concerned with crisis as that which breaks into history, and ruptures history, a pre-history, in effect, seen as a previously smooth continuity

---

1. I focus in this chapter on Benjamin's "Theses on the Philosophy of History" (1940) and Koselleck's "Crisis" (2006).

of events that has been disrupted or distorted by a crisis-moment. My claim is that the rhetoric of the unprecedented can be interpreted through what I call a *historiography of the transcendent*, by which I mean a conceptualization of what is unexpected as a kind of transcendence. The moment in which the transcendent—or the crisis—erupts into history is the moment the transcendent becomes amenable to rational discourse. As rational the transcendent can be capitalized, monetized, and profited from.

For Benjamin, if the unprecedented has entered history it is no longer unprecedented. The radicality of Benjamin's conception of historiography is in the tension of his theological outlook of messianism with the historicality of the possibility of the "messiah's"—or what I gloss as the transcendent, or the crisis-moment's—rupture into history.[2] What this means is that the expected can never be unexpected—the messiah is expected, but cannot therefore be historical, because what is historical is in danger of being lost to what is "present."[3] In keeping history present, what has occurred in history can only be kept present insofar as the present makes it so—that is, present. The introjection of the messianic into this discussion appears to be a way of retaining the unexpected, that is, the unprecedented *as such*, or *away* from the "Antichrist," or "conformism." Thus any claim that the unprecedented, unexpected, or radically other has entered into history is a rhetorical gesture towards repetitive iterations of the status quo, or conformism. In this way, Benjamin's work allows us to see the attendant claims of profiting from crisis as profiting from the rhetorics of crisis.

By contrast Koselleck offers a differing view: that crises are indeed still possible within history, even as ontological events, events that change the meaning of what "is" at the level of "decision" that crisis represents. Benjamin's interpretations of what I am glossing as the expected-unexpected is helpful in seeing the limits of the so-called "opportunities" with crises as iterations of what has already occurred, as "status quo," but that Benjamin's view is perhaps limited

---

2. Benjamin writes: "A chronicler who recites events without distinguishing between major and minor ones acts in accordance with the following truth: nothing that has ever happened should be regarded as lost for history. To be sure, only a redeemed mankind [sic] receives the fullness of its past—which is to say, only for a redeemed mankind has its past become citable in all its moments. Each moment it has lived becomes a *citation à l'order du jour*—and that day is Judgment Day" (Benjamin 1986, 254). A redeemed humanity is a completed, fulfilled, expiated humanity, and to be able to receive the fullness of past means to receive the inheritance of the past fully. But this is not amenable to the unredeemed creatures that we are. So, because we are unredeemed, and perhaps fractured and incomplete, we cannot know the past fully, or, it cannot be citable for us "in all its moments" (ibid.).

3. Further: "To articulate the past historically does not mean to recognize it 'the way it really was' (Ranke). It means to seize hold of a memory as it flashes up at a moment of danger [Hegel]. Historical materialism wishes to retain that image of the past which unexpectedly appears to man singled out by history at a moment of danger. The danger affects both the content of the tradition and its receivers. The same threat hangs over both: that of becoming a tool of the ruling classes. In every era the attempt must be made anew to wrest tradition away from a conformism that is about to overpower it. The Messiah comes not only as the redeemer, he comes as the subduer of the Antichrist" (Benjamin 1940, 255).

precisely in this way. While the radicality of the faith in a to-come that never arrives positions us to remain at a distance from the actualization of change, and keeps us, perhaps, skeptical and critical, there still remains the fundamental historiographical question of how it is—if it is—that societies change, and how or toward what purposes we can represent this change.

Koselleck's vision of the nature of crisis as transformative along political and social lines allows us to orient ourselves toward a more historicist view of the development of events. Koselleck's view, however, may be limited by the reliance on the kind of causality attending to the emergence of the event, and the subsequent fallout of that event. What, it seems, an improved version of both theorists' understanding of crisis requires is a great dose of theoretical humility: change does occur, *contra* Benjamin, but how this change occurs is not entirely knowable, *contra* Koselleck. At best what we are left with is a familiar and uncomfortable position of anticipation combined with a recognition of the arbitrariness of the identification of causes and effects. Finally, I think what this spells out is that the kind of things we choose to identify as causes of the COVID-19 crisis, and the kinds of things we choose to identify as consequences of it, indicate the kind of orientation *we* as individuals take toward social and political questions that matter for any desire to see meaningful transformation of exploitative systems and political injustice. In other words, what we choose at this critical juncture points to the kind of world we intend to see birthed out of this crisis/noncrisis.

Koselleck

My interest in the concept of crisis in general is based on the question of the mechanisms or principles of historical change. For Koselleck, one answer to the question of how change happens in history is precisely through crisis. Koselleck offers a genealogy of the term crisis, in his article entitled "Crisis" (Reinhart 2006). The literature on Koselleck's, and Benjamin's, view of history is extensive and I do not pretend to be comprehensive of the thought of either figure in this chapter. Instead, what I want to do here is set out some ideas in the direction of thinking about the concept of crisis in terms of the influence that the political and theological valences of this term have on a less explored idea of crisis's relevance, that is, to its economic valence.

Is COVID-19 an economic crisis? Is this the "first time" that a health crisis has taken on such economic significance? The influence of COVID-19 on the economy is clear: with a slowdown or in some cases a complete stop on the exchange of goods and services, the economy suffers since it is based upon this primary mode of action. But this is a superficial level of influence: what of the scores of workers whose shift to work-from-home has spelled the end of their daily commute into the office? Or what about the minimum wage workers, mostly women in the hospitality services such as restaurant work, who refuse to return to thoroughly exploitative, abusive along gendered lines, lines of work? It seems that the COVID-19 crisis has, in part, generated an "opportunity" for the meaning of work to be re-thought.

Koselleck's point, as I take it here, is not that the dimensions of crisis, be they political, theological, medical, psychological or existential, exist in isolation from others, but, instead, that these different dimensions each become relevant at different times and for different conceptual reasons. That is, for example, what Koselleck describes as a transition from a "medical" to an "economic" view of the word crisis is made possible because of the extension of the concept of crisis's semantic range to include economics. This is a kind of argument by analogy, that medical crisis is akin to economic crisis insofar as both have in common a necessary causal relation: certain conditions will produce inevitable outcomes, and what is needed to know these outcomes is what the initial conditions of the crisis are. This argument—summed up rather quickly—is that there are precipitating events that accumulate over time and reach such a critical mass that a "crisis" necessarily occurs. This view implies that we can know the causes of crises, if we only identify, and in this instance retrofit, enough relevant preceding causes to indicate that the crisis can or would have been likely to occur. Likewise, after the crisis has occurred or reached its critical point, a series of "fall out" events occur, which are likewise traceable to the crisis. Everyone's least-favorite catchline today is: "Due to COVID." But can we know what is really due to COVID?

Benjamin

William Schinkel, in "The Image of Crisis: Walter Benjamin and the Interpretation of 'Crisis' in Modernity," claims that Koselleck's idea that "through its [crisis's] diagnostic and prognostic substance [it is] indicative of a new consciousness" is "outdated" (Schinkel 2015). He writes, "Today, no use of 'crisis' carries such deep connotations of change. Calling some state of affairs a 'crisis,' is, quite the opposite, a move toward stabilization of the existing" (ibid., 38). Schinkel wrote this article in 2015. I wonder if his views would change now given the many rhetorical discussions around the COVID-19 crisis pertaining specifically to whether we ought to "return to normal" or use such an opportunity to generate a new world full of new expectations and means for accomplishing our goals. Many discussions do relate to how long until we return to "normal," but there is indeed a growing recognition, I would argue, that there is no such thing as any "return" in this case—"change" after this crisis must happen.

What is more troublesomely problematic about Schinkel's claim that the "old" meaning of crisis as revolutionary no longer obtains is the lack of evidence he gives for this claim. Schinkel simply asserts that this is the case, that crisis *only* relates to how long it might take to "get back to normal," without any concomitant discussion of the aftermath of this "return," or what this, as we just so easily call it today, "new normal" might look like. The idea that there is a "new" normal to be found seems to challenge Schinkel at the level of popular rhetoric. While for a time the "new normal" referred to the preventative measures that we adopted in order to stymie the tide of COVID-19 case count, at this point I would argue that the "new normal" after COVID relates to the economic impact the pandemic has had upon us. By economic, I do not simply mean the exchange of goods, but a more classical sense of the organization of home—the organization of our communities, of how we relate to each other in small and large groups, of who we are in relation to others in terms of the moment of crisis; all of these issues are now in redevelopment precisely because of this crisis.

And yet I hesitate to claim, given prior considerations, that the COVID-19 crisis is a *cause* of these periods of renegotiation—is at all demonstrable or provable that they are? We may say with the logicians that the COVID-19 crisis may have been a necessary but not sufficient condition—that something radical "needed" to happen, but it alone is not sufficient to carry out such a renegotiation of a troubled world grappling with legacies of colonialism, gender-based violence, exploitation and so on. The sufficient condition is, perhaps, the nascent, often suppressed, often apparently impossible and inaccessible, desire for change—and crisis is an opportunity to express that desire manifestly.

Indeed, Schinkel seems to exemplify a kind of pessimistic, ironically very modern (because he denies that modernity is sufficiently radical) malaise about the meaninglessness of crisis in our time: "Similarly, with the 'crisis of modernity,' and the 'crisis of representation', one could say that the revolutionary uses of 'crisis' in political history have been lost" (Schinkel 2015, 38). But why could one say this? What evidence is there that the revolutionary use of the word crisis—an idea undeveloped in his article—has been lost? Can we not generate examples of revolutionary crisis in from the 2010s, even? What of the Arab Spring, the popular protests in Hong Kong, or movements local to Turtle Island, Idle No More, or Black Lives Matter? It seems to me as if in our inability—out of privilege or lack of an ability to creatively imagine what it might be like for others to experience crises for *ourselves* Schinkel has taken a nihilistic tact toward the value of crisis as a heuristic tool for understanding historical change: as Nietzsche understood it, nihilism as the *devaluation* of the highest values, or, as one might gloss it, the evacuation of significance from meanings previously held dear. There is some truth to the idea that crisis has become a moot point in historiography—and indeed Koselleck himself anticipated some of this overcoming of the concept. But the concept, if we are to critique it, should not be seen as no longer existing, as having dissipated, but as, as with all things, transformed. And by taking this approach, we can understand more of what it means to live in the times we do, facing the challenges we face. At least, that is the goal.

Schinkel interprets Benjamin as viewing modernity's crises as "eternal returns of the same," arguing that what returns is not the same event, but the same experience of shock from the event. While Schinkel's work profitably illuminates the recurrence of crisis as a key concept in modernity, and this is observable in economic terms, I think that this view might profit from Koselleck's idea of crisis as an analytic concept used to interpret historical events. Rather than seeing crisis as something that can be accounted for in terms of precipitating causes, or as seeing crisis, after it occurs, as causing certain events to subsequently occur, instead, we ought to look at the rhetoric of crisis and what is being identified as precipitation and what is being identified as consequence. In so doing, we limit the need to either judge crisis as "legitimate" or as "*truly* challenging to the status quo" and instead see crisis as a collective historical tool that social groups use conceptually to make sense of moments of change. While we can call into question whether this change truly changes anything (or what difference a difference makes, to paraphrase Jonathan Smith), nevertheless the idea of crisis has legs of its own, apart from any one actor's intention, and does seem to point toward something that alters the psychical and material landscape of our social lives. To deny that crises do this would seem to escape into the dream image, not of progress, that Schinkel claims we ought not to, but of the denial of the possibility of progress and of crisis as a way of describing its possibility.

Zoe Anthony is assistant professor of philosophy and religion at the University of Tampa. She researches and teaches in the areas of nineteenth- and twentieth-century Continental philosophy, philosophical and religious ethics, and method and theory in the academic study of religions.

References

Benjamin, Walter. 1986. "Theses on the Philosophy of History." In Walter Benjamin, *Illuminations*, translated by Harry Zohn. New York: Schocken Books.
Koselleck, Reinhart. 2006. "Crisis." Translated by Michaela Richter. *Journal of the History of Ideas*, 67(2): 357–400.
Schinkel, Willem. 2015. "The Image of Crisis: Walter Benjamin and the Interpretation of 'Crisis' in Modernity." *Thesis Eleven*, 127(1): 36–51.

Chapter 7

Black Fires

Crisis as Nadir and the Memory of Racial Violence in the South

Aaron M. Treadwell

From the genesis of the trans-Atlantic trade, religion has stood as a fundamental tool of survival for African people. Throughout the Diaspora, the syncretic traditions experienced by black people cultivated nuances and theological shifts in their faith. Theoretically speaking, black religion has a duality that can be defined as abstract and interconnected. Regionally and culturally, persons in the Diaspora cultivated theological systems that relied on previous traditions of the past, alongside a current reaction to cultural norms in their present. Hindsight has allowed the field of black religion to define this process of acculturation as an organic tradition of survivalism. As one's esoteric concerns change, so must the application of faith.

By the late nineteenth century, the black church continued to be a voice of resistance against the crises of the post-Reconstruction era, which has been labeled "the Nadir of race relations" (Logan 1954). African Americans were forced to ask questions of theodicy, which has been paraphrased by William R. Jones as "Is God a White Racist?" or "Why can a Good and all-powerful God, allow racism, oppression, and murder to attack his people." These conversations were had in private and in public, and the perception of a black pastor was often dictated by their ability to mediate such concerns.

Viewed in terms of the rhetoric of crisis, "Nadir" as a label for this era implicitly argues that there has not been a season in American history where citizens had faced more trouble and danger than from 1877–1915. To be clear, over 4,000 African Americans were lynched in the so-called Nadir, and the majority of these acts of terrorism took place regionally in the southern states. It was in this environment that pastors sought to protect their membership by circumventing a theology that could provide hope and resistance to members. Some pastors were rebellious in their sermonic response to violence and preached the second amendment from the pulpit. "The Negro must do like all other races. He must fight for his rights. Nothing shorter than a Winchester or a Gatling gun will stop this *lynching*" (*Christian Recorder*, May 25, 1893). Many black pastors took a dogmatic and pious approach to protect their members, praying that the God of Moses would soon judge and wreak havoc on those who sin.

> There are those who insist that fire must be fought with fire in the case of colored men whose kind are constant suffers from the bloody violence of mob. They advocate the gospel of the Mosaic regime which required eye for eye, tooth for tooth, life for life. To do this, whoever would be for the race to believe its past record as a long suffering, hardy and ascendant people. While a defense of family, life and friendship should be made, even at the cost of life, the idea of any general peace uprising in any section, is to be deprecated under any and all circumstances.
> (*Christian Recorder*, August 16, 1894)

The commonality between examples is that both pastors sought to create solutions for protection, which included publicly addressing the issue at hand. The history of black churches responding to lynching is well documented in the field. "Tongues of Fire: Theological Protectionism," an article published in the *Journal of African American History*, documents over 50 published black Church responses to lynching during the Nadir era.

Though the historical trend of lynching decreased in the 1950s, American terrorism still continued to haunt the black communities of the southern United States. Though lynching had decreased, racism had become more deeply embedded in the culture and politics of the U.S. Thus, we may ask, was the "Nadir period" actually the lowest point in U.S. race relations? For whom? How is it measured? What is at stake in identifying, or trying to identify, when race relations were better or worse? In the American imagination, lynching is a national cultural trauma and a site of racial terror. This article will argue that among political disenfranchisement stood a physical replacement to lynching, colloquially called church burning, or arson.

There are hundreds of recorded arsons in the annals of African American history, and many of the targeted buildings were black churches. Outside of the documented attacks of obvious arsons are hundreds of "open cases," or likely arsons. The adverb "likely" arson is vital to this analysis, and in addition many of the fires experienced by black churches are recorded as accidents. The word likely was often used to avoid legal ramifications in the community, while acknowledging the obvious conditions of the fire. One black church in middle Tennessee was burned just days after the Pastor's son integrated a local high school. The police report was filed as a "mysterious accident" (*Nashville Banner*, June 22, 1963; *Chattanooga Daily Times*, June 9, 1963). One black church in Perry, Florida was burned down after a member decided to run for mayor. This congregation's fire was cited as a "likely arson." Both congregations eventually moved from their original locations, and members cited racial tension as a major part of their eventual relocation. Even in recent oral interviews, members still maintain a worry for future reprise.

In the summer of 1962, there were numerous cases of terrorism in Southern Georgia. These acts of violence became national news, and would receive a response from J. Edgar Hoover, John F. Kennedy, Martin Luther King Jr., and Jackie Robinson. This article will examine the cause and effect of these individual acts of terrorism, including a detailed investigation into why there were attacks against black churches in the area. During this season of chaos, there were six black churches that faced arson, and these cases are still impacting the community today. We might even call it a crisis. At the epicenter of black resistance during the Civil Rights Movement, black churches like those in Georgia often found themselves as initial targets for racial violence. In the bloody history of racial terror and black resistance,

Preparing for Theological Resistance in Georgia

In his inaugural presidential address to Morehouse College, Benjamin E. Mayes stated in 1940 that "I wouldn't go to a segregated theater to see Jesus Christ himself" (Kuhn, et. al. 1990, 302). When looking at the purpose of this statement, it should be identified as both a theological claim and an act of theological resistance. For Mayes, in order to acknowledge the scriptural truth of *imago-dei,* or "being made in the image of God," black people in Georgia had to recognize that segregation had the ability to damage to their spirit. In addition to this reflection, Mayes encouraged the act of theological resistance towards segregation, by instructing black church goers to reject laws, customs, and teaching all through the instrument of the black church.

Mayes surely wasn't the first nor last person in Georgia to theologically speak out against racism. Bishop Henry McNeal Turner made an entire career of preaching "God is a Negro" throughout the late-nineteenth and early-twentieth-century Georgia. Rev. Dr. Martin Luther King, Jr. frequently challenged racism with theological resistance by preaching public speeches against public transportation, voting, and education. Black liberation sermons in the black church tradition have historically been the organ for black consciousness, and by the mid-1950s black Georgians were in desperate need of encouragement and direction to resist white supremacy (Johnson 2013, 207–225).

Black churches often turned to theological resistance in order to survive the reality of racial oppression, both physically and mentally. By 1940, Black people in the state of Georgia had formed nearly one-third of the state's population, but were overwhelmingly disinherited (Owen 1951, 144–147; Pyles 1967, 15). The oppression faced by these persons varied in the states ecosystems. The rural parts of central and southwest Georgia were dominated by farming, and the fertile land was primarily owned by white large-farming families (plantations). Within this region, black people only owned six percent of the land, leaving the majority of the population to share cropping (U.S. Census Bureau 1943). In the northern region, small-scale mining was the driving economy, yet black people were predominately left out. The southeastern island region was dominated by the Gullah and Geechee peoples, who although economically and institutionally saw little to no regional development they would merit high levels of self-sufficiency. Finally, the majority of black people in the state lived in urban areas that experienced far superior waves of success over Jim Crow.

As argued by Tolnay and Beck, the rural black population were often the recipients of violence during the Jim Crow era. This was often due to a lack of institutional protection, and sheer numbers of black residents to protect themselves

(Beck and Tolnay 1997; Tolnay and Beck 1995; Wilmore 1972). Southern Georgia, soon became a hunting ground for black people who sought resistance, and churches often were the initial targets within rural Georgia. A precursor for violent acts of terrorism was often in response to black organization and social-political progress. Churches were often at the forefront of violence due to the visibility of their edifice, and the agency that it provided its membership. Acts of intimidation could be physical, civil, and mental. Black Codes and later Jim Crow laws restricted black political mobility, and racist propaganda and negative theological literature caused mental harm.

Georgia records highlight a major growth of black churches in the mid-twentieth century, whereas these numbers did not equate to black people receiving acceptance from local white residents. Many white preachers in the area were writing and preaching that black people were connected to the Hamitic curse in order to demean black spiritual credibility. This theological over-sight argued that black people were a cursed race which deserved to be enslaved and oppressed (Johnson 2016). In the 1940s, economic success for Georgia African Americans proved to be dangerous, and numerous acts of violence were used to strip thriving black communities. Black Georgians earned on average less than half of white people, and the state allocated four times less on black education. Financial inequality also bled into medical disadvantages, as black children were twice as likely to die in childbirth, and three times more likely to die from health complications.

Social advancement in Georgia, especially within the southern rural cities, crumbled under the leadership of Governor Eugene Talmadge. Under his leadership, black protest culture would collapse in Georgia, and NAACP branches fell from fifty-five to under twenty by the 1950s. Labeled as the "all time Georgia champion of white supremacy," the governor's four-point legislative program all but assured that white supremacy had a home in Georgia (Bluestein 2007). This program included a poll tax, poll test, and discriminatory practices against impoverished rural communities—the majority of these populations being black. For example, some counties required voters to "sign a pledge in support of white supremacy" to vote (Tuck 1980, 76). The disenfranchised policies of poll taxing and poll test were monitored and assisted by the Ku Klux Klan, and the organization was protected by Talmadge's administration. Dr. Samuel Green, who was the Grand Dragon for the state of Georgia, was the lieutenant colonel and aide-de-camp for Talmadge, and this political support provided open range against black bodies and their parent institutions (Payne 2007, 27).

Just six months into Talmadge's term, over a dozen violent racial attacks were reported. Klan activities in the state targeted black social advocates, and often included cross-burnings and public displays of terror in response. The cross-burnings were often done to stop black suffrage attempts, and historically these acts were successful. "Blood will flow in the streets if the Negro votes," argued one Democratic party leader on the eve of the Democratic primary of 1948 (Tuck 1980, 78; NAACP 1948). Acts as such warrant Georgia's history concerning disenfranchisement, especially within rural Georgia. By the 1950s, the Klan in Georgia continued to thwart the black vote. By 1952, black disenfranchisement in the state was statistically leading every southern state outside Alabama and Mississippi. Part of the problem rested within the renewed presence of the Georgia Klan, as it was allowed to cooperate within the protection of Governor Talmadge. If change was to happen in rural Georgia, black people knew that there would be a heavy sacrifice to be made. This burden soon became carried by social-political local black churches, as they attributed their sacrifice to a faith that supported civil liberation.

The battle against segregation and disenfranchisement in rural Georgia became chaotic by the 1960s. The media coverage of restaurant sit-ins and bus boycotts caused a heightened consciousness within black and white communities. Due to rural Georgia's notorious history with white supremacy, the Student Nonviolent Coordinating Committee (SNCC) and the Congress on Racial Equality (CORE) pinpointed this region as a focal point for voter registration drives. Strategically, their intentions were good but socially these organizations had overlooked the systematic power of terrorism within this region. Upon arriving to rural south-east Georgia, many activists would find that many of the rural black population were not receptive, due to fear of reprisal. Black activism in these regions had become a death wish in the eyes of many residents.

By March 1960, Atlanta and Savannah were participating in sit-ins, and in 1961, Albany joined the movement for freedom, whereas minimal examples of activism would take place in rural Georgia. Martin Luther King Jr., a notable leader of the Civil Rights Movement (CRM), helped to encourage over 7,000 Georgians to demonstrate state-wide, whereas these acts were urban protests (SRC 1961). These demonstrations did impact black voting surges in cities like Albany, Atlanta, Augusta, Columbus, Savannah, and Macon, and they also ushered in the presence of voter registration campaigners, including SNCC and Core into the state. Yet, little to no progress was being made within rural Georgia prior to the 1960s, and this was due to the hostile environment and the fear of black residents.

As black voting surged in urban Georgia, protest and voting registration had a unique hill to climb in the rural regions. When SNCC launched a project to bring voting opportunities to rural Georgia in 1962, many black people knew that actual warfare would soon follow. Rural locations were heavily influenced by Ku Klux Klan leadership, and racial violence was at a historical high. "Terrible Terrell" and Lee County, were known for having police forces that had been heavily infiltrated by terrorist, causing observers to assess that "the negroes of this Georgia Town are Scared;" and for good reason (*Southern School News*, April 1958, 13). At the first sign of social-political activism in rural Georgia, few friends of the movement would be found. One of the loan friends to the CRM in rural Georgia was the black Church, and it soon became ground zero for retribution violence.

The Southwest Georgia Project

The "Southwest Georgia Project" of SNCC selected rural counties, Lee and Terrell, to address black disenfranchisement. These particular communities had a reputation as places "where it is still literally true that Negroes have no rights which the white man has to respect" (*Student Voice*, 16 December 1964; Harmon 1996, 325). Both counties had a federal history of voting restrictions before the 1962 SNCC project, including a run in with federal district judge William Bottle in 1960. Bottle issued an injunction against Terrell for blocking voters, but this charge was unsuccessful.

On their own front, SNCC workers decided they would try their hand in changing the voting landscape in disenfranchised locations like Terrell County. The organization tried recruiting local students to protest in the area, including recruiting students on school grounds. Lee and Terrell high schools were on high alert and took precautionary methods by expelling two students that had previously been arrested for campaigning. In an interview with Terrell County residents, members were adamant that their parents were hesitant to support the voting drive.

> Everyone was on high alarm, and many of us were scared. Most of the black parents wouldn't even allow their children to attend school the next day, all in fear that we'd be harmed, or worse. Most of the black students didn't attend school for some time, and even though the school systems were promising us that we'd be safe, our parents didn't want to take chances.
>
> (Interview recorded by Aaron M. Treadwell, 2021)

In response, even though SNCC received minimal participation, the white supremacist community attacked them at full throttle. First, the school systems were forced to ostracize any and all persons who supported the suffrage drive. Any student who was hinted at participating with SNCC remained expelled from school, and all SNCC workers were banned from school grounds. Second, violence was used in this season to invoke fear and deter the voting drive. One of the SNCC workers, Jack Chatfield, was shot in the arm. Other workers received numerous threats, including a violent episode at the Mt. Olive Baptist Church in Sasser, Georgia. It was in this church that SNCC was having organization meetings. When the sheriff, Z. T. Matthews, along with several "gun-toting, swearing deputies" entered the church, they reportedly began to threaten the congregation. The sheriff was overheard saying "we want our colored people to go on living like they have for the last hundred years." Surely the physical, mental, and theological comforts of the Mt. Olive Baptist congregation was shaken at this experience. Additional acts of local chaos would continue over the next two months (*Student Voice*, October 1962, 1–4).

SNCC workers continued to organize and fight for voting rights within Terrell County even after the aforementioned attacks. They continued to raise funds, and eventually published a special issue of the *Student Voice* for distribution in the Albany-Terrell-Lee communities, and one particular quote got everyone's attention.

> We do not have the money to pay for gas or wear and tear. We can see no other way out than to attempt to raise money by washing cars, dishes, floors and windows, cutting grass, or any other chore around the house. We do not have money for

transportation in general, into and from these counties ... We are not supermen. We are only young people with a determination to be FREE and to be FREE NOW!

(*Student Voice*, October 1962, 1-4)

Shortly after the publication, Sheriff Matthews and Terrell County residents responded with violence, and were cited as saying that people must put this movement down. For Matthews, challenging systemic oppression equated to being an outlaw—and this made social-political theology an enemy of the state.

Documented Church Violence

The initial black church in the rural Georgia arson-spree was Shady Grove Missionary Baptist Church, in Leesburg, on August 15, 1962. Shady Grove was targeted due to its public relationship with the Student Nonviolent Coordinating Committee (SNCC). This relationship included opening the sanctuary to host meetings and voting drives. In the police records, the fire was initially identified as faulty wiring and or lighting. After an FBI investigation, J. Edgar Hoover acknowledged possible arson, and arrested two white men with the fire. Jack Smith and Douglas Parker were charged in October, two months after the incident. The charges were "conspiring against the rights of citizens," whereas arson was not included. Martin Luther King would respond to the event in an SCLS newsletter in September, and the article was titled "The Terrible Cost of the Ballot":

> Tears welled up in my heart and my eyes not long ago as I surveyed the shambles of what had been the Shady Grove Baptist Church of Leesburg, Georgia. I had been awakened shortly after daybreak by my executive assistant, the Rev. Wyatt Tee Walker, who informed me that a SNCC (Student Nonviolent Coordinating Committee) staffer had just called and reported that the church where their organization had been holding voting clinics and registration classes had been destroyed by fire and/or dynamite.
>
> Lee County is one of the three southwest Georgia counties where for years an attempt to register to vote has been tantamount to inviting death. As I stood there sensing the intense heat from the smoldering remains, there came to mind all of the protestations of these segregationists, the conservative Whites, the liberals, and many Negroes who have not yet grasped the meaning of nonviolent direct action.

(*Greenville Sun*, October 5, 1962, 1)

In response to the Shady Grove arson, hundreds of black people in the area also found themselves jailed. Most of these arrests were for "community disturbance," and all culprits were connected to the SNCC integration protests.

The second arson happened on September 1, 1962, as three white men and one white youth committed arson on the I Hope Baptist Church in Dawson, Georgia. Unlike the Shady Grove incident, this was a legally documented arson. The guilty party admitted that "They just decided to burn them one" (*Knoxville News Sentinel*, September 18, 1962). The vandals were Glenn Roland, 55; his son, Melvin Earl Roland, 21; Marvin Allen Milner, 31; and a 16-year-old youth who was un-named. Sheriff Z. T. Matthews of Terrell County, GA., said the four arsonist "admitted setting fire to the Negro I Hope Baptist Church three miles north of Dawson in the early morning of Monday ... They were drinking beer and just decided to burn the church" cited the FBI (*Greenville Sun*, September 18, 1962; *Chattanooga Daily Times*, September 20, 1962, 21). The admitting party were questioned by FBI Director J. Edgar Hoover, but it was said no evidence of Federal violations were at play. These men did not face criminal prosecution. It should be stated that there was no federal hate crime legislation against racial attacks at that time.

Beyond the simplistic testimony, a historical battle for racial freedoms was taking place in the Dawson community. Georgia was overseeing a Federal Appeals Court to outlaw racial discrimination in public schools. The arsonist surely attempted to make a point, whereas they targeted a black church and not a school. What is interesting is that unlike the Shady Grove congregation, I Hope Baptist Church did not open its doors to SNCC. According to members, the pastor and leadership had voted against being socially political due to the dangers associated with agitation. Still, the decision to remain silent did not protect this black congregation, and their entire sanctuary would succumb to the fire.

The I Hope Baptist Church would set off a local and national alarm for chaotic white terrorism in rural southern-Georgia. White allies began to write and publicly condemn the unfortunate trend of black church-burning taking place in the state (*Chattanooga Daily Times*, September 20, 1962, 21). Nationally, Attorney General Robert F. Kennedy sent a verbal report to President Kennedy citing the FBI probe concerning the Shady Grove and I Hope fires. The Justice Department said that the fires would be investigated to determine to see if they were a direct attack against voter registration (*Knoxville News Sentinel*, September 18, 1962). Yet, even with the testimonies of the arsonists, the Dawson sheriff and community did not seek full legal recourse. Instead, the Dawson community led by Mayor Carl Roundtree, said that "white people of Dawson and Terrell County would rebuild I Hope Baptist Church." Roundtree went into more detailing, telling the editor of the Dawson newspaper that,

> The white people of this town and country want to rebuild this church themselves. I'm going to serve as chairman of a committee to accept contributions for rebuilding this church. But we don't want any help. We feel that since this particular church was burned by people who live in Dawson and Terrell County, it's our job to do this. We're glad to do it—to show people throughout the nation that we deeply resent this shameful act.
>
> (*Chattanooga Daily Times*, September 20, 1962, 12)

The third and fourth churches to face arson was the Mount Mary Baptist Church and the Mount Olive Baptist Church. Both congregations were arsoned on September 9, and both were located in Terrel County. Mount Mary Church, located in Dawson, Georgia, was very active in the voter registration campaign. This church hosted the drives and the activist. A local paper would describe this relationship as, facilitating "the mingling of white and Negro members of the Student Non-violent Co-ordinating Committee, the group which has spearheaded the registration efforts" (*Knoxville News Sentinel*, September 10, 1962, 2).

Mount Olive Baptist Church located nine miles down the road in Sasser, Georgia, was also connected to voting drive. Mount Mary and Mount Olive's community had experienced recent incidents of gunfire attacks before the September 9 arson. Four local black residences had been shot at, earlier in the week. In addition, it should be noted that the I Hope Baptist Church had faced arson just eight days prior. Further incidents surrounding the black Sasser community in the month of September included local white people fighting FBI agents who were identified as encouraging the voting drive, and the aforementioned shooting of SNCC member John Chatfield.

The culmination of these acts forced SNCC to appeal to President John F. Kennedy, saying "the unwarranted attack upon an agent of the FBI is only indicative of the lawlessness rampant in Southwest Georgia" (*Student Voice*, October 1962, 1–4). The activist organization had been in Terrell County since November 1961 and had charged that several of their meetings over the previous year had been "broken up by law enforcement officers." Neither the President nor a representative responded to this particular lament, but it would catch the attention of the national media (ibid.).

One figure who did respond to the cries of SNCC was world-renown superstar Jackie Robinson. Robinson, born in Cairo, Georgia, would soon become a national voice against terrorism within rural Georgia. He would chair a national fund to rebuild the Mount Mary and Mount Olive Churches and set a goal of $25,000. "It is a sad situation when even the most rabid segregationist would stoop this low to defy the wrath of God and burns His house," argued Robinson (*JET*, September 20, 1962, 30). Heavyweight champion Floyd Patterson was also a part of the fund drive. The drive also included a public cry for President Kennedy to come to Terrell and Lee Counties. According to Robinson, "the Ku Klux Klan and the segregationists make a mockery of democracy," and black churches in the area were all under immense danger (ibid.). Even outside cities expressed a distaste against the actions of Terrel terrorism. Atlanta Governor Ernest Vandiver offered a $250 state reward for information concerning the arson, justifying the state's responsibility to provide protection for black churches, including those who supported social-political activities like CRM participation (*Chattanooga Daily Times*, September 12, 1962, 4).

Aforementioned support for black churches to operate as voting sites still did not mesh with rural terrorist in southern Georgia. Five days after the Mount Olive and Mount Mary events, Peyton African Methodist Episcopal (AME) Church became the fifth black church to face arson. On September 14, 1962, in Clyattville, Georgia, "inflammable material was thrown through a window of the church. Somebody threw a Molotov cocktail into Peyton AME Church in attempt to destroy it." Due to Peyton's structure, and because the cocktail was made with an inflammable liquid, "a few seats and parts of the floor were scorched," but the church overall held strong (*Knoxville News-Sentinel*, September 16, 1962, 10).

According to the Sheriff J. L. Futch, this was a shocking turn of events since "racial trouble was low" in Lowndes County, when compared to Terrell and Lee. In addition, the Sheriff stated that the counties were separated by 100 miles.

It should be noted that there are also strong similarities in both cases. First, Peyton and the Mount Olive and Mount Mary Churches did have a public relationship with integration efforts. Second, all of the targeted churches received verbal warnings prior to arsons, suggesting that black churches were aware of the danger of accepting "troublemakers" who were coming to assist with voting. Local white churches, which had been silent, even decided to pen a formal resolution in response to the Peyton fire. "In a formal resolution, the Albany Ministerial Association said it feels that the presence of the northern ministers, 'would be in no wise constructive and might well undermine the continuing efforts of this body and of concerned individuals in this area'" (Knoxville News-Sentinel, September 16, 1962).

St. Matthew was the sixth black church in South Georgia targeted by arson, on September 25 in Macon, Georgia. Similar to the I Hope Baptist Church, St. Matthews was cited as being a careful church, and not political; this was according to the Senior Pastor, Rev. C. J. Andrews. "All I know is that I just don't understand how it could have started." The Church "had not been used for any integrationist activities" (*Knoxville News-Sentinel*, September 25, 1962). Pastor Andrews wanted to be public that the church wouldn't declare the fire an arson or terrorist attack. This could have been due to unwanted publicity or fear of reprisal. The fire department did mention that "the cause had not been determined several hours after the fire." With that said, there is literature signifying the benefits of keeping silent in the face of attacks and that de-escalating an event had provided many a false sense of security from reoccurring danger.

Why the Black Church?

The relationship between church attacks and the presence of voting drives was in high correlation in 1962 rural southern-Georgia. It should be noted that political activities within a particular church did not guarantee that non-political black churches were safe. The arson attacks against St. Matthew Baptist Church and I Hope Baptist Church, exhibit a risk that any black church participating in social-political activity could put an entire community at risk. In 1961, a year prior to the South Georgia arsons, the largest black Christian denomination in the world split due to the threats of social-political theology. From the National Baptist Convention schismed the Progressive National Baptist church, as leaders Benjamin Mayes, Martin Luther King, and others left the conservative denomination due to its refusal to accept the dangerous theological practice of a social-political gospel.

The decision to utilize a dangerous theology has received attention in the historiography concerning black reprise. It has been cited that many denominations and communities internally pleaded and even reprimanded congregations who utilized a social-political theology (Wilmore 1972, 163–221). The application of this theology includes preaching against racism, hosting conversations concerning racism, and providing avenues that encourage agitation against social issues within the community. In Tallahassee, Florida, when a black pastor led a

Conference against racism, a group of black protestors attempted to burn down the church (Rivers and Brown 2001, 50). The same AME Church in the Florida panhandle would vote twenty years later against using any and all examples of social-political theology. According to the AME Florida Conference leader, Charles Pearce, the benefits of preaching politics were outweighed by the dangers. During a meeting, the Elder put forth the direction that nobody would "be admitted hereafter into the Conference as long as the "ministers were involved in political pursuits." According to the Jacksonville newspaper, AME ministers even went public with such sentiments by 1881. "Ministers and delegates now seem to confine themselves to their church work and nothing more, which is gratifying to all Christians;" noted the writer. One can only assume all black parties did not share these sentiments, since black political activism was being removed from churches due to the aftereffects of white terrorism, and its history of causing trauma and the internalization of fear into a community's theology (Brown 1994, 286–287; *Jacksonville Daily Florida Union*, December 6, 1881).

In an interview, many members of the I Hope Conference argued that the attacks did decrease the prevalence of social action preaching in black Terrel churches. According to members, I Hope Baptist Church rebuilt its sanctuary in its original lot, and publicly let the community know its stance on preaching politics—they would not.

> The church did nothing political in the first place. We never had SNCC in our sanctuary, or on church grounds. The pastor was vocal with the police that we were not a part of the franchising activities, and we did not preach "politics in service." In fact, we never even preached about the fire, in lieu of word getting out.
> (Interview recorded by Aaron M. Treadwell, 2021)

This particular rhetoric is in line with south Georgia's arson-ed churches. They all rebuilt their edifices in the same location and crafted an explicit anti-political stance. When asked why they refused to mention their church getting burned down in sermons and prayers, the congregation's answer was simple—"we were scared" (ibid.).

The psychological and theological aftermath of the violence from the so-called Nadir era deserve close interpretation. Fear can impact one's grappling with theodicy, causing terrorized persons to ask why bad things happen to good people. If considered in terms of crisis, the decades after the four-thousand lynchings of the Nadir era did not result in a period of stasis, peace, or normalcy; indeed, it resulted in more violence, arson, and a culture of mistrust and skepticism among religious social circles. This mistrust might have best been depicted by Rev. Dr. Martin Luther King Jr., when he described Sunday as being "one of the most segregated hours in America" (King 1960). In the American memory, lynching is the key site of racial terror. But racism and violence did not abate after lynching declined and remembering the church burnings of the 1960s calls into question identification of low points and nadirs.

As for Hope Baptist Church, the current congregation mentioned that membership did not go down immediately due to its arson, but currently the church is struggling to hold on: "Our pastor died from COVID last year, and right now we are just a small congregation that is mending for ourselves." The congregation did mention that they did not feel comfortable reaching out for assistance from their predominately white community. The good in I Hope's story is the comradery they've made with the other three local arsoned black churches—Mount Olive Baptist Church, Mount Mary Baptist Church, and Shady Grove Baptist Churches. Annually, the four churches have a joint worship service, commemorating their ability to survive continuous crises: "At one point we were afraid to address our past, but by joining together in this service, it gives us the confidence and ability to come together and grieve and lift up our spirits."

Aaron M. Treadwell is associate professor of History at Middle Tennessee State University (MTSU). His research interests include violence against African Americans, the Second Amendment's support within black churches, Southern history, African-American biographies, and the theological shift of Afro-Spirituality in the nineteenth century.

References

Beck, E. M. and Stewart Tolnay. 1997. "When Race Didn't Matter: Black and White Mob Violence Against Their Own Color." In W. Fitzhugh Brundage (ed.), *Under Sentence of Death: Lynching in the South*, 132–154. Durham, NC: University of North Carolina Press.

Bluestein, Greg. 2007. "Ex-Governor Investigated in 1946 Lynchings." Retrieved from https://web.archive.org/web/20150716023003/http://www.nbcnews.com/id/19251476/ns/us_news-life/t/ex-governor-investigated-lynchings (accessed February 10, 2022).

Brown, Canter. 1994. "Carpetbagger Intrigues, Black Leadership, and a Southern Loyalist Triumph: Florida's Gubernatorial Election of 1872." *The Florida Historical Quarterly*, 72(3), 275–301.

Elliott, Ward E. Y. 2014. *The Rise of Guardian Democracy*. Cambridge, MA: Harvard University Press.

Harmon, David Andrew. 1996. *Beneath the Image of the Civil Rights Movement and Race Relations: Atlanta, GA 1946–1981*. New York: Routledge.

Johnson, E. 2013. "Is the Negro Like Other People? Race, Religion and the Didactic Oratory of Henry McNeal Turner." In J. Adekunle (ed.), *Converging Identities: Blackness in the Modern African Diaspora*. Durham, NC: Carolina Academic Press.

Johnson, Sylvester. 2016. *The Myth of Ham in Nineteenth-Century American Christianity*. New York: Palgrave Macmillan.

King, Jr., Martin Luther. 1960. "Meet the Press." Retrieved from https://kinginstitute.stanford.edu/king-papers/documents/interview-meet-press

Kuhn, Clifford M., E. Joye, and E. Bernard West. 1990. *Living Atlanta: An Oral History of the City 1914–1948*. Athens, GA: University of Georgia Press.

Logan, R. W. 1954. *The Negro in American Life and Thought: The Nadir, 1877–1901*. United States: Dial Press.

NAACP. 1948. "Records of the National Association for the Advancement of Colored People." News release, December 2. Retrieved from https://findingaids.loc.gov/exist_collections/ead3pdf/mss/2008/ms008007.pdf

Owen, Hugh Carl. 1951. "The Rise of Negro Voting in Georgia: 1944–1950." Thesis, Emory University.

Payne, Charles M. 2007. *I've Got the Light of Freedom*. Berkeley, CA: University of California Press

Pyles, Charles Boykin. 1967. "Race and Ruralism in Georgia Elections, 1948–1966." Thesis, University of Georgia.

Rivers, Larry Eugene, and Canter Brown, Jr. 2001. *Laborers in the Vineyard of the Lord*. Gainesville, FL: University of Florida Press.

SRC. 1961. "Student Protest Movement: A Recapitulation, September 1961." Series XVI, Reel 220, no. 223. Bethesda, MD: University Publications of America.

Tolnay, S. E. and E. M. Beck. 1995. *A Festival of Violence: An Analysis of Southern Lynchings, 1882-1930*. Urbana, IL: University of Illinois Press.

Tuck, Stephen G. N. 1980. *Beyond Atlanta: The Struggle for Racial Equality in Georgia 1940-1980*. Athens, GA: The University of Georgia Press.

U.S. Census Bureau. 1943. "1940 Census of Population: Volume 4. Characteristics by Age. Marital Status, Relationship, Education, and Citizenship." Retrieved from www.census.gov/library/publications/1943/dec/population-vol-4.html (accessed on September 20, 2024).

Wilmore, Gayraud, 1972. *Black Religion and Black Radicalism*. New York: Doubleday.

Chapter 8

Force of Law

Resources in Derrida for Rethinking Policing

Karen Zoppa

> Law was not created with us in mind: it's not created for our safety; it's created to enforce colonialism; it's created to enforce capitalism.
>
> (Taylor 2021)

The current crisis in law enforcement is a crisis of faith, according to the critique of law/enforcement offered in Jacques Derrida's "Force of Law: The Mystical Foundations of Authority." His analysis of the filiation of law to enforcement argues that law is founded both in an inescapable violence and in an authority that is founded on nothing more than its credibility, that is to say, the faith granted to its inscriptions. In its current iteration in North America, the law and its enforcement is founded upon a theory of justice that violates the integrity of the other, of "otherness" as such, in privileging a fictional ideal person equal before a universalizable law. Such an ideal, rather than serving the cause of justice, undermines it by erasing difference and, thus, the particular situated singularity of those subject to the law and its enforcement. It supplies an ideal of the subject before the law that is ultimately unenforceable, since no such homogenous ideal person exists. Derrida offers a remedy for this problem at the theoretical heart of the current crisis by recalling a different iteration of justice, one that places "the other," which is to say "otherness" as the ubiquitous identity of each person, at its axis,[1] while insisting that we take seriously the "mystical foundations" of our public institutions, in order that we might displace these untenable fictions. To displace these fictions requires acknowledging the different logic always unfolding in our assumptions and institutions, that the latter may be justified and guided toward acts of justice that accommodate the other, as such, rather than negating otherness, as is the current practice.

---

1. The critique offered here assumes the dominance of "English Speaking Justice" in the global-capitalist world, a theory of justice founded in the liberal tradition of English Empiricism, especially John Locke, Thomas Hobbes, David Hume and more recently systematized in John Rawls's *A Theory of Justice*. For a concise summary and critique of this philosophical legacy and its influence on Rawls, see Grant (1985); for a more expansive summary and critique, see Habermas (1996). The following analysis depends on readings of the liberal enlightenment tradition that cannot be adequately defended here, but which aims to offer a coherent structural critique of the current crisis.

Derrida's critique of law and force is part of his larger project, to demonstrate the instability of the traditional metaphysics of Being and its chain of filiations, particularly the binaries of Being/becoming; eternal/finite; absolute/contingent. The former in each pair supply the premises for the authority of our institutions, including the current inscription of the law. His readings repeatedly demonstrate the contradictions inherent in any paradigm or position, that is, those powers of composition which are always already dismantling the position. In disclosing this perpetual dialectic, Derrida enjoins our civilization to rethink its premises: to dismiss the untenable premises of the eternal and absolute in order to rethink those positions worth nurturing from this inheritance. In this particular case, his analysis reveals the error of predicating absolute universalizable moral positions destined for an abstract ideal subject, a subject constructed in the image of its makers—white male property owners—at the exclusion of the multi-valent "others." To rethink the foundation of the law is to rethink the police as enforcers of such law: what role, if any, will police play in a law that is written for others as such, a law that is responsive to otherness, and by implication, context? What is clear is that if we are charged with changing the law because it is no longer viable, we inevitably change policing. In other words, the crisis in policing is a symptom of a bigger crisis, the crisis in the authority of the law as such.

The current iteration of justice at stake in this crisis is entangled with the "globalatinized capitalism" that permeates our contemporary world. Derrida has argued that contemporary capitalism is itself an iteration of "religion," founded on those same two forces that are at play in "religion," faith and knowledge.[2] The faith and knowledge that are the sources for religion and capitalism also underwrite the law and, by extension, its enforcement. The effect is that any decision about policing is necessarily a decision about law, and the capitalist states the law supports. Derrida argues that the "mystical foundation for authority" for both law/enforcement and religion (including capitalism) is the originary faith which enables all human relationships (Derrida 2002a, 72). This faith is, on the one hand, the necessary condition for any justice to come; while, on the other hand, it also enables the law and its enforcement, for good or evil. Such a play of faith raises questions that both limit and liberate possible responses to this crisis.

The crisis facing nations that inherit colonialism and its offspring, capitalism, demands decisive change in our current conception of policing and law. The murder of George Floyd by a Minneapolis police officer ignited broad protest against racialized police violence and a demand for justice. This violence, which Derrida categorizes as the most visible operation of violence in law/enforcement

---

2. See Derrida (2002, 1995) for Derrida's analysis of religion as an iteration of capitalism in texts by Kant, Hegel, Kierkegaard and Bergson, and its tropes of authority, responsibility, sacrifice in a reading of Jan Patocka, Heidegger and Kierkegaard. The play of faith and knowledge in founding and reproducing religion is mirrored in the founding and reproduction of law: faith is the performance that maintains the credibility and authority of knowledge: an attempt to indemnify and keep unscathed, static, absolute, those things faith agrees to believe, usually those metaphysical and moral claims of the tradition. This chapter does not address the play of "knowledge" in the construction of law and order due to limitations of length.

(Derrida quoted in Campos-Salvaterra 2019, 157), has led to a range of responses among both activists and scholars of criminology, from the demand for the outright abolition of police, as such, to the more pragmatic defunding police movement,[3] which are reviewed briefly here.

Defund, Abolish, Revolt

The defunding movement has many iterations, most focusing on harm reduction in the wake of ubiquitous racialized police violence. Koziarski and Huey observe that "sectors of this movement call for the removal of the police from social issues through divestment in the police and greater investment in preventative social services" (Koziarski and Huey 2021, 12), which must not be allowed to absolve police from responsibility for their unjust and unlawful enforcement practices. They promote "evidence-based policing" as "a means to identify police practices that are effective, ineffective, or even harmful, but such research can be used to hold the police accountable for ineffective efforts and to inform budgets and resourcing needs" (ibid.). At the same time, they conclude that at best, while such adjustments to police responsibility and protocols may result in some harm reduction, it does not address the structures that underwrite contemporary law and enforcement.

At the other end of the spectrum, abolitionist theorists analyze the crisis in policing within the context of a critique of capitalism and colonialism. As McDowell and Fernandez note, there exists a range of positions within the abolitionist camp, especially among criminologists, from liberal to radical. They cite at least five strategies that result from a liberal abolitionist perspective, including: "decarceration (away from prison), diversion (away from the institution), decategorization (away from offender typologies), delegalization (away from the state) and deprofessionalization (away from the expert)" (McDowell and Fernandez 2018, 378).

McDowell and Fernandez critique these strategies as deficient because they leave the legal system itself in place, thereby neglecting the deep structures that uphold the current practices, a view supported in Derrida. Supporting the position of radical abolition, they observe that some "argue that to even speak of "police brutality" is itself an oxymoron; a misidentification of the problem (act versus structure) that runs the risk of entrenching rather than disrupting the very violence activists seek to eliminate" (ibid., 380). They promise instead to support a radical program:

---

3. See McDowell and Fernandez (2018) for a comprehensive account of abolition theory in scholarship and activism; Joseph-Salisbury et al. (2021) for a review of racialized police bias, consequences and activism in the United Kingdom; and Koziarski and Huey (2021), which argues for the more pragmatic defunding position, with particular attention to the Canadian context.

(1) aiming directly at the police as an institution; (2) dismantling the racial-capitalist order; (3) adopting uncompromising positions that resist liberal attempts at co-optation, incorporation, and/or reconciliation; and (4) creating alternative democratic spaces that directly challenge the legitimacy of the police.
(McDowell and Fernandez 2018, 388)

In other words, they argue that nothing short of a revolutionary turn away from capitalism and its colonial inheritance can eliminate the harms of the contemporary order.

British scholar Joseph-Salisbury and colleagues adopt a similar position:

> we take seriously demands to first defund and later abolish the police. By defunding, we refer to the systematic redirection of funding (and power) away from the police, and instead towards community and social support mechanism. By abolition, we refer to the prospect of first imagining and then creating futures beyond policing.
> (Joseph-Salisbury et al. 2021, 2)

This position offers a horizon for the abolitionist movement, located in an undefined but improved future. They share Angela Davis's definition of abolition, one that is "not "a negative process of tearing down" but rather, one of "re-imagining institutions, ideas, and strategies, and creating new institutions" (ibid., 8). However, abolition as a "re-imagining" of responses to harms and inequality as well as an "enacting of new forms of justice" begs the question: what do we mean by justice? What is the relation of justice to law and its enforcement? What kind of justice can we imagine apart from law?

Critics of these various reform positions agree that the crisis in policing is embedded in a larger civilizational crisis, one that must be critiqued structurally. Such critiques of our current inscriptions of justice, law and enforcement draws our thinking toward Derrida, who engages them in "Force of Law: The Mystical Foundations of Authority" (Derrida 2002b). Within the recent European tradition, he reads, on the one hand, a distinction between law and justice and, on the other hand, their reciprocal entanglement. He reflects on the ways that the law, always founded in violence, necessitates enforcement. I want to focus on Derrida's reading of "force" "law," and "justice" in order to outline some limits and possibilities for decision in this crisis of policing.

Justice, Not Fairness

"Force of Law," from a colloquium entitled "Deconstruction and the Possibility of Justice" at the Cardozo Law School,[4] observes that *deconstruction* only appears to

---

4. Derrida practices philosophy by responding to texts, according to the logic of deconstruction. As he formulates it in *Dissemination*: "A text is not a text unless it hides from the first comer, from the first glance, the law of its composition and the rules of its game. A text remains, moreover, forever imperceptible. Its laws and rules are not, however, harbored in the inaccessibility of a secret; it is simply that they can never be booked, in the present, into anything that could

not address justice: "what one currently calls deconstruction, while seeming not to "address" the problem of justice, has done nothing else while unable to do so directly but only in an oblique fashion" (Derrida 2002b, 237). Such obliqueness is a corollary of one of his main observations, that justice is not necessarily the law. In Part I of "Force of Law," Derrida makes explicit

> a difficult and unstable distinction between justice and law, between justice (infinite, incalculable, rebellious to rule and foreign to symmetry, heterogenous and heterotropic) on the one hand and, on the other, the exercise of justice as law, legitimacy, or legality, a stabilizable, statutory and calculable apparatus [*dispotif*], a system of regulated and coded prescriptions.
>
> (Derrida 2002b, 250)

He presents a concept of justice that contrasts the prevailing classic liberal view of justice, founded in the tradition of the social contract, which assumes the capacity of the subject to calculate their own self-interest in seeking fairness.[5] The liberal account of justice is, in part, a source of the current crisis in law enforcement, as it privileges the ideal subject, equal before a universalizable law. In doing so, it violates the concept of the integrity of the other, any other, as such, by submitting to the identity logic that demands the other be made the same, treated the same. This account of justice seems to have lost the credibility of its "mystical foundation of authority" for those who have been treated unjustly in its name and in their otherness. It also has lost credibility among its enforcers who, when presented with the dissonance between the ideal of the current law and the actuality of those many singularities subject to the law, seem to ignore the law as such.

In remedy, Derrida proposes a theory of justice that resonates more with the Judaic figure of *zedek* (justice, charity, equity), the equity that exceeds calculation, than with the classic liberal view. Citing Levinas, he evokes justice as "an infinite right" whose basis is not the abstract category of humanity but rather "the other," where "*equité* is not equality, calculated proportion, equitable distribution or distributive justice, but rather, absolute dissymmetry" (Derrida 2002b). This "idea of justice" which demands singular decision is at the same time infinite

---

rigorously be called a perception" (Derrida 1981, 10).

Such texts exemplify the process Derrida names deconstruction, in which they are, "constantly composing with the forces that tend to annihilate it" (quoted in Kamuf 2006, 878). In other words, a text is always in the process of displacing and contaminating itself, and it defies any attempts at linear summary and analysis. Instead, one engages in a performance of reading the text through one of its "threads," in order to expose its composition and displacement. The result of Derrida's careful readings requires a reader of Derrida to follow a similar practice. Because deconstruction is a process operating independent of the reader, and Derrida's readings thus do not produce summative analysis, I cannot summarize "Force of Law." However, I can pull the threads embedded in the title that inhabit a philosophical analysis of authority and justice, one that is instructive for the response to the policing crisis and the aporia or undecidability at its center.

5. The most vivid example of this is John Rawls, *A Theory of Justice*, the most recent iteration of the social contract theory of justice.

and irreducible, because it is owed to the *singular other*, a demand for "the gift without exchange, without circulation, without recognition or gratitude" (ibid., 254). Derrida recognizes this account of justice as a kind of "madness," and perhaps "mysticism," not amicable to a regulatory idea of law, a justice which constantly demands that the one who must decide stands at the edge of the precipice. However, such an idea of justice is welcome as it serves the "classical emancipatory ideal" which needs to be re-thought and re-elaborated in the face of the problematic analyzed here (ibid., 258).

Justice, according to this tradition, is always directed to the other, the other who is always to come, the other who disrupts both self-identity and the desire to make the other the same. To do justice is to respond to the infinite appeal of the other whose right, according to Levinas, is "practically an infinite right" (Levinas quoted in Derrida 2002b, 250). Of this justice, Derrida asserts

> Law is not justice. Law is the element of calculation, and it is just that there be law, but justice is incalculable, it demands that one calculate with the incalculable; and aporetic experiences are the experiences, as improbable as they are sometimes necessary, of justice, that is to say of moments in which the *decision* between just and unjust is never insured by a rule.
>
> (Derrida 2002b, 244)

The aporetic moment of justice operates in a space where no transgression is possible, outside the originary violence of the law. At the same time, justice is addressed in the singular, the idiomatic. The problem is "how to reconcile the act of justice that must always concern singularity, individuals, groups, irreplaceable existences, the other or myself as other, in a unique situation, with rule, norm, value or the imperative of justice that necessarily have a general form, even if this generality prescribes a singular application in each case?" (Derrida 2002b, 245). How to "write" a law that can name what is "acceptable"—by naming what is not acceptable—at the same time that these categories are always iterating according to the time/space/ singularity of the social context? This question weighs upon us, always, but here is limited to the North American social contract context of English speaking law.

Derrida has Kantian ethics in mind when he addresses the problem of the singularity of decision in the context of a putative universalization of the law. "One must know that this justice always addresses itself to singularity, to the singularity of the other, despite or even because it pretends to a universality" (Derrida 2002b, 246). Can one calculate a maxim for a singular situation that will be meaningful in all other like situations? Clearly impossible, since the same situation is always already different, "crossed by historicity," "opened to what is Other," in the very "irreducible alterity of time" (Campos-Salvaterra 2019, 159) and as such our maxim will of necessity be inflected and iterated.

By contrast, the prevailing account of justice-as-fairness undoes the movement of differentiating the other by insisting on treating each subject as an ideal person, equal before the law, a law which prescribes universalizable aims for singular situations.⁶ Thus, the appeal of the singular other—which operates at the heart of the Judaic account of justice—is neutralized by a law founded on the classic liberal account of justice, which posits the fiction of equality of persons before the law and seeks a universalizable decision. In such a situation, the singular appeal of the other cannot be addressed by the machinery of law underwritten by classic liberal account of justice. This dissonance demands redress: another inscription of law, informed by a different account of the person is required. That said, whatever version of justice is authorized, justice is distinct from law, and yet law must act in its name. This entanglement introduces the following anomaly: law necessarily requires enforcement; moreover, the law is founded in an originary violence: thus, if the law is founded in force, and operates with force, is justice not also implicated in this violence? Is it still just?

Justice Appeals to Violence

Citing Kant, in a discussion of the English phrase, "to enforce the law," Derrida notes that it "reminds us that if justice is not necessarily the law [*le droit ou le loi*], it cannot become justice legitimately or *de jure* [*de droit ou en droit*] except by holding [*detenir*] force or rather by appealing to force from its first moment, from its first word" (Derrida 2002b, 238). This is because at the beginning of justice "there will have been speech, language, *logos, and* "this is not necessarily in contradiction with another *incipit*, which would say, "in the beginning there will have been force" (ibid.). Here, Derrida invokes another guiding figure to his thought, the exercise of force in language that he calls *différance*. Derrida's reading of force as "violence" locates it wherever there is a violation of the indemnified. In its Latin etymology, the *Oxford English Dictionary* states that "violate" connotes "to disturb the sanctity of, profane, to treat without respect, to pollute, defile, to spoil, sully, to treat with violence, to outrage, to dishonour, to ravish, to transgress against, infringe, to injure." The derivative noun, "violence" also suggests in use "to restrict, constrain, or alter unnaturally; to distort the meaning of." All of these operate in Derrida's reflections on violence and span a range of contexts, from the abstract and linguistic to the immanent and visceral. In *arche*-writing, his term for the original ruling principle involved in the written as such, we see in the very first grapheme the "violation" of spoken meaning, of the "proper" meaning, since writing—in the first instance—always already awaits a later reader, a different context, another meaning. Thus, the originary meaning is transgressed, disturbed, altered. Hence, the violence of *arche*-writing is the violence of disruption. Derrida argues in "Signature, Event, Context":

---

6. It must be acknowledged that this liberal "person equal before the law" who is judged under "the veil of ignorance" is itself a kind of legal fiction which masks the privileging of those who govern and write the law: in North America, generally powerful male landowners of European descent. The law as such does not have the "other," any other—whether non-European, non-male, disenfranchised or dispossessed—in mind when it writes "universalizable" laws; and such an aim is in itself doomed—according to the critique of "presence"—because of the heteronomic logic of *différance*.

This structural possibility of being severed from its referent or signified (and therefore from communication and its context) seems to me to make of every mark, even if oral, a grapheme in general, that is, as we have seen, the non-present remaining of a differential mark cut off from its alleged "production" or origin. And I will extend this law even to all "experience" in general, if it is granted that there is no experience of pure presence, but only chains of differential marks.

(Derrida 1982, 318)

These chains of differential marks are themselves a kind of violence—in their performance of severing the word, the name, the *meaning* from its original context of time and space—and are implicated in every decision, decision itself a severing. In extending it "even to all 'experience' in general," it follows that this law, at work in all our relationships, is also at work in the production and reproduction of law. As Valeria Campos-Salvaterra has observed:

> If violence is originary, as Derrida concludes, then any attempt to criticize it must always be based on the arche-violence of meaning, with the consequence that any planned escape from violence and hence a pure non-violence is simply not possible. Derrida's point is that, rather than thinking in terms of a violence/non-violence dichotomy, we must recognize that violence lies at the "foundation" of all meaning but takes on different configurations. There is then an "economy of violence" in which violence is understood in terms of differential and multiple becomings rather than static and binary categories and oppositions.
>
> (Campos-Salvaterra 2019, 148)

These "different configurations" range from the violation of meaning in language production—the violence that disrupts language from its destination as naming presence toward its mode of re-presentation—to the violence of law breaking and its counter-violent expiation by its enforcers, the police. Campos-Salvaterra observes a three-part schema: originary or arche-violence, tied to language; moral violence, tied to prohibition and its cycle of founding and preserving law; and empirical violence, the "most visible" violence which acts as a counter-violence against moral violence (ibid.).

The second level, moral violence is "less visible but has been treated by the critical tradition—especially Walter Benjamin—as an aggressive gesture that violently cuts right from wrong, good from evil, with no other foundation than the force of the cutting itself," which Derrida calls a "tautological performance" (Derrida 2002b, 238).[7] This "moral violence" at the origin of law is authorized simply in this original act of force of severing the permitted from the prohibited. Such severing, which is to say such discrimination, is the condition for the possibility of meaning, as well as for all identity, definition, difference, justice and injustice. Such severing is the means by which the other is identified as such, without which the

---

7. It is worth noting that the French word *fond, fondment*, which abound in the French version of this text, connote both "to found," as in a foundation for the object of discourse, as well as "to justify," to give an account of before one who decides. The pun is impossible to render in translation.

singularity of each other is not possible. But it can also act as the means by which the other is excluded, denied, and dispossessed of that "infinite right" to justice.

The Mystical Foundation of Authority

This is perhaps exemplified in the following examples. Derrida reads this entanglement of law and justice in two fragments from Pascal and Montaigne. Pascal declares, "Justice, Force—It is right that what is just should be followed; it is necessary that what is strongest should be followed" (quoted in Derrida 2002b, 238). Contrasting what is "just" with what is "Necessary," the former implies *a priori* that it must be followed and thus enforced, while the latter implies enforcement is a necessity. The fragment explicates this relationship between justice and force, observing "it is necessary then to combine justice and force; and for this end make what is just strong, or what is strong just" (ibid.). Pascal's problematic conclusion states that because "the necessity of force is implied, then, in the *juste* of *justesse*," it follows that "thus being unable to make what is just strong, we have made what is strong just" (ibid., 239), a classic displacement of one term by the other, of justice by force. Pascal then refers to "the mystical foundation of authority," quoting Montaigne, who wrote:

> Laws are now maintained in credit, not because they are just, but because they are laws. It is the mystical foundation of their authority; they have none other ... Whosoever obeyeth them because they are just, obeyes them not justly the way as he ought.
>
> (Derrida 2002b, 239–240)

The distinction between law and justice proceeding from Montaigne's quotation asserts that law, in and of itself, is not necessarily just: laws are obeyed simply because they have authority. This authority is located in the word *credit*: "The authority of the laws rests only on the credit that is granted them" (ibid., 240). It is here that we find an intersection between the force of law and religion: both originate from two sources: faith—here, the credit one grants laws, beyond reason, beyond ontology; and knowledge—those commitments that are held unscathed, protected, indemnified and holy.[8]

---

[8]. Derrida unfolds this analysis of religion most explicitly in "Faith and Knowledge: The Two Sources of Religion at the Limit of Reason Alone." In it, he argues that what we call "religion" is the particular iteration of response to the Other—through faith and through knowledge (the indemnification of the Other's appeal)—unique to the "globalatinized" world of today: the colonial capitalist offspring of Imperial Rome. The "law" as such in this current context, is inherited from Judaism and Hellenism, filtered through Imperial Rome and begotten in the currents of the contemporary hegemony of global capitalism through the mechanisms of colonialism. As such, "religion" in some ways can only refer to Christianity's many iterations, but has been imposed through colonialism on the cultures of non-Europeans. Derrida's observations are not unique—they are affirmed in Masuzawa and Fitzgerald, among others. However, in "Faith and Knowledge," he locates this analysis in the philosophical texts of the Enlightenment and early twentieth century—especially Kant, Hegel, Bergson, and Heidegger.

Derrida finds in Pascal's thought "a desedimentation of the superstructures of law that both hide and reflect the economic and political interests of the dominant forces of society" (Derrida 2002b, 241). Even more compelling are the deep structures revealed in this play of force and law, which indicate "a performative force, that is to say always an interpretive force and a call to faith" (ibid.). How so? In the same way that one is gathered and bound to the holy and sacred, made *religious* (Derrida 2002a, 70–72), by promising to believe the truth that the other has promised to tell, by granting the other and their story credit, *fiabilité*, a promise to believe: faith.

The faith which founds both law and religion, and which provides the legitimacy for their enforcement, is itself grounded in the originary violence of language: in the founding operation by which it establishes *definitions,* and so violates the integrity of speech itself. Violence is also operating in the founding of law, which proceeds from language, the *logos,* and in the setting of its bounds. This is not necessarily unjust, as this operation, which

> amounts to founding, inaugurating, justifying law, *to making law*, would consist of a *coup de force*, of a performative and therefore interpretive violence that in itself is neither just nor unjust and that no justice and no earlier and previously founding law, no pre-existing foundation could, by definition, guarantee or contradict or invalidate.
>
> (Derrida 2002b, 241)

This is because within the founding of law, the origin of its authority rests on nothing but itself, on its *fiabilité*, on that credit which we agree to grant it. This is the mystical foundation of authority: it is founded on faith, not reason, even if reasons can be shown for that faith. As he observes in "Faith and Knowledge," the faith at issue not only operates as a source of religion, but also in the fiduciary and legal. It is an elementary act of faith, the

> irreducible "faith," that of the "social bond" or of a "sworn faith," of a testimony ("I promise to tell you the truth beyond all proof and all theoretical demonstration, believe me, etc."), that is of a performative of promising at work even in lying or perjury and without which no address to the other would be possible.
>
> (Derrida 2002a, 80–81)

The content of this reciprocal promising, to tell the truth, to believe what is told, is the fundamental action that enables all of our relations and institutions, and underwrites both the figure of religion and the figure of law. It is however, precisely that, a performative, and its *fiabilité* is itself founded in the experience of such promising. Paradoxically, this act of faith that is the source of both law and religion is also that which opens it to justice. Of the laws credited by faith, Derrida notes that "this is not to say they are themselves unjust, in the sense of 'illegal' or 'illegitimate.' They are neither legal nor illegal in their founding moment" (Derrida 2002b, 242). He continues: "They exceed the opposition between founded or unfounded, or between any foundationalism or anti-foundationalism," because the terms of their authority reside only in the credit afforded them by us (ibid.).

The terms of this faith are apophatic—hidden, unspoken, unseen, uninterpretable, undecidable. In short, mystical.[9] The credit we afford law is thus entirely performative and relational, and subject to iteration, a fact displaced by the universalizable ends of the classic liberal theory of justice, but served by Derrida's proposed iteration of justice.

The crisis emerging from police violence is itself a symptom of a more structural crisis, the cessation of faith in the authority of the law as it is currently inscribed. The justice that authorizes the law has lost credibility, in part because it displaces the singularity of the other with an unenforceable ideal. It also no longer operates effectively among those who must enforce its laws. The police as an institution is bound to the law: no law without enforcement, and police enforce the law within the register of violence. But the current crisis reflects more than simply the inevitable play of police/enforcement: in the erosion of faith in the authority of the law and the justice that underwrites it, the police now arrogate that authority to themselves, and respond ad hoc to the appeal of the other.

Force of Justice

The elimination of violence from law/enforcement is not possible, according to this genealogy. The law as inscription originates in the originary violence of language, which enables all other violences. However, violence operates in degrees and in different contexts, as we have seen, founding both the possibility of meaning and identity while it can also serve to oppress.

Reading Benjamin's *Zur Kritik der Gewalt*[10] in Part II, Derrida observes that the violence that founds the law and the violence that preserves the law is indistinguishable. Although Benjamin tries to maintain a rigorous distinction between the founding violence of states with the preserving violence of states, the two violences "contaminate" each other and exchange places in a perpetual economy. The ubiquity of this violence expresses itself most forcefully in what Benjamin argues is the failure of modern democracies, wherein the police "are the state,"

> no longer content to enforce the law and thus preserve it: the police invent the law, publish ordinances and intervene whenever the legal situation is unclear to guarantee security—which is to say, these days, nearly all the time. The police are the force of law [loi], they have force of law, the power of the law. The police are ignoble because in their authority, "the separation law founding violence and law preserving violence is suspended." ... The possibility—which is also to say the

---

9. "Mystical" from the Greek *muein*, to close the eyes and lips, thus *mustikos*, an initiate. The "foundation" of mysticism connotes both that which exceeds articulation, the ineffable, non-rational and at the same time, the *religious*—one bound to the secret, to not revealing what is said and done. See Liddell, Scott, and Jones (1996). Derrida observes this in "Force of Law" (Derrida 2002b, 269).

10. First published in 1921. See Derrida (2002b, 263, note 26) for a full bibliographical entry. The German *gewalt* connotes "force," but in a number of registers, including the legal force or authority of the state as well as moral and empirical violence.

ineluctable necessity of the modern police force, ruins, in sum—one could say deconstructs—the distinction between these two kinds of violence that nevertheless structures the discourse that Benjamin calls a new critique of violence.
(Derrida 2002b, 277)

Derrida, in 1992, is responding to the 1921 Benjamin text with observations that remain disturbingly fresh for the public imagination today. The police "arrogate the law" in their function as enforcement for the law, perform the violence necessary to preserve the violence that is the law, but a violence in a register that, as we have recently witnessed, produces "evil," in its use of lethal force. Instead of enforcing the law, they make the law, arrogating the power of the legislative to their executive function, and worst of all, "the police violence of democracies denies its own principle, making laws surreptitiously, clandestinely," with the result that "there is not yet any democracy worthy of its name" (ibid.), only fallen states in which the enforcement now legislates the law. Benjamin ends his text with an exhortation:

> But one must reject [Verwerflich aber] all mythical violence, the violence that founds the law, which one may call governing [schaltende] violence. One must also reject [Verwerflich auch] the violence that preserves law, the governed violence [die verwalteteGewalt] in the service of the governing.
> (Benjamin quoted in Derrida 2002b, 292)

Derrida is not endorsing this view, but he is interested in showing how Benjamin's critique of violence deconstructs itself in the movement of his discourse. He finds powerful resources in Benjamin for thinking about law and force, even though ultimately, Derrida judges that he is too "archeo-eschatological" for his taste (Derrida 2002b, 298). Still, he hovers over the analysis of what Benjamin calls "something rotten in law" (ibid., 273), the "governed violence in the service of the governing," a condition that is increasingly familiar in many precincts today. The injunction in Benjamin that moves Derrida is how to respond to the lessons to be drawn from evil—that is to say, lethal force—"*from all the exterminations of history:*"

> we must think, know, represent for ourselves, formalize, judge the possible complicity among all these discourses and the worst (here, the "final solution"). In my view, this defines a task and a responsibility the theme of which I have not been able to read in either Benjaminian "destruction" or Heideggerian "Destruktion."
> (Derrida 2002b, 298)

This is Derrida's injunction to us, in this crisis, to respond to "this task and responsibility," to ultimately judge the complicity among all these "exterminations of history" that violate the integrity of singular lives, black lives, indigenous lives, "other" lives, violations that call for justice. The analysis of the violence that structures the force of law is a step in this response.

Frazer and Hutchings note that the ubiquity of Derrida's schemes of violence—originary, moral, and empirical—"are to some extent ameliorated by the second kind of distinction he draws: an evaluative distinction between better and worse, greater and lesser violence. Derrida insists that 'true violence' is a breach of integrity" (Frazer and Hutchings 2011, 11). These degrees of violence suggest a just response to the current crisis in law enforcement: to respond by taking responsibility. As they observe, while Derrida is never in favor of violence, he demands from everyone an avowal of this violence, an accepting of responsibility for our crediting that which is founded in the originary violence of language:

> he affirms his commitment to understanding violence as the violation of integrity, and his view that law requires such a violation. And so too does any concrete articulation of the aspiration to justice, since any such articulation necessarily does violence to integrity, reducing the unique and singular to other terms. In this context, what becomes important is not the (necessarily doomed) quest for a non-violent politics but refusing to disavow one's own violence and, more generally, not denying the risks of violence inherent in political action.
> (Frazer and Hutchings 2011, 11–12)

They show that for Derrida, an elimination of violence is not possible, but taking responsibility for it, avowing it, and responding to the appeal of the other, is part of the performance of justice, as such. Likewise, Campos-Salvaterra proposes that by reading how violence deconstructs itself at the origin of language as well as law/enforcement, we have a unique conceptual tool with which to approach "questions of violence:"

> If violence is a condition of possibility, one must also accept that it is also a condition of the impossibility of meaning, classification, and naming in general. This means that the same violence that produces meaning is that which interrupts that production. The production of meaning is then always crossed by historicity and, thus, opened to what is Other, to the irreducible alterity of time. Ultimately, the non-static, historic, and dynamic way of understanding violence makes it impossible to engage in a classic critique. Instead, violence has to be economized: for Derrida, the least violence must always be chosen—without a repeatable formula and regarding every different context as unique.
> (Campos-Salvaterra 2019, 159)

Within the economy of violence, the axiom, "the least violence must always be chosen—without a repeatable formula and regarding every different context as unique" might operate in the service of that iteration of justice which must address the singularity of the other.

Derrida's text suggests that the problem with policing is not simply the structure of the historic context of colonial capitalism and its abuses of the other, nor the embedded systems of racialized discrimination and patriarchal privileging, although these are implicated as well. His reading of violence shows that this crisis proceeds in part from the very structure of language—in its competing desires to first name and then represent—as well as the institution of law/enforcement. This analysis points out to those who would in varying degrees defund the police that we will still contend with the originary violence of the law, which remains in need of enforcement. As his reading of Benjamin reveals, the two violences—originary and preservative—are merely one inevitable circulating economy. This text also points out to the abolitionists that even if we abolish the police, the force of law, founded in the originary violence of language, remains. To abolish the police entails that we abolish the law which it enforces. Can we structure a society without law? Can we structure anything without language, itself founded in originary violence? What is the shape of "law" that can anticipate and welcome the other as its axiom? Perhaps the salient lesson here is that whatever decision is taken, it can only hope to achieve lesser degrees, non-evil degrees, of violence, never the elimination of violence, as such.

On the other hand, the "task and responsibility" Derrida enjoins us to undertake demands response. He invites us to a reciprocal revolution: to aim at a lesser violence, as well as to consider a theory of justice that privileges the appeal of the other. To lessen violence is a decision that might still cultivate the other theory of justice: one that affirms the response to the infinite appeal of the other, singular and non-universalizable. Benjamin, in his critique of violence, wanted to prove "that a non-violent elimination of conflicts is possible in the private world when it is ruled by the culture of the heart, cordial courtesy, sympathy, love of peace, trust, friendship" (Derrida 2002b, 284). Such a culture is ruled by an openness to the other which holds the infinite hope for justice in its custody. But can such a "private culture of the heart" reach into the conflicts of the public domain?

It may take a revolution. It may take another theory of justice: "infinite, incalculable, rebellious to rule and foreign to symmetry, heterogenous and heterotropic." It may be that the task and responsibility of evaluating and judging the complicity in all the recent texts of evil in our world—lethal racialized violence, gendered violence—will inform a response to the other, can allow the other—who is always to come (*l'avenir*)—to guide the prescriptions of law, and support "a universalizable culture of singularities."

Karen Zoppa earned her PhD from the Department of Religion at the University of Manitoba. Her research focuses on Critical Theory of Religion in relation to contemporary philosophy and literature. She teaches Humanities at the University of Winnipeg.

References

Campos-Salvaterra, Valeria. 2019. "The Original Polemos." In Gavin Rae and Emma Ingala (eds.), *Meanings of Violence: From Critical Theory to Biopolitics*, 148–166. Abingdon: Routledge.

Derrida, Jacques. "Faith and Knowledge. The Two Sources of Religion at the Limit of Reason Alone." In Gil Andijar (ed.), *Acts of Religion* . New York: Routledge, 2002.

Derrida, Jacques. "Force of Law: The Mystical Foundation of Authority." In Gil Andijar (ed.), *Acts of Religion* . New York: Routledge, 2002.

Derrida, Jacques. 1982. "Signature Event Context." In Jacques Derrida, *Margins of Philosophy*, trans. Alan Bass, 309–330. Chicago, IL: University of Chicago Press.

Frazer, Elizabeth and Kimberly Hutchings. 2011. "Avowing Violence: Foucault and Derrida on Politics, Discourse and Meaning." *Philosophy and Social Criticism*, 37(1): 3–23.

Grant, George Parkin. 1985. *English Speaking Justice*. Toronto: House of Anansi Press.

Habermas, Jurgen. 1996. *Between Facts and Norms. Contributions to a Discourse Theory of Law and Democracy*. Cambridge, MA: MIT Press.

Joseph-Salisbury, Remi, Laura J. Connelly, and Peninah Wangari-Jones. 2021. "'The U.K. Is Not Innocent': Black Lives Matter, Policing and Abolition in the U.K." *Equality, Diversity and Inclusion*, 40(1): 21–28. https://doi.org/10.1108/EDI-06-2020-0170

Kamuf, Peggy. 2006. "Composition Displacement." *MLN*, 121(4): 872–892.

Koziarski, Jacek, and Laura Huey. 2021. "#Defund or #Re-Fund? Re-examining Bayleys Blueprint for Police Reform." *International Journal of Comparative and Applied Criminal Justice*, 45(3): 269–284.

Liddell, Henry George, Robert Scott, and Henry Stuart Jones. 1996. *Greek–English Lexicon*, 8th edition. Oxford: Clarendon Press.

McDowell, Meghan G., and Luis A. Fernandez. 2018. "'Disband, Disempower and Disarm': Amplifying the Theory and Practice of Police Abolition." *Critical Criminology*, 26: 379–391.

Taylor, Ella. 2021. "Racism and Policing in Canada: What Is to Be Done?" Webinar, Critical Dialogues on Policing in Canada, University of Winnipeg, June 18. Retrieved from www.youtube.com/watch?v=kXksnPUxb5M&t=1s (accessed September 25, 2024).

Chapter 9

When Is a Crisis a "Turning Point"?

Andrew Durdin

Crisis is a rather congested term, which, in turn points to an equally congested conceptual intersection. One need only search Google News to find that "crisis" is attributed to a vast range of social and political issues. It refers to different sorts of tensions, transitions, possibilities, inequalities, misfortunes, etc., and tends to mark often disparate issues as of the utmost importance and in need of urgent attention. Yet, what's not clear is that if one were to distill how crisis is being used in all these instances, that it would add up to anything more than a general gloss that something consequential (and usually bad) is about to happen. Such a definition of crisis though—as simply denoting moments of consequence—does not do much to help untangle the various valences and usages of the term. Such moments, however defined, are ubiquitous in everyday life and present themselves at almost every level of society. One would need to add an extra layer of definitional precision to crisis to frame these sorts of moments in analytically interesting ways.

This is all to say, that such a heavily burdened term as crisis might have little to offer in terms of analytic purchase. Of course, there are ways around this problem. One solution would be the standard constructivist response to the difficulties of defining any capacious interpretative term—whether crisis, or religion, culture, identity, or whatever. That is, whatever crisis *is*, it is best characterized by a range of decentering predicates such as "multiple," "fragmented," "fluid," "contested," "negotiated," etc. Rather than define crisis in one way then, we ought to explore the various rhetorics of crisis deployed by differently situated groups and pay attention to the various contexts in which they do so. Another solution is to give up on crisis as a term of analysis altogether and either redistribute its various meanings into other more refined terms, that can get at more specific contexts, or reframe it as evidence of some larger social-scientific issue.

Both have their benefits and drawbacks that I won't dwell on here. What I suggest instead, and what I think the chapters in this section invite us to do, is to make efforts to internally nuance the term, to strive to create some self-consciously structured typology of crisis in order to make it a nimbler tool for social analysis. The idea of crisis as "turning point" is suggestive, in part, of how such a task might be undertaken. The chapters here have convinced me that at least one potentially useful way of clarifying crisis theoretically is in terms of scale. Specifically, the gradation of crisis as turning point suggests value in thinking at the level of structure, the macroscopical, and long-term trends rather than merely at the level of periodic tensions and upheavals, the microscopic, and the short term. Such an orientation would attempt to isolate and explain situations, events, and stimuli that would account for large consequential social changes, i.e., those impactful moments in history where things ceased being one way and fundamentally started being some other way, for better or for worse.

Another way to set this point into relief is to say that while the rhetoric of crisis inflects almost every social and political issue today and indeed reflects very real material and social hardships for differently situated people, many, if not most, crises are not turning points. If crisis is typically defined in terms of the opportunities they present, or as moments of decision-making, not all of them will be equally consequential. Some are wasted, opportunities lost, squandered, or perhaps the wrong decision is made—i.e., decisions that play right back into the hands of the status quo. Indeed, it is easy to get the impression that, these days, the more things seem to get thrown into crisis the more things come out the other side still pretty much the same. However, I suggest turning points are those rare revolutionary crises that lead to some shift in the *longue durée*, where one episteme gradually gives way to another, or when structural contradictions end up displacing one regime with a new one.

Admittedly, what counts as consequential or important—that is, the scale by which we measure impactful change—is a matter of perspective. There is no doubt that the COVID-19 pandemic or the 2008 financial crash had (and continues to have) unexpected and lingering effects on a wide range of social institutions and peoples. How these will continue to play out is anybody's guess, which is actually my point. Put simply, I suggest that the task of investigating crises as turning points is not profitably pursued by journalists, pundits, and critics of contemporary society and culture; that is, those who interrogate the present, or recent history, and make predictions about what will happen, or is likely to happen, in the future. Rather, the job of identifying and analyzing consequential change at a structural level requires distance and hindsight, dealing not in possibilities or opportunities, but in actualities and *faits accomplis* and inquiring how those came about and what their impact has been. In other words, theorizing crisis as turning point is a task for historians. Historiographic discourse's *raison d'etre* is standing back from things, but obviously never being completely detached from them, and drawing on different accounts in order to speak to a larger picture, to attempt a wider perspective, and to assess systemic issues and their significance. Such after the fact designations are not, to be sure, obvious. They are argued, debated, modified, and at times also rejected. However, those who study the past are arguably in a better position to examine and judge when a crisis is a turning point or just more of the same.

It is with these patchy (and inadequately elaborated) ideas in mind that I turn to the three chapters all of which are, in their own way, interested in identifying crisis and asking questions about the decisions, impacts, and legacies of the crises they discuss. Zoe Anthony's chapter seems to be asking similar questions about historiography to those I'm driving at, but with a particular skepticism about identifying the causes of a given crisis. On my reading, her analysis investigates various discursive claims about crisis as unprecedented and the conceptual accouterments that are packed into these. Playing Benjamin and Koselleck off each other is an interesting way to go about making this point. If Benjamin's rhetoric of expected-unexpected is a way for him to argue that the invocation of crisis is just another mode by which the powerful reproduce the status quo (thus, there are no real crises and things don't really change), then Koselleck wants to say something quite the opposite: societies change, crises play a role, and we can identify their causes. Anthony takes a sort of fallibilist position between these two thinkers: "[C]hange does occur, contra Benjamin, but how this change occurs is not entirely knowable, contra Koselleck." That is, we are entitled to say we know change occurs even if we cannot prove it through strictly empirical means. My question then is: how much can we know about the empirical causes of historical change? It's not "entirely" knowable, yes, but can we be more precise about what we can know? I press this point because to say something about the rhetorical claims different people make about crisis is indeed interesting, but it seems that part of making sense of these needs to be done over and against material and social factors, one of which is being able to identify historical cause and effect—or at least a range of circumstances or conditions. Finally, Anthony's idea of economizing of crisis seems promising and I hope she pursues this elsewhere.

Aaron M. Treadwell's chapter, a brief history of Nadir-era church burnings in Georgia, presents a dazzling array of data of what he terms "terrorism" against black Georgians and its relationship to black liberation theology. I think the Nadir of race relations in the United States could potentially be a really interesting period in which to think through different scales of crisis. As Treadwell very clearly lays out, the social torture endured by black Georgians during this time was thoroughly threatening, destabilizing, and marginalizing at all almost every level of existence. But was this a period of crisis as turning point? If one's everyday life is defined by social marginalization, is one then living in a period of crisis or simple stasis. Indeed, is the Nadir period just the status quo we situate between crisis points of post reconstruction and the nascent civil rights movement? All this is idle speculation by a non-specialist, but it does raise the issue of the importance of the historian in sifting evidence, coordinating events, and assessing how one period fits into larger contexts of historical continuity or discontinuity. Yet, if we think of crisis as so many points of opportunity that speckle any given social situation (rather than as a turning point), Treadwell's analysis of Nadir-era Georgians is nonetheless instructive. For Treadwell, it was black churches that offered solace and solutions for the impossible situation in which so many black Georgians found themselves. And it was on this score, that I would have liked to hear more about the precise relationship between the arsons Treadwell lays out in such detail and black liberation theology. The chapter begins with a general discussion but never circles back around. Specifically, I'd be interested to hear more about the category of "theological resistance," and what analytic work it does in the chapter. Undoubtedly pastors used their pulpit to provide encouragement and the energy to "fight on," but so have many pastors across Christian history. What is it about the kind of resistance preached and carried out by these individuals that is clarified by qualifying it as theological? As it stands, the chapter seems more about economic and political forms of resistance, especially surrounding voting rights. Indeed, several of the examples of arson seem to have been retaliation against local black initiatives pushing for voting rights rather than anything specifically theological.

Finally, there is Karen Zoppa's probing reading of Derrida on authority, violence, and religion. Zoppa argues that Derrida's notion of "crisis of faith" can help us make sense of the current law enforcement crisis. Despite Zoppa's admirable job of reading and synthesizing some of Derrida's thoughts into a manageable framework that she applies creatively to the concrete situation of police violence, I remain skeptical that Derrida helps us understand or concoct solutions to police violence. Let me say why. To begin with, in terms of my own sensibilities (political, analytic, etc.), I very much favor an approach that identifies underlying exploitative structures of social problems and aims to eliminate them. For instance, I don't think race- or gender-based economic disparities will go away if we just have more people of color or women working for Goldman Sachs. Making sure we have an equal number of white bankers as we do black bankers, or male bankers as we do female bankers will not fix the fact that Goldman Sachs is indicative of a financialized banking system, an enduring economic structure, that summarily screws more folks of color and women than it promotes. All to say, I have no issue with structural abolition. However, there is a point at which taking aim at the "deep structures" becomes a fool's errand if they are imagined as too deep and too engrained to be abolished or eliminated. And this is my problem with Derrida's "Force of Law": he creates a series of homologies to track violence as a violation of the indemnified all the way back to language itself, whereby language and writing become themselves acts of violence. Now set as critique of presence and the Western metaphysical tradition of philosophy these have provided fruitful insights, but if our goal is to get police to stop beating the shit out of people, Derrida's insights hold little practical utility. By placing violence at such a primordial level, it becomes not a question of eliminating violence but rather haggling over just how much violence is acceptable. To be sure, I am not suggesting that Derrida's economizing of violence is the only thing standing between the society we have now and realizing some pacificist utopia, rather I am dubious of the analytic and more importantly the political implications of making violence foundational to human sociability.

Zoppa's chapter begins with the idea of structure and police violence as structural, but on the other end of her Derrida reading it becomes much less clear what is to be done about the crisis of police violence. Again, I think this is because Derrida has tied us in a philosophical knot that precludes eliminating the root causes of particular violent structures. It sounds like the best that we can do is by way of "taking responsibility for it, avowing it, and responding to the appeal of the other." Or to put it a different way: if Derrida's appeal to an infinite, incalculable idea of justice is couched in aspects of the Jewish tradition, the idea of challenging police violence simply by taking responsibility sounds thoroughly Christian. On my reading, this view suggests that in order to combat police violence—especially in its racist application—one must prioritize feeling the contrition for one's own racial sins, confess them, and hope for some kind of forgiveness. Now, don't get me wrong, understanding the way one might be complicit in reinforcing unequal social structures on an everyday, casual level is important and it's important to come to grips with things like "privilege." That's not really what I'm talking about here. What I have in mind is the posturing of so many New York Times-reading white liberals who will trip over themselves for, as one social scientist puts it, the "Protestant rush of professing their intrinsic racial sinfulness, since to do so leads to a sense of absolution and not having to do much else." In the meantime, the structures of police violence remain untouched (Reed 2017).

A final point: I disagree with Zoppa on just what the nature of the crisis of law enforcement is. The crisis as I see it is not that police have shifted from law enforcers to becoming a law in and of themselves. Rather the police are doing what they've always done in the capitalist system that created them—protecting the private property rights of the ruling class. This is what modern police forces were created to do. In fact, the function of the police is part and parcel with much of the larger state bureaucratic edifice we've concocted over the last century, also designed to reinforce various exclusive claims to land. Thus, to quote the late, great David Graeber: "Police are bureaucrats with weapons" (Graeber 2015, 73). Those most likely to lack exclusive property claims, especially in the United States, have been non-white people and for this, and other reasons, they have always been disproportionately the target of police violence. This is to say that the crisis in law enforcement may not be the kind of crisis Zoppa thinks it is. The crisis, as I see it, is that the affluent middle class have become horrified by the usual means in which the police have traditionally protected and ensured their class status and interests. From time to time, the middle class has remembered that police beat up poor people (disproportionately black people) and in these moments they usually become livid like they've just learned about it for the first time before drifting on to other matters. The intense outcry over the murders of George Floyd and Breonna Taylor (two of many victims) has been particularly encouraging, and indeed in one sense it is a crisis, a moment of decision and opportunity. Whether it is a turning point remains to be seen.

Andrew Durdin is assistant professor in the Department of Religion at Florida State University. His work focuses on critical approaches to the study of religion with an emphasis on the Roman imperial period, the modern historiography of ancient religions, and magic and religion in the ancient and modern world.

References

Graeber, David. 2015. *Utopia of Rule: On Technology, Stupidity, and the Secret Joys of Bureaucracy.* London: Melville House.
Reed, Adolph. 2017. "Monumental Rubbish: With the Statues Torn Down, What Next for New Orleans?" Retrieved from www.commondreams.org/views/2017/06/25/monumental-rubbish-statues-torn-down-what-next-new-orleans

Part III

Lexicon

Crisis as Method in the Study of Religion

Chapter 10

The Crisis of World Religions and the Critique of Essentialism

Michael P. DeJonge

Within the theoretically fragmented field of religious studies, there is nonetheless an ever-widening consensus that the "world religions paradigm" (hereafter WRP) is in crisis. This once-stable paradigm, which has done much to organize teaching and research in religious studies, has fallen under sustained criticism, and it remains unclear what, if anything, will replace it. One prominent line of criticism accuses the WRP of "essentialism." As Kevin Schilbrack rightly points out, such criticism "draws on the widespread philosophical rejection of essentialism" (Schilbrack 2010, 1127). This chapter elaborates on this point by reading the crisis of WRP against the background of the crisis of substance metaphysics that has generated the philosophical rejection of essentialism.

In what follows, I argue that the philosophical rejection of essentialism that fuels critics of WRP is embedded in a broader critique of the substance metaphysics in which essentialism is most at home. When compared with this philosophical rejection, essentialism critiques of WRP are often imprecise and superficial: imprecise in their accounts of essentialism and superficial in their reception of this philosophical rejection. Deeper engagement with this philosophical rejection of essentialism would encourage naming essentialism specifically as an ontological doctrine and rejecting essentialism by appropriating a non-substance metaphysics.

What Is Essentialism?

Later I will argue that essentialism critiques of WRP tend to be imprecise in not registering that essentialism is an ontological doctrine. Here I want to motivate attention to that issue by showing in a preliminary way the lack of clarity surrounding essentialism in religious studies. Clarity is, of course, relative; whether an account of something is sufficiently clear depends on the goal in mind. I take it that the goal of essentialism critics is, in part, to theorize in an anti-essentialist way. So, the standard for clarity with respect to an account of essentialism is whether it says clearly enough what essentialism *is* (so we can avoid being essentialists) and what it *isn't* (so we can become anti-essentialists). Given space constraints, I can only provide a general account of the unclear character of essentialism critiques.

In general, it is difficult to derive from essentialism critiques of WRP what exactly essentialism is supposed to be. This is because, first, "essentialism" is often used without definition or elaboration, as if its meaning is self-evident. Second, when essentialism is defined or elaborated, there is no apparent consensus in meaning among various critics. For example, in the edited volume, *After World Religions*, which sets for itself the goal of moving beyond the "uncritical essentialism" of the WRP, I find three substantive discussions of essentialism. In one case, essentialism has to do with ascribing agency to religion rather than to humans; in a second case, the meaning of essentialism is hard to discern; in a third, essentialism has to do with relating particular religions to the general category of religion (Cotter and Robertson 2016).[1] The reader is left, then, with a confused impression of what essentialism is supposed to be. Third, and most important, even when essentialism is defined or elaborated, any clarity dissolves if we try to derive from that elaboration some concrete suggestions for being anti-essentialists.

Let me illustrate this last point with one representative example. Tim Murphy's "'God' Is Not One, But 'Religion' Is," reviews Stephen Prothero's world religions book, *God Is Not One*, charging it with essentialism. Murphy does not offer a definition of essence or essentialism, but it is clear from his piece that he sees essentialism operating in two ways: generally and particularly. Generally, essentialism is when particular religions (such as Christianity or Buddhism) are treated as belonging to the general category of religion. Particularly, essentialism is when particular religions are treated as unified and coherent. Being anti-essentialist, then, partly involves rejecting essentialism at both the general and particular levels. Murphy judges Prothero to be successful in doing so (Murphy 2011, 20).

But Murphy thinks something more radical is involved in rejecting essentialism: "De-essentializing religion has radical consequences, however. If there is no essence to religion, then 'religion' can—must?—be seen as a constructed category, not an invariant given, rooted in human nature or existence" (Murphy 2011, 21). The opposite of essentialism here is constructionism. To avoid essentialism, we apparently should stop treating things as having essences, instead treating them as constructions. In accord with this suggestion, the next section of Murphy's piece treats "'Religion' as a Constructed Category."

It is common to think that the opposite of essentialism is constructionism, as if affirming constructionism means rejecting essentialism. But this is a changing of the topic. The question of whether a thing has an essence is different from the question of whether that thing is constructed. Indeed, Aristotle—the prototypical theorist of essentialism—sees no problem with treating constructed things also as things with essences, since the origin of a thing makes no difference for the question of whether a thing has an essence. To take his favorite example of a statue, there is no contradiction in affirming that a statue is constructed *and* affirming both levels of what Murphy identifies as essentialism: that the particular statue

---

1. For the goal of overcoming essentialism, see Cotter and Robertson (2016, 13). For the three accounts of essentialism, see ibid., 9–10, 64–65, 177.

has an essence, and that it belongs to the general category of statue. Essentialism and constructionism are not mutually exclusive.[2]

Perhaps Murphy could offer a supplemental argument showing how constructionism does not on its own entail anti-essentialism but does do so when combined with another position. This may be possible, but this only confirms that, with constructionism, Murphy has not named an alternative to essentialism. His account of essentialism, then, is unclear in that we glean no concrete guidance for becoming anti-essentialists. The most concrete guidance on offer is, "Be good constructionists," but being good constructionists does not in any straightforward way ensure that we won't be essentialists.

In presenting this example from Murphy I have already begun to suggest an account of essentialism, and I will elaborate that in the next section. My point for now is that this example is representative. In essentialism critiques of WRP, we often get some idea of what essentialism might be, but the accounts of essentialism are ultimately unclear insofar as the attempt to derive from them an anti-essentialist theoretical roadmap leaves us empty handed. Being better constructionists, or attending more to complexity and contestation (e.g., Hughes 2011), or granting agency to humans rather than to religions (e.g., Cotter and Robertson 2016, 9–10; Smith 2011, 18–19) does not directly avoid essentialism.

Essentialism

We need, then, a more precise account of essentialism. I propose these definitions: An "essence" is that by virtue of which a thing is the thing that it is. "Essentialism" is the position that there are things with essences. "Anti-essentialism" is the denial that there are things with essences.

What is involved in the essentialist claim that there are things with essences? Because an essence is that in virtue of which a thing is what it is, to say that there are things with essences is to say that there are things that are what they are in virtue of themselves. The contrast to "in virtue of themselves" here is "in virtue of their relationship to other things." So, essentialism is the claim that there are things that are what they are in virtue of themselves rather than in virtue of their relationship to other things.

This general account of essentialism can be specified in various ways. Plato's theory of forms, for example, provides a paradigmatic specification of essentialism. According to this view, particular things (such as Socrates and Plato) are what they are not in virtue of themselves but in relationship to general things (such as the form of being human). In other words, particular things are not things with essences, but the forms, which are general things, are essences. In the Platonic version of essentialism, it is the *general* things (the forms) that have essences.

Aristotle also offers a paradigmatic specification of essentialism, one that differs from Plato's. For him, particular things have essences. Socrates is what he is because of his own essence, his being human. General things, including kinds

---

2. For more on this point, see, for example, Witt (1995, 324–327).

(such as being human) and properties (such as being pale), do not have essences but rather are what they are because of their relationship to particulars that do, such as Socrates, who is human and pale. In the Aristotelian version of essentialism, it is the *particular* things that have essences.[3]

At this point, then, we have a definition of essence and essentialism, and two examples (in Plato and Aristotle) of ways to be essentialist. Now let's get to the point we are so eager for in religious studies: How can we reject essentialism? Since essentialism says there are things with essences, we need to deny that there are things with essences. How might we do that?

Rejecting Essentialism

One strategy for rejecting essentialism can be illustrated by John Locke, whom we can read as objecting to an Aristotelian version of essentialism.[4] According to Aristotle's account, a changing thing is a hylomorphic compound of matter (*hulē*) and form (*eidos* or *morphē*), and the essence of a changing thing is its form. A changing thing can both change and remain what it is when the essential form persists through accidental change. So, Socrates might spend the day in the marketplace and change from pale to dark, but the form of Socrates—his being human—would persist. In this way, Socrates remains what he is by virtue of his essence, which is his form. Note, too, that the form tells us which of Socrates' properties are essential and which are accidental. His being human means he must remain human (remain rational, remain an animal, etc.) to remain who he is, but his paleness or darkness is an accidental property. This Aristotelian idea of an enduring essential form of a changing thing came to be called a "substantial form" in the Latin reception of Aristotle.

Locke rejects the idea of a substantial form. Instead of saying that a changing thing has a form which dictates which of its properties are essential and therefore endure through change, Locke argues that all of a thing's properties belong to an essence-less or form-less substance. For him, a changing thing consists only of an underlying but essence-less substance and the properties that accompany it. Essences are not in the picture.

Locke provides us with an actual option for rejecting essentialism. Unlike suggestions to be good constructionists, or to attend more to complexity and contestation, or to attend more to human agency, Locke's account of an essence-less substance directly challenge essentialism. It offers a real alternative to essentialism, that is, a position the adoption of which entails the rejection of essentialism. So, at this point we also have an example of what *isn't* essentialism.

Now, while Locke is helpful for providing an actual alternative to essentialism, no one in religious studies is an anti-essentialist because of their passion for

---

3. This is, in any case, one contested reading of Aristotle, advanced by, for example, Politis (2004) and Witt (1989). The preceding several paragraphs can be derived from Politis (2004, ch. 9).
4. Interpretations of Locke vary on this issue (see Jones 2020). I present one interpretation for the purpose of illustrating a way to reject essentialism.

eighteenth-century empiricism. Our inspirations for anti-essentialism are more recent and "critical": poststructuralism, postcolonial theory, feminist theory, etc. These movements reject essentialism in a more fundamental way than Locke does, challenging not only an essentialist account of things but also the very metaphysics in which that account traditionally appears. To show this, I first need to return to Aristotle's essentialism, this time presenting it in the broader context of his metaphysical project.

Essentialism and Substance Metaphysics

In *Metaphysics*, Aristotle says he is doing first philosophy or first science. Science, for him, is about explanatory knowledge, so metaphysics as first science provides the most fundamental explanatory knowledge. Moreover, he treats metaphysics as the most general science, one concerned not with certain classes of things (as when biology concerns living things, or physics concerns changing things) but with all things. Metaphysics, for Aristotle, is the most fundamental and most general explanatory knowledge.

It had been established by Parmenides and accepted by Aristotle's teacher Plato that the most fundamental principle or explanation of all things is "being" (*to on*), since everything that is is. Following in this tradition, Aristotle treats metaphysics, the most fundamental and most general science, as the science of being. Therefore, the guiding metaphysical question is, "What is being?"

How do we ask this question, "What is being?" Or, of what do we ask it? Aristotle evidently thinks that we ask this question of "beings," "things," or "things that are" (all translations of *ta onto*). So, Aristotle refers the metaphysical question "What is being?" to "beings" or "things," asking: "What is it for a thing to be?" Asked in the most fundamental and most general way proper to metaphysical questioning: "What is it for *any* thing *ultimately* to be?"

In answering this question, Aristotle says there are two ways for things to be. In one case, a thing is what it is in virtue of itself, as when Socrates is Socrates by virtue of his very own being human. In the second case, a thing is what it is in virtue of something outside of itself, as when the paleness of Socrates is what it is only because Socrates is pale. That first kind of thing—the kind that is what it is in virtue of itself—Aristotle calls *ousia*, and this has come to be translated as a "substance."

Now we can bring back the concept of essence to show how it fits into this broader metaphysical framework. Recall that an essence is that which makes a thing what it is. Based on this, we can say that a substance is precisely a thing with an essence. Recall, too, that essentialism is the position that there are things with essences. Since substances are things with essences, essentialism means affirming that there are substances.

It is not just that the concept of essence "fits into" this metaphysics. Beyond this, the concept of essence is the answer to Aristotle's metaphysical question. If we ask, "What is it for *any* thing *ultimately* to be?," the answer is: "A thing is what it is because of an essence, either its own essence (in the case of things that are substances) or that of another thing (in the case of non-substances)." Essence is the lynchpin of Aristotle's metaphysics.[5]

Based on this, I want to say that conversations about essentialism in Religious Studies would be deepened if it were recognized, first, that essentialism is an ontological doctrine. That is, essentialism, most properly considered, is an account of things (*ta onta*) and thinghood. Essentialism provides an answer to the question, "What is it for a thing to be?" This is important because many discussions within religious studies treat under the label of essentialism issues that are downstream from this ontological point, and which may or may not logically follow from essentialism.

For example, it is common to call the overdetermination of particulars by generals "essentialism."[6] If a particular such as "Hinduism" is overdetermined by the general "religion," or if the particular "Hindu person" is overdetermined by the general "Hinduism," scholars detect essentialism. But the discussion of Plato and Aristotle above shows that essentialism (the claim that there are things with essences) does not in itself imply a particular configuration of generals and particulars. Rather, the relationship between generals and particulars is shaped by further theoretical decisions about what *kinds* of things have essences. If, as with Plato, generals have essences and particulars do not, then general categories have priority over particulars. But this priority is reversed with Aristotle's essentialism. So, if scholars find, say, the particular "Hinduism" overdetermined by the general "religion," they are not reacting to essentialism per se but to a specific configuration of it, e.g., Plato's. Discussions of essentialism would become more precise, then, if scholars distinguished between essentialism and those ideas that may or may not follow from it.

Based on the above discussion of Aristotle's metaphysics, conversations about essentialism in religious studies would be deepened if, second, it were recognized that essentialism, as an ontological doctrine, has its traditional home in a substance metaphysics. By "substance metaphysics" I mean exactly the line of thinking traced above in Aristotle, where the general metaphysical question (What is there?) is treated as a question of being (What is being?), which in turn is referred primarily to things (What is it for a thing to be?) and answered in terms of "substance" and "essence." The defining feature of a substance metaphysics, to my mind, is the referral of the metaphysical question to *things*.[7] If we ask, "What is there?," a substance metaphysics answers, "there are things." Essentialism is at home in a substance metaphysics because it is only after the metaphysical question has been referred to things that the logic of essence can arise.

---

5. The above few paragraphs can be derived from Politis (2004, 1–22).
6. See the previously mentioned examples from Murphy (2011, 177).
7. For this reason, a substance metaphysics could more properly be described as an ontological metaphysics, i.e., a metaphysics oriented to things and thinghood. But the label "substance metaphysics" is more common, and I adopt it here.

Rejecting Substance Metaphysics

This characterization of essentialism as an ontological doctrine within substance metaphysics suggests two strategies for rejecting essentialism. The first is to leave the context of substance metaphysics (i.e., a thing-focused metaphysics) intact while offering a non-essentialist ontology (i.e., an account of things without reliance on the concept of essence). This is the option represented by Locke's essence-less substance theory.

The second, more radical option involves rejecting essentialism by challenging the very project of substance metaphysics. This means challenging the idea that the question of metaphysics should be referred above all to things or thinghood, asserting instead that being or fundamental reality is other than things. It is this more radical rejection of essentialism that is at work in the critical theories that are being appropriated by essentialism critiques within religious studies.

Let's look at three (non-mutually exclusive) options for rejecting substance metaphysics, for offering a metaphysics not focused on things. One option is a process metaphysics, which argues that processes, not things, are metaphysically basic. Aristotle's substance metaphysics treats being as simple, grounded as it is in the self-identical, unchanging essence of things. Such an approach privileges being understood as "is," relegating being qua "becoming" to a process that happens to things. A process metaphysics flips this priority, treating being primarily as becoming, as a process that under certain conditions stabilizes into things. The pre-Socratic philosopher Heraclitus is a forebear of this process view, which was revived to some degree by Hegel and Whitehead, and then more thoroughly in contemporary philosophy of science (e.g., Seibt 2020).

Another option is an event metaphysics, influentially developed by Martin Heidegger. He revisits the "ontological difference" between being and beings, objecting to the Aristotelian referral of the question of being to beings/things. Instead, he treats being as a primordial, forever-recurring event which precedes and discloses beings. Again, this flips a basic priority. Events do not happen to things, as with Aristotle. Things are eventful happenings (e.g., Beistegui 2004, 112–113).

A third option is a differential or relational metaphysics. Aristotle's metaphysics privileges substances, those beings that are what they are by virtue of their own essences. Such beings are identical with themselves. Only on the basis of this self-identity do relations of difference emerge—difference is ultimately only the difference *between* things. A differential metaphysics reverses the priority of things over difference, instead treating difference as prior to and *constitutive of* things. No thing is what it is in virtue of itself; every thing is what it is on the basis of differential relations (Cisney 2021). The linguist Saussure influentially articulated this differential logic (if not a differential metaphysics), writing, "in language there are only differences *without positive terms*" (Saussure 1959, 120).[8]

---

8. Also, "language is a form and not a substance" (Saussure 1959, 122).

112 • *Discourses of Crisis and the Study of Religion*

If we take poststructuralism as a prominent example of those critical theories inspiring anti-essentialist arguments in religious studies, and if we take Derrida as a representative of poststructuralism, we can see elements of all three of these approaches involved in his rejection of essentialism. Appropriating Saussure's differential logic to continue Heidegger's critique of the metaphysical tradition, Derrida develops the metaphysical "principle" of *différance*, according to which things appear by virtue of the eventful, processive play of differential relations. For him, there are no things or essences, or, at least, none that cannot always be deconstructed in terms of their constitutive differences. This is a radical anti-essentialism grounded in a rejection of substance metaphysics (Derrida 1982).

It is this more radical style of essentialism critique—one that challenges not just an essentialist ontology but also a substance metaphysics—to which critics of essentialism within Religious Studies persistently refer. Yet on this count, the rejections of essentialism within Religious Studies tend toward superficiality. In general, critics of essentialism within Religious Studies do not present essentialism as an ontological doctrine, and they do not register that the critical rejection of essentialism derives its power from its critique of substance metaphysics.

Again, limits of space require me to illustrate this general point with one representative example. In Leslie Dorrough Smith's contribution to the Prothero book review forum, she, too, charges *God Is Not One* with essentialism. In making this case, she rightly approaches the crucial alternative between essence and difference. The key to overcoming essentialism, she says, is to attend to difference. This is promising as far as it goes, and it tips a hat in the direction of the more radical style of essentialism critique. But the level at which she urges Prothero to attend to difference is never anything other than differences *between things* (e.g., between religions, between people), an idea perfectly at home in substance metaphysics. Lost is the sense that the concept of difference driving the radical critique of essentialism is pre-ontological—a difference not *between things* but *constitutive of things* (Smith 2011).[9] This is one example of how essentialism critiques within religious studies risk superficiality in light of the sources that inspire them.

Conclusion

Essentialist critiques of WRP within religious studies reflect widespread reactions elsewhere in the humanities and social sciences against perceived essentialism. Although there are a number of political and moral impulses driving such critiques, the critique itself is properly ontological. In this way, the crisis of WRP reflects the broader crisis of substance metaphysics. Unless essentialism critiques of WRP attend to this broader crisis, they risk conceptual imprecision and superficiality. Absent a more precise account of essentialism, it is often unclear whether the aspects of WRP under critique are even helpfully labeled in terms of

---

9. Note that Judith Butler, whom Smith cites, sees that rejecting essentialism involves rejecting "the metaphysics of substance" (see Butler 2006, 22).

essentialism. And without a more fundamental reception of the radical style of essentialism critique, it is often unclear how essentialism critics escape their own critiques. A more thoroughgoing reception of the rejection of substance metaphysics is required in order to say if and in what sense WRP is essentialist.

Acknowledgements

I thank Alex Levine for helpful comments on a previous draft of this chapter.

Michael P. DeJonge is James F. Strange Chair of religious studies at the University of South Florida. He is the author of *Bonhoeffer's Theological Formation* (Oxford University Press, 2012), *Bonhoeffer's Reception of Luther* (Oxford University Press, 2017), and *Bonhoeffer on Resistance* (Oxford University Press, 2018).

References

Beistegui, Miguel de. 2004. *Truth and Genesis: Philosophy as Differential Ontology*. Bloomington, IN: Indiana University Press.
Butler, Judith. 2006. *Gender Trouble: Feminism and the Subversion of Identity*. New York: Routledge.
Campbell, Richard. 2015. *The Metaphysics of Emergence*. New York: Palgrave Macmillan.
Cisney, Vernon. 2021. "Differential Ontology." In *The Internet Encyclopedia of Philosophy*. Retrieved from https://iep.utm.edu/.
Cotter, Christopher R. 2016. and David G. Robertson (eds.). *After World Religions: Reconstructing Religious Studies*. New York: Routledge.
Derrida, Jacques. 1982. "Différance." In Jacques Derrida, *Margins of Philosophy*, trans. Alan Bass. Chicago, IL: University of Chicago Press.
Hughes, Aaron W. 2011. "Religion Is Not Simplistic: Some Critical Thoughts on Stephen Prothero's God Is Not One." *Bulletin for the Study of Religion*, 40(2): 9–14.
Jones, Jan-Erik. 2020. "Locke on Real Essence." In Edward N. Zalta (ed.), *The Stanford Encyclopedia of Philosophy*. Retrieved from https://plato.stanford.edu/archives/spr2020/entries/real-essence/.
Murphy, Tim. 2011. "'God' Is Not One, But 'Religion' Is: A Critical Reading of Stephen Prothero's God Is Not One." *Bulletin for the Study of Religion*, 40(2): 19–25.
Politis, Vasilis. 2004. *Routledge Philosophy GuideBook to Aristotle and the Metaphysics*. New York: Routledge.
Saussure, Ferdinand de. 1959. *Course in General Linguistics*. New York: Philosophical Library.
Schilbrack, Kevin. 2010. "Religions: Are There Any?" *Journal of the American Academy of Religion*, 78(4): 1112–38.
Seibt, Johanna. 2020. "Process Philosophy." In Edward N. Zalta (ed.), *The Stanford Encyclopedia of Philosophy*. Retrieved from https://plato.stanford.edu/archives/sum2020/entries/process-philosophy
Smith, Leslie Dorrough. 2011. "On Works of the Imagination: A Critical Consideration of Stephen Prothero's God Is Not One." *Bulletin for the Study of Religion*, 40(2): 14–19.
Witt, Charlotte. 1995. "Anti-Essentialism in Feminist Theory." *Philosophical Topics*, 23(2): 321–44.
Witt, Charlotte. 1989. *Substance and Essence in Aristotle: An Interpretation of "Metaphysics" VII-IX*. Ithaca, NY: Cornell University Press.

Chapter 11

Enlarging Religious Studies, Wither-ing Neoliberalism

Matt Sheedy

In July of 2021, the story of three billionaires flying into space—Richard Branson, Jeff Bezos, and Elon Musk—captivated mainstream news outlets and social media alike. Whereas legacy media mostly lauded these efforts as the start of a new and bold frontier, the commentary on social media tended to mock the hubris of these oligarchs looking to feed their egos amid numerous global crises. In a month full of wildfires and record-breaking temperatures in the Pacific North West, unprecedented flooding in parts of Western Europe, the ongoing pandemic, and global economic unrest, the triumphal praise from establishment powers for this cosplay of the uber-rich appeared to many as a caricature come to life, un-ironically parading itself before our eyes.[1] And then, we moved on, as the "Twittering Machine" drew our attention to the next worthy spectacle.[2]

In *The University in Ruins* (1996), Bill Readings argues that the modern University has experienced three main ideas: "the Kantian concept of reason, the Humboldtian idea of culture, and now the techno-bureaucratic notion of excellence" (loc. 345). The crux of Readings's argument is that state investment in the production of national culture has declined since the early 1990s, especially in universities, which had, until this time, served as a central conduit.[3] In its place, a corporatized, multinational "ideology of excellence" has emerged that follows market logics rather than national interests. What links Branson, Bezos, and Musk to Reading's observations should be apparent to the attentive reader—namely, that the corporate-lead "techno-bureaucratic notion of excellence" has only

---

1. During the first few months of 2022, the film *Don't Look Up* topped the charts on Netflix and caused a stir among media pundits and politicians alike. Suffice it to say, the lines between the reality that I describe in the opening paragraph and the satire depicted in the film are not that far apart.
2. I borrow this term from Richard Seymour's book of the same name. As he describes it: "In 1922, the surrealist Paul Klee invented the Twittering Machine. In the painting, a row of stick-figure birds clutches an axle, turned by a crank. Below the device where the voices squawk discordantly is a reddened pit. The Museum of Modern Art explains: 'the birds function as bait to lure victims to the pit over which the machine hovers.' Somehow, the holy music of birdsong has been mechanized, deployed as a lure, for the purpose of human damnation" (Seymour 2019: 15).
3. For a wide-ranging analysis of the effects of these changes on the production of literature in Canada, see McGregor, Rak, and Wunker (2018).

intensified since the 1990s,[4] and remains one of the most dominant ideologies informing mainstream cultural, economic, and political life today.

In this chapter, I address the theme of crisis in the study of religion through the broader lens of neoliberal ideology, which I combine with a discussion of Scott Elliott's 2013 volume *Reinventing Religious Studies: Key Writings in the History of the Discipline*, covering forty years of debates in the Council of Societies for the Study of Religion (CSSR) *Bulletin*, from 1969 to 2009. One thing that is clear when looking back on this period is that a feeling of crisis has always been lingering in the field, though the terms and conditions have decidedly changed. Previous crises in religious studies have primarily focused on who gets to determine the shape and identity of the discipline, with theology and its various sublimations playing the heel. In our current era, the very existence of the field as a tenuous member of the humanities and social sciences is under increasing pressure, and this time the power to contest our disciplinary identity may be largely out of our hands. Or is it? That is the primary question that I wish to provoke here.

One through-line linking the emergence and development of the study of religion with our current state of crisis is the birth of an era that many have referred to as neoliberal capitalism, which is commonly thought to have gained political power in the mid-1970s. I will have much more to say on this concept in due course, though to start I offer a provocation of sorts to set the stage for what is to follow.

Writing in his book, *The Age of Precarity: Endless Crisis and the Art of Government* (2021), Dario Gentili makes the following observation:

> The neoliberal economic crisis does not produce a "state of exception" but, to employ an expression used by Walter Benjamin in 1940, has turned "the exception into the rule." The neoliberal art of government's contribution to this configuration of crisis consists in the model of political judgment it produces. In fact, even though the form of a judgment for or against remains, its outcome is never a final or conclusive decision as it had been in the modern period, when it could restore or overthrow the existing order to resolve the crisis. The political judgment of neoliberalism is, rather, a judgment that helps preserve the order, or, to put it another way, administers it. In short, neoliberalism rules by means of the forced decisions brought about by crisis within the given order.
>
> (Gentili 2021, loc. 90)

To put it plainly, neoliberalism thrives on a state of permanent crisis, and replicates itself by administering *temporary* solutions to the various crises that it helps to bring about. For Gentili, the idealization of the "self-employed entrepreneur" is one outcome of this form of governance, as precarity has become a way of life that encourages survival within the market order above all else. This

---

4. To this "techno-bureaucratic" idea, I would also add the growth of techno-utopian thinking. As Marantz (2019) puts it, common sense assumptions of techno-utopianism are reflected in the ethos: "The best stuff spreads. … New technologies will disrupt old hierarchies, and this disruption will ultimately redound to the good" (209).

is just as true for those working in permanent jobs with benefits as it is for the un- and under-employed precariat since neoliberalism incentivizes individualism over solidarity and collective organizing. One can get along or move on. This new normal is at odds with older models of the university, academic guilds, and knowledge production (e.g., Readings's Humboldtian idea of culture) that have traditionally relied upon forms of apprenticeship supported through government funding and philanthropic grants. As sources of funding dry-up, the ideal of blending canonical learning (i.e., teaching formative thinkers and paradigms) with novel innovations is increasingly likely to cede ground to research deemed useful for corporate interests. Following this logic, the disciplines and sub-disciplines best suited to survive without corporate backing will be those that are institutionally supported by niche benefactors.[5]

To the extent that this thesis on the effects of neoliberalism is accurate, or at least partially accurate, it is worth asking what these trends can tell us about the type of crisis that we face? To what extent are we at fault for not innovating with the times? Or are we perhaps victims of larger social forces that are mostly out of our hands? What kinds of methods, theories, and critiques do we need to focus on, or perhaps re-engage within the history of our discipline in order to better position ourselves to weather these growing storms?

A Brief Map of Some Neoliberal Territories

Most academic treatments of neoliberalism begin with a nod to the "origin" of this idea, its various developments, followed by reflections on its particular character and continued persistence through numerous crises. For example, in *Neoliberalism: A Very Short Introduction* (2021), Steger and Roy point out that the term was first coined in the aftermath of World War I by a group of "moderate" German professors linked to the Freiburg School who wished to revive "the classical liberal ideal of minimal state interference in the economy" (xv). More specifically, as Cahill and Konings (2017) observe, early uses of the term came from scholars who wanted to recover liberal economic principles in the face of growing socialist forces (17). They also note formative debates during the interwar period featuring prominent thinkers like Ludwig von Mises and Friedrich Hayek, who were two of the founding members of the Mount Pèlerin Society in 1947, which is frequently cited as a key moment in the intellectual development of neoliberal ideas (see Phillips-Fein 2019). Those present at Mont Pèlerin, Switzerland, were especially concerned with the influential economic theories of John Maynard Keynes, among many others, who argued that governments should actively intervene in the economy through the creation of state programs, jobs, and expenditures (including universities).

---

5. Consider the dramatic growth of positions in Islamic Studies following the 9/11 attacks, which are now waning, and the scarcity of jobs in once thriving sub-disciplines, such as American religions. By comparison, a steady-stream of positions in pastoral work and theology have shown few signs of atrophy, due, in part, to the strength of ecclesiastical institutions.

The term *neoliberalismo* was adopted by Latin American economists in the 1970s, and was given a shot in the arm after two Mont Pèlerin members were awarded the "Nobel Prize" in economics—Freidrich Hayek in 1974 and Milton Friedman in 1976—thus helping to legitimize this particular brand of economic theory.[6] In the late 1980s and early 1990s neoliberalism became a popular buzz word among leftist activists to describe the "Washington Consensus," corporate globalization, and a hyper-individualized form of consumer culture.[7] According to Springer, Birch, and MacLeavy (2016), the term caught on globally following the Zapatista uprisings in Chiapas, Mexico in 1994, in response to the signing of the North American Free Trade Agreement (NAFTA).

The 1970s are commonly understood as the "first wave" of neoliberalism, when Latin American states like Chile and Argentina became laboratories for the deregulation of post-war social welfare provisions in favor of market-based solutions. The "second wave" of neoliberalism is associated with the policies of Bill Clinton and Tony Blair, whose "third way" programs "sought to reconcile middle-class concerns with business interests" (Steger and Roy 2021, 43).[8] Important to the emergence of this "second wave" was the impact of Ronald Reagan and Margaret Thatcher, who began to dismantle the welfare-state in the U.S. and the U.K. on the heels of numerous economic crises throughout the 1970s.[9] The "third-wave" of neoliberalism is linked to the Obama administration and its failure to impose anti-trust laws regulating the monopoly practices of the financial sector following the Global Financial Crisis of 2008. Although Steger and Roy don't use the term "fourth wave," they do speak of our current moment as an era where neoliberalism is increasingly under attack through forms of populism and "anti-politics," where the latter is described as a reactionary force since it does not offer any kind

---

6. As Mirowski (2016) points out, there is no Nobel prize in economics, but only a "Bank of Sweden Award in Economic Sciences in Honor of Alfred Nobel" that is awarded at the same time and place. Mirowski observes that the creation of this "ersatz" prize was pushed by the "Neoliberal Thought Collective" who understood the symbolic capital that such an association would bring about (loc. 3564).
7. According to Steger and Roy: "The Washington Consensus is often viewed as synonymous with neoliberalism. Coined in the 1980s by the free-market economist John Williamson, the term refers to the lowest common denominator of policy advice directed at mostly Latin American countries by the IMF, the World Bank, and other Washington-based international economic institutions and think-tanks. In the 1990s, it became the global framework for economic development" (Steger and Roy 2021, 19).
8. Steger and Roy note two pivotal policy moves under the Clinton administration that would solidify modes of neoliberal governance into the future. The first was the 1999 Financial Services Modernization Act, "which removed long-standing legal divisions between the activities of commercial and investment banks as well as those between insurance companies and brokerage houses" (Steger and Roy 2021, 42). The second was the repeal of the Glass-Steagall Act in 1999, "which was signed into law by President Roosevelt in 1933 to prohibit commercial banks from engaging in investment activities on Wall Street" (ibid., 104). This move led to a "frenzy of mergers" of financial services firms who dramatically increased speculative practices.
9. This includes dramatic spikes in oil prices and subsequent shortages, and "the simultaneous occurrence of runaway inflation and rising unemployment ('stagflation')" (Steger & Roy: 10).

of alternative—only varieties of nativism and ethno-nationalism (see Hochuli and Hoare 2021).[10]

The growth of critical commentary on neoliberalism jumped considerably from the early 1990s to 2010,[11] with a wide range of political and scholarly analysis trying to make sense of what this term signifies as a description of contemporary political, economic, and ideological trends.[12] One of the first popular academic treatments of neoliberalism came from David Harvey (2005),[13] who defines it as a theory of political economy that sees human flourishing as best embodied in institutions that promote "strong private property rights, free markets, and free trade" (loc. 103), and where the role of the state is limited to facilitating these aims.[14] For Springer, Birch, and MacLeavy (2016), "most scholars tend to agree that neoliberalism is broadly defined as the extension of competitive markets into all areas of life, including the economy, politics, and society" (loc. 582). At that same time, they note that the term risks becoming "a totalizing rhetorical signifier" rather than a useful concept to interrogate social life (ibid., loc. 873). Similarly, for Venugopal (2015) neoliberalism carries "an inordinate descriptive and analytical burden in the social sciences" (169), which leads him to argue that all that can be usefully salvaged from the term is "a broad indicator of the historical turn in macro-political economy" (186). For England and Ward (2016), "neoliberalization" is a form of statecraft that "includes recasting the state's responsibilities ... for the collective well-being of its citizens and, as such, there is a shift in the responsibilities between the state, the market, communities and families" (loc. 2224).

---

10. As Centeno and Cohen (2012) put it: "With the 2008 financial crisis, faith in the liberal world economy collapsed, but financial-systemic problems made it difficult to engage the crisis with midcentury, big government solutions" (323).
11. Venugopal (2015) makes note of the following trends in scholarly papers dealing with neoliberalism: "Between 2005–09, there were more than 5,600 Google Scholar entries in English with the term 'neoliberal' or 'neoliberalism' in the title, almost double that of the previous five-year period 2000–04, and a ten-fold increase over 1990–94" (165).
12. Springer, Birch, and MacLeavy (2016) detail a wide range of scholarship analyzing neoliberalism in relation to areas such as: biotechnology, cities, citizenship, development, discourse, gender, homelessness, labor, migration, nature, race, sexualities, violence, and more (loc. 567).
13. By "popular academic treatments" I mean books by well-known academics whose central focus is on neoliberalism. Earlier academic texts that discuss neoliberalism can be found before this time, especially in work that deals with the influence of Michel Foucault, especially his 1978–1979 lectures compiled in *The Birth of Biopolitics* (2010). See Barry, Osbourne, and Rose (1996) for a treatment of this topic during the mid-90s.
14. Arguably the first popular non-academic book on neoliberalism was *The Shock Doctrine* by journalist Naomi Klein (2007), where she highlights the influence of Milton Freedman and the Chicago School of economics in making use of crises in order to push forward unpopular policies that roll back state provisions in favor of privatized market schemes (e.g., foreign ownership of resources, and charter schools).

Some scholars are more normative and descriptive in their definitions of neoliberalism,[15] while others have proclaimed it dead, such as Manuel Aalbers (2013), who argues that "it is often not so much deregulation that we see, but rather re-regulation" (1084). This line of argument suggests that contrary to popular opinion, neoliberalism is not about gutting the state in order to unleash the "invisible hand" of the free market, but instead points to a re-organization of laws and resources that intervene on behalf of the private sector and multinational corporate interests over state-centered provisions (see also Cahill and Konings 2017; Hancock 2020).

There is much more that can be said about neoliberalism that cannot be covered here. What most interests me about the confluence of neoliberalism and the study of religion is twofold. First, thinking about neoliberalism as an ideology that shapes subjectivities and social structures is important for any discipline in the humanities and social sciences. While neoliberalism is sometimes invoked in the study of religion, I do not see much engagement with the type of questions and theories laid out above. Second, if neoliberalism reflects, to quote Wendy Brown (2019), "a bundle of policies privatizing public ownership and services, radically reducing the social state, [and] leashing labor" (17), then it stands to reason that we ought to engage more critically with those forces that threaten the future of our discipline.[16]

As I turn now to Elliott's volume dealing with forty-years of scholarly reflection on the reinvention of the study of religion, I pose the following question: to what extent has the current crisis in religious studies been thought about in relation to neoliberal ideologies, along with its conceptual and material effects on the future of the field? What elements of past critique ought we to salvage and what needs to be more carefully scrutinized if we are to have a shot at getting out of this mess in the next 5, 10, or 20 years with our shirts still on our backs?

---

15. Birch (2015) describes it in terms of five processes or policies: "privatization of state-run assets (firms, council housing et cetera); liberalization of trade in goods and capital investment; monetarist focus on inflation control and supply-side dynamics; deregulation of labour and product markets to reduce 'impediments' to business; and, the marketization of society through public–private partnerships and other forms of commodification" (loc. 157).

16. On this topic, Edward Nik-Khah (2016) examines the influence of Chicago School economist George Stigler, whose ideas eclipsed those of Milton Friedman in the eyes of their Chicago School colleagues by the early 1980s. Stigler was particularly interested in university education and wanted to "spin off teaching from research" in order to "free elite scientists from such teaching responsibilities" (ibid., loc. 1064). Junior scholars "would provide the "semi-skilled labor of research," while tenure would be "removed altogether" (ibid., loc. 1130), replaced by patronage from corporations and pro-market foundations, who, he maintained, would be "uncontaminated by the egalitarian views of the government and the public at large" (ibid., loc. 1138).

Revisiting the Reinvention of the Religious Studies

Writing in 1996 at a jointly sponsored NAASR (North American Association for the Study of Religion) and SSSR (Society for the Scientific Study of Religion) meeting, Darlene Juschka remarks:

> One foot still in theology (to interpret data religiously) and the other sliding between humanities and social sciences (to interpret religious data), religious studies has suffered from an identity crisis since its conception. This crisis has meant that it has cloistered itself from other university disciplines. Neither theology nor a humanity or social science, it stands alone, and will, in the face of downsizing, fall alone.
>
> (Elliott 2013, 211)

At least two things strike me about this statement. First, one gets the sense that little has changed since 1996 when it comes to the types of crises that critical scholars in the critical study of religion (e.g., members of NAASR) have raised concerns about. Although it may be true that other sub-fields have emerged in the interim to tip the balance away from theology (e.g., the Cognitive Science of Religion),[17] the question of unifying the field through shared methods and theories remains as divided as ever. Second, it may come as a shock to younger scholars to hear that downsizing in the humanities was a concern as far back as the mid-1990s. More surprising still is a remark by Russell McCutcheon on the same panel from 1996, where he ends his piece by quoting then-colleague Charles Hedrick writing in 1976 about the looming job crisis, "the need to bridge the gap between the academic community and the rest of the world," and the importance of graduate schools taking the lead in finding positions for their graduates (208). For McCutcheon, what is most disturbing is that this statement from 1976 could have been written in 1997 (when his paper was published in the *Bulletin*), while noting that little has been done in the intervening 21 years to remedy the crisis.

It is perhaps no coincidence that government investment in academic institutions began to erode in the mid-1970s as neoliberalization began to take hold. Few, however, have made this connection in scholarly representations of the study of religion, nor traced the relationship between changing political and economic structures with paradigm shifts in the field. While a thorough analysis of such trends is beyond the scope of this chapter, I want to explore the idea of reinventing religious studies as a process that is tied to crises occurring outside of academic networks, and think about how neoliberal modes of governmentality have shaped both our thinking, priorities, and (in)abilities to address the various challenges that we face. This includes the reduction in tenured and secure academic positions, the rise in contingent labor, and ongoing cutbacks to the humanities in particular.

---

17. For example, The International Association for the History of Religion (IAHR) conference in Toronto in 2010, entitled, "Religion: A Human Phenomenon," prominently featured CSR scholarship (on panels and in keynote addresses), as did the North American Association for the Study of Religion (NAASR) in Atlanta in 2015.

Elliott's volume opens with a commissioned essay by Harold Remus reflecting on the CSSR from 1969 to 2009 and its role in bringing together numerous professional societies interested in shaping the field as a discipline distinct from theology. As one example, Remus points to conversations among Council members in 1973 on "new" and "emerging areas," such as New Religious Movements, Native American, Women's, and Afro-American Studies (Elliott 2013, 19). Of more general concern at the time was the matter of how to transform religious studies into a "humanistic enterprise," along with choosing what methods and theories ought to be centered in the interest of unifying the field (ibid., 23). Claude Welch's 1970 piece echoes this call for unifying religious studies through the development of journals and graduate programs, while stressing the need for "more adequate interpretation of the scholarly study of religion to government agencies" (ibid., 33). While it could be argued that the discipline has succeeded in developing the study of previously marginalized areas, such as gender, race, and non-normative traditions, the challenge of unifying the field remains unresolved. Debates over areas studies, "critical," or "big tent" approaches continue unabated,[18] as does the question of whether and/or how to communicate with government agencies and the broader public.

The 1960s is noted by several scholars in this volume as a formative period for the discipline finally coming into its own, while at the same time marking choices that may not, in retrospect, have led to the best possible outcomes. For example, in his 1970 contribution, John F. Wilson observes that concerns over the prevalence of "special pleading" and the challenge of promoting more objective methods for the field seem to have declined, while area studies, including a growing focus on "Eastern Wisdom," have expanded considerably (Elliott 2013, 35). For these and other reasons, Wilson fears that "commitment ... under the guise of 'existential relevance'" has eclipsed the ideals of working toward "objectivity" and "neutrality" (36). Writing over ten years later, Carl A. Raschke (1983) argues that the "demise of traditional religious authority" (51) during the 1960s was replaced by a more individualistic and experimental ethos, including "a romance with the archetypal and archaic" (ibid., 54). For Raschke, these cultural trends coincided with the development of descriptive and phenomenological approaches to the study of religion, which eclipsed theology proper (ibid., 52).[19] Raschke effectively links these cultural trends with paradigm shifts in religious studies in a way that

---

18. A critique of the "big tent" approach was the theme of the 2015 NAASR meeting in Atlanta. As the call for papers states: "When Is the Big Tent Too Big? We seek papers that critically assess the strengths and weaknesses of the 'big tent' philosophy that governs professional organizations, publishing, and departments in religious studies and biblical studies. This 'big tent' mixes etic and methodological naturalist perspectives with emic, confessional, and theological approaches to religion along with opportunities for interfaith dialogue. Contributors to this session identify the impact the Big Tent has on the secular study of religion and sacred texts and its status within the large world of secular disciplines of the humanities and social sciences" (NAASR Note 2015).
19. Commenting on the legacies of the 1960s on the field, Jacob Neusner writes in 1977 that understanding religious studies as part of the humanities means opening up to "the human-meaning of being-religious in the lives of ordinary folk, not only virtuosi" (Elliott 2013: 40).

seems obvious in retrospect. Here we might ask what kind of reflection is taking place in our current moment in relation to cultural and political trends? More on this below.

Another common theme in the annals of the CSSR *Bulletin* is the problem with religious studies relying too heavily on "imports" from other fields, such as Victor Turner, Mary Douglas, and Clifford Geertz.[20] While Ninian Smart (2014; first published in 1979) acknowledges that Mircea Eliade has made waves outside of religious studies proper, he sees a need to move beyond Eliade's influence and export theories that we are particularly adept to lead in, such as comparative ethics, the history of religions, and addressing the insider/outsider problem. Smart ends his piece by reflecting on the state of universities in 1979, noting how they are not increasing in size, that "religious studies is not laser technology" and doesn't acquire funding easily, while concluding with a warning that "we're shrinking almost, if we don't watch out. And the only way in which we may develop research in new directions is from sources outside our institutions" (ibid., 50).

Writing in 1970 on teaching religion at the university, Robert Bellah draws attention to the crisis "of boundaries and separations in the academic world," which he attributes to "specialization and differentiation" that threatens to tear our "whole culture ... apart at the seams" (Bellah 1970, 94). For Bellah, taking an inductive approach to the discipline that centers the experiences of students is one way to move beyond this impasse. In reply, James Dittes (1971) argues that Bellah is overstating the case and suggests that we can be more attentive to the kind of arrogant reductionism found in the social sciences without playing into humanistic stereotypes that may result in others not taking the study of religion seriously (98). In a conceptually related piece from 1981, John Whittaker takes exception with Bellah's stance and asks whether there is such a thing as "religious experience" that we can define in a neutral or objective way? Fast forward to a series of responses to Robert Minor and Robert Baird's 1983 contribution on teaching religion, which foregrounds the existential relevance of learning about different cultures and traditions, we see a discussion on the difference between teaching religion versus teaching *about* religion, and how these boundaries might be navigated at state versus religiously affiliated schools once again come to the fore.

These early contributions in the CSSR *Bulletin* presage future debates that are still with us today, and include: objectivity versus experience and special pleading; straddling the boundaries between humanistic and social scientific research; the insider/outsider problem; as well as striking a balance between studying older versus modern traditions and contemporary concerns. While the question of what defines the field of religious studies (as distinct from theology) has not disappeared, it is clear that advances have been made when it comes to the deployment and development of critical methods and areas of study, such as the post-9/11 rise in studies of secularism and non-religion.[21]

---

20. Walter Capp also makes this argument (Capp 1978, 43–45).
21. See Charles Elliott Vernoff's essay "Naming the Game: A Question of the Field," for a more thorough analysis of leading methods and theories in the field from the vantage point of 1983.

At this point, at least two things are clear from these early contributions. First, defining the field as distinct from theology has been a perennial concern since the 1960s, as has the tension between certain varieties of humanism (e.g., centering experience and existential concerns) and more rigorous social scientific approaches. Needless to say, as austerity continues to spread, careful consideration of the (perceived) social legitimacy of what we do and how we do it is more important than ever. Second, there appears to have been a shift in how we view the problem of unifying the field. Whereas earlier debates focused on which methods and theories will help us to clearly define ourselves as a discipline in order to secure a stable academic future, current discussions of crises don't seem to have a lot to offer beyond talk of greater diversity within the academy, reactions to Trumpism, modest nods to adjunct and contingent labor (see Daley-Bailey 2016), and expressing concerns over the climate emergency.[22]

All of this prompts the question, has the pursuit of creating a secure and distinct field of religious studies been the X factor in getting us this far, or is there perhaps something else that we have ignored? Has the ever-growing trepidation over the future of religious studies amidst broader political trends been addressed in a systematic way since we first heard rumbles of austerity back in the mid-1970s, or do we still find ourselves having barely moved on these considerations, as McCutcheon lamented back in 1997?

In the roundtable discussion featuring Juschka, McCutcheon, along with Brain E. Malley, and Gustavo Benevides, we find the most pointed and contemporaneous critique of neoliberalism in the Elliott (2013) volume, with themes including critical scholarship versus caretaking, identity politics, and the role of social movements outside the university informing what we do. For McCutcheon, religious studies ought to be viewed "not as a special case but as one among a number of fields engaged in the theoretically based study of human beliefs, behaviors, and institutions" (Elliott 2013, 207), thus suggesting (at least to my mind) the need for more collaboration with social scientific areas of study. For Juschka, the relative success of identity politics in dismantling "grand narratives" has been tempered by populist trends throughout the 1990s, where the centering of the particular interests of distinct groups—e.g., women, racialized, or queer communities—has overtaken efforts to unify the field through shared methods and theories. Importantly, she urges scholars to connect "economic and political activity off campus with those on campus" in order to "better understand the difficulties we presently face" (ibid., 212).

It is noteworthy that the final section in Elliott's volume, dealing with Islam and 9/11, reflects a more direct engagement with the kind of pressing public concerns that Juschka and many others raise dating back to 1970. Even here, however, it remains an ongoing debate as to whether the study of Islam has become "critical," or whether the disproportionate attention that has been paid to it since 2001

---

22. See, for example, recent conference themes, keynote addresses, and initiatives of the American Academic of Religion, the world's largest religious studies organization, at www.aarweb.org.

has been squandered in favor of more apologetic concerns.[23] Relatedly, it is worth asking why the work of the late Jonathan Z. Smith, who is among the most influential scholars of religion over the last half century, has not been widely exported to other fields? Despite the efforts of many to promote his work (see Braun and McCutcheon 2008, 2018; Crews and McCutcheon 2020), it would appear that even J. Z. hasn't cracked the barrier of cross-disciplinary dissemination with his novel approach to classification by means of, to quote him from Elliott's volume, "description, comparison, redescription, and rectification" (Elliott 2013, 140).

One of the more interesting and politically relevant contributions in Elliott's volume is an essay by Tim Jensen, originally published in 1998. Jensen highlights some of the successes that he and his colleagues have had in promoting the study of religion "as a historical and social construct" (Elliott 2013, 162) in Denmark, which they have presented in newspapers, to businesses, and to government agencies—even going so far as place a sociologist of religion (who replaced the Bishop of Copenhagen) in the Ministry of Ecclesiastical Affairs (ibid., 167). As a small and relatively homogenous country, Denmark has certain built-in advantages (and perhaps necessities) when it comes to integrating academic study with business and government agencies. The fact that such a model exists, however, and has successfully pushed a critical, secular study of religion is an experiment that deserves closer attention as a way to combat the effects of neoliberalization.

Reconsiderations

While Elliott's volume is only a sample of some of the more pressing debates that occurred in the study of religion over what is now more than half a century, it nonetheless provides a snapshot of what piqued scholars' interests, revealing both battles won, those currently being waged, and battles still to come. In many ways, the problems with theology in the early days of the field have been resolved, though much remains to be hashed-out when it comes to how we position ourselves in relation to it. A glimpse at job postings in 2021/2022 reveals a steady stream of pastoral and theological positions as compared to a slow drip in the study of religion. Perhaps it's time to reconsider this relationship and ask what, if anything, might be done to collaborate with theology in mutually productive ways, while still remaining autonomous domains?

Another topic worthy of consideration is how the surge of identity politics through the advent of social media has created new modes of mythmaking, especially when it comes to questions of race, gender, and sexual identities. Although these are often volatile, hot-button topics, much of the discourse on these questions resembles debates in the study of religion between critical and apologetic approaches that favor special pleading. While it is true that a certain sector of scholarship has leaned into identity-related questions when theorizing religion, it strikes me that there is room to push this work further and perhaps even export

---

23. See Aaron Hughes's *Islam and the Tyranny of Authenticity* (2015) and my own edited volume, *Identity, Politics, and the Study of Islam* (2018) for a debate on these questions.

some of our expertise when it comes to walking the tightrope between insiders and outsiders, priests and heathens, as Ninian Smart (albeit with a different set of concerns) called for over forty-years ago.

Turning to theories of neoliberalism, we would do well to consider how this mode of discourse and ideology critique aligns in important ways with the study of religion, including questions of morality and mythmaking. For example, in *The Countercultural Logic of Neoliberalism* (2020), David Hancock describes how Friedrich Hayek believed that in order to defeat socialism and Keynesian ideas, capitalism would have to create its own heroes and mythologies within popular culture—an idea that was championed by neoconservative thinker Irving Kristol in the 1970s, who borrowed this idea from Hayek (Hancock 2020, 73). Hancock elaborates:

> Important to this has been the development of entrepreneurial celebrities. Lionised for their risk-taking, they have escaped from the dour, conservative stereotypes of finance ... and in Donald Trump we have the personification of the rejection of conservative values in entrepreneurial celebrity and the dominance of a libidinal spirit that gives him great authenticity to millions of Americans.
> (Hancock 2020, 74)

For Hancock, the countercultural logic of neoliberalism has been most effective when it comes to overturning traditional bourgeois morality in favor of a culture of transgression that was first popularized during the 1960s (see Nagle 2017). Importantly, he argues that such transgression transcends traditional left/right political and economic ideologies and uses "th[is] aesthetic to sell a now precariatised life-world as the ultimate expression of personal freedom" (Hancock 2020, 9).[24]

Wendy Brown picks up on a similar theme in her book *In the Ruins of Neoliberalism*. While Brown highlights the role of Hayek in promoting markets and morals as "the foundation of freedom, order, and the development of civilization" (Brown 2019, 12), she also notes that his vision of neoliberal reason stressed the value of "traditional hierarchies," and patriarchal "family values."[25] Jessica Whyte echoes this theme in *Morals of the Market* (2019), noting that members of the Mont Pèlerin Society maintained that "family values, Christianity, and 'Western civilization' (loc. 181)" were foundational to the organization of neoliberalism as an ideological framework. She also observes that Hayek's "morals of the market" "required that moral obligations are limited to the requirement that we refrain from harming others, and do not require positive obligations to others" (ibid., loc. 232). In a similar vein, Melina Cooper (2016) marks the development of these ideas by examining the influence of Chicago School economist Gary Becker, who sought to end "welfare as we know it" and "enforce kinship obligations as an alternative to the redistribution of income by the state" (loc. 1569).

---

24. For a book-length analysis of these ideas coming out of 1960s sub-cultures, see Fred Turner's *From Counterculture to Cyberculture* (2006).
25. For a thorough treatment of this idea, see Jaime Peck's *The Construction of Neoliberal Reason* (2010).

One final study of note is Suzanne Schneider's *The Apocalypse and the End of History: Modern Jihad and the Crisis of Liberalism* (2021), where she offers a novel and persuasive interpretation of jihadi violence by placing neoliberalism at its core. As she writes:

> It is a central premise of this book that jihad became unmoored from its traditional keeper, the state, over the course of the last century. In this chapter I argue that a new ideological scaffolding has emerged to match this reality, one in which individuals—as believers, soldiers, and martyrs—have moved center stage. ... [T]he primacy of the individual in both moral and political terms reflects something novel within militant thought: namely, a sense of disenchantment with both politics as usual and establishment forms of collective resistance.
>
> (Schneider 2021, loc. 800)

Tracing the ways in which forms of jihad have long been the domain of Islamic jurists and viewed as "a communal obligation" (ibid., loc. 492), Scheider argues that modern-day jihadis linked to groups like ISIS reflect a "realignment back to [neo]liberal sentiments," since these groups reject the authority of the state and elevate "the individual as primary political subject" (ibid., loc. 501). In the spirit of neoliberal ideology, she claims that this "new jihad offers ... the apparition of personal agency amid an ever-growing sense of collective futility" (ibid., loc. 811).

Without making any strong proclamations about the character and effects of neoliberalization, I propose that theorizing this concept reflects an effort to name a tradition of thinkers, policies, institutions, and ideologies that have had a considerable impact on the modern world. It is also evident that the type of morality and myth-making that neoliberal ideology is commonly associated with can offer a useful analytic lens for thinking about the production of modern subjectivities, including ideas about the individual, freedom, and the role of the state.[26] Indeed, the curious blend of traditional morality with cultures of transgression that is said to characterize neoliberal forms of governmentality is an area ripe for exploration in the study of religion. Lastly, the link between neoliberalism and market-based solutions has clear implications for the future of the study of religion, which has been among the more vulnerable disciplines to cutbacks and austerity measures, especially following the 2008 Global Financial Crisis.

One final note that was not addressed in Elliott's volume is the role of social media in transforming scholarship on religion and the opportunities it may yet afford us. For a time, it seemed that blogging was a new and fruitful horizon for religious studies, though attention has lapsed in recent years, perhaps lost in the glut of information bursting from all sides.[27] Given the lacks jobs in religious

---

26. Sociologists of religion have long theorized about the relationship between state provisions and religiosity (see Beckford 2012; Bruce 2002; Norris and Inglehart 2004), though few have made explicit or sustained connections with neoliberal ideology.

27. I edited the *Bulletin for the Study of Religion* blog (an heir of the *CSSR Bulletin*) from 2012 to 2018, and witnessed first-hand how the enthusiasm and collaborative energy that blogging initially inspired began to wane in the later years of the 2010s.

studies, the humanities and much of the social sciences, we would do well to make better use of younger scholars, whose proximity to new cultural trends, native slag, sub-cultures, and technologies, gives them a tremendous advantage over many older scholars who naturally lose the thread of connectivity to the rhythms and lifeworlds of those who swim in these waters each and every day.

If our new, digital horizons have come to resemble Paul Klee's Twittering Machine (see note 2) under the lure of neoliberal reason, greater awareness of its effects on our discipline is a crucial first step toward steering the systems and subjectivities that it has created in more productive directions. In addition, what if the rich, yet often ignored history of religions is one of those nascent forces waiting to be revived? What if the new horizons of social media can help bring this about, while granting younger generations a key role in the process with their own skill sets in collaboration with the old guard? And what if the question of unifying the field has finally found a common goal in developing methods and theories that speak back against neoliberalization as a threat to our collective survival and, perhaps, can help us to rebuild beyond the fog of perennial crises?

Matt Sheedy holds a PhD in the study of religion and is a visiting professor of North American Studies at the University of Bonn, Germany. His research interests include critical social theory, theories of secularism and atheism, as well as representations of Christianity, Islam, and Native American traditions in popular and political culture. He is the author of *Owning the Secular: Religious Symbols, Culture Wars, Western Fragility* (Routledge, 2021).

References

Aalbers, Manuel B. 2013. "Neoliberalism is Dead ... Long Live Neoliberalism." *International Journal of Urban and Regional Research*, 37(3): 1083–1090.
Barry, Andrew, Thomas Osbourne, and Nikolas Rose. 1996. *Foucault and Political Reason: Liberalism, Neo-Liberalism, and Rationalities of Government*. Chicago, IL: The University of Chicago Press.
Beckford, James A. 2012. "SSSR Presidential Address Public Religions and the Postsecular: Critical Reflections." *Journal for the Scientific Study of Religion*, 51(1): 1–19.
Bellah, R. N. (1970). *Beyond Belief: Essays on Religion in a Post-Traditionalist World*. Berkeley, CA: University of California Press.
Birch, Kean. 2015. *We Have Never Been Neoliberal: A Manifesto for a Doomed Youth*. Washington, DC: Zero Books.
Braun, Willi, and Russell T. McCutcheon (eds.). 2008. *Introducing Religion: Essay in Honor of Jonathan Z. Smith*. Sheffield: Equinox.
Braun, Willi, and Russell T. McCutcheon (eds.). 2018. *Reading J.Z. Smith: Interviews and Essays*. New York: Oxford University Press.
Brown, Wendy. 2019. *In the Ruins of Neoliberalism: The Rise of Antidemocratic Politics in the West*. New York: Columbia University Press.
Bruce, Steve. 2002. *God is Dead: Secularization in the West (Religion in the Modern World)*. Oxford: Blackwell Press.
Cahill, Damien, and Martijn Konings. 2017. *Neoliberalism*. Cambridge, MA: Polity Press.
Centeno, Miguel A., and Joseph N. Cohen. 2012. "The Arc of Neoliberalism." *Annual Review of Sociology*, 38: 317–340.

Cooper, Melinda. 2020. "Neoliberalism's Family Values: Welfare, Human Capital, and Kinship." In Dieter Plehwe, Quinn Slobodian, and Philip Mirowski, Philip (eds.), *Nine Lives of Neoliberalism*, loc. 1553–1952. London: Verso.

Crews, Emily D., and Russell T. McCutcheon (eds.). 2020. *Remembering J.Z. Smith: A Career and Its Consequences*. Sheffield: Equinox.

Daley-Bailey, Kate. 2016. "For the Good or the 'Guild': An Open Letter to the American Academy of Religion." *Bulletin for the Study of Religion*, 44(4): 4–9.

Dittes, J. E. (1971). Typing the Typologies: Some Parallels in the Career of Church-Sect and Extrinsic-Intrinsic. *Journal for the Scientific Study of Religion* 10(4): 375–383. https://doi.org/10.2307/1384784

Elliott, S. S. (2013). *Reinventing Religious Studies: Key Writings in the History of a Discipline*. Abingdon: Routledge.

England, Kim, and Kevin Ward. 2016. "Theorizing Neoliberalization." In Simon Springer, Kean Birch, and Julie MacLeavy (eds.), *The Handbook of Neoliberalism*, loc. 2017–2329. New York: Routledge.

Gentili, Dario. 2021. *The Age of Precarity: Endless Crisis as an Art of Government*. London: Verso.

Hancock, David. 2020. *The Countercultural Logic of Neoliberalism*. New York: Routledge.

Harvey, David. 2005. *A Brief History of Neoliberalism*. New York: Oxford University Press.

Hochuli, Alex, and George Hoare. 2021. *The End of the End of History: Politics in the Twenty-First Century*. Winchester: Zero Books.

Hughes, Aaron. 2015. *Islam and the Tyranny of Authenticity: An Inquiry in Disciplinary Apologetics and Self-Deception*. Sheffield: Equinox.

Klein, Naomi. 2007. *The Shock Doctrine: The Rise of Disaster Capitalism*. Picador: New York.

Marantz, Andrew. 2019. *Antisocial: Online Extremists, Techno-Utopians, and the Hijacking of the American Conversation*. New York: Penguin Books.

McGregor, Hannah, Julie Rak, and Erin Wunker. 2018. *Refuse: CanLit in Ruins*. Toronto, ON: Book*hug.

Minor, Robert, and Robert Baird. 1983. "Teaching About Religion at the State University: Taking the Issue Seriously and Strictly." *Council for the Study of Religion Bulletin* 14(3): 69–72.

Mirowski, Philip. 2013. *Never Let a Serious Crisis Go to Waste: How Neoliberalism Survived the Financial Meltdown*. London: Verso.

Mirowski, Philip. 2020. "The Neoliberal Ersatz Nobel Prize." In Dieter Plehwe, Quinn Slobodian, and Philip Mirowski (eds.), *Nine Lives of Neoliberalism*, loc. 3501–4091. London: Verso.

NAASR Note. 2015. "When is the Tent too Big?" Retrieved from https://naasr.com/2014/12/28/naasrsbl-call-for-proposals

Nagle, Angela. 2017. *Kill All Normies: The Online Culture Wars from Tumblr and 4-Chan to the Alt-Right and Trump*. Winchester: Zero Books.

Nik-Khah, Edward. 2020. "On Skinning a Cat: George Stigler on the Marketplace of Ideas." In Dieter Plehwe, Quinn Slobodian, and Philip Mirowski, Philip (eds.), *Nine Lives of Neoliberalism*, loc. 816–1186. London: Verso.

Norris, Pippa, and Ronald Inglehart. 2004. *Sacred and Secular: Religion and Politics Worldwide*. Cambridge: Cambridge University Press.

Peck, Jamie. 2010. *Constructions of Neoliberal Reason*. New York: Oxford.

Phillips-Fein, Kim. 2019. "The History of Neoliberalism." In Brent Cebul, Lily Geismer, and Mason B. Willliams (eds.), *Shaped by the State: Toward a New Political History of the Twenty-First Century*, 347–362. Chicago, IL: University of Chicago Press.

Plehwe, Dieter, and Quinn Slobodian (eds.). 2020. "Introduction." In Dieter Plehwe, Quinn Slobodian, and Philip Mirowski (eds.), *Nine Lives of Neoliberalism*, loc. 121–393. London: Verso.
Purcell, Mark. 2016. "Our New Arms." In Simon Springer, Kean Birch, and Julie MacLeavy (eds.), *The Handbook of Neoliberalism*, 613–622. New York: Routledge.
Raschke, Carl A. 1983. "The Future of Religious Studies: Moving Beyond the Mandate of the 1960s." *Council for the Study of Religion Bulletin* 14(5): 146–148.
Readings, Bill. 1996. *The University in Ruins*. Cambridge, MA: Harvard University Press.
Schneider, Suzanne. 2021. *The Apocalypse and the End of History: Modern Jihad and the Crisis of Liberalism*. London: Verso.
Seymour, Richard. 2019. *The Twittering Machine*. London: The Indigo Press.
Sheedy, Matt (ed.). 2018. *Identity, Politics, and the Study of Islam*. Sheffield: Equinox.
Smart, Ninian. 2014. "History of Religions." In Scott Elliott (ed.), *Reinventing Religious Studies: Key Writings in the History of a Discipline*, 46–50. New York: Routledge.
Springer, Simon, Kean Birch, and Julie MacLeavy. 2016. "An Introduction to Neoliberalism." In Simon Springer, Kean Birch, and Julie MacLeavy, (eds.), *The Handbook of Neoliberalism*, loc. 551–996. New York: Routledge.
Steger, Manfred, and Ravi K. Roy. 2021. *Neoliberalism: A Very Short Introduction*, 2nd edition. Oxford: Oxford University Press.
Turner, Fred. 2006. *From Counterculture to Cyberculture: Stewart Brand, the Whole Earth Network, and the Rise of Digital Utopianism*. Chicago, IL: The University of Chicago Press.
Venugopaul, Rajesh. 2015. "Neoliberalism as a Concept." *Economy and Society*, 44(2): 165–87.
Vernoff, Charles Elliott. 1983. "Naming the Game: A Question of the Field." *Council on the Study of Religion Bulletin*, 15(4), 109–112.
Whyte, Jessica. 2019. *The Morals of the Market: Human Rights and the Rise of Neoliberalism*. London: Verso.

Chapter 12

Pop Goes the People
Populism, Panics, and Pandemics

Carmen Celestini

On March 17, 2020, the premier of Ontario declared a state of emergency, and the province was placed into lockdown. As I was then teaching there, I soon found myself in a state of lockdown longer than any other in North America (Levindon-King 2021). The crisis created by the COVID-19 pandemic, at times, was overwhelming, and I was locked in my home for what felt like an eternity. Certainly, I recognized the privilege of my position of having the luxury of a spacious home, the ability to remain working, and the distractions and contact that technology afforded me, and yet the perpetual state of my world being reduced to the walls of my home and the few blocks in my neighborhood I would walk each day became almost suffocating.

Outside the walls of my pandemic existence, as people reacted to the preventative measures of the pandemic, the world had collided into my research of conspiracy theories, populism, Christian apocalyptic thought, and right-wing extremism. These measures and the pandemic itself, easily melded into the conspiratorial world that the mainstreaming of conspiracies, such as QAnon, and extremism had been creating.

The culmination of all these divergent publics came to a crescendo with the events of January 6 on Capitol Hill. My teaching and my research had moved from the margins to the mainstream. This unprecedented global crisis intermingled the political with the pandemic and spilled over into a crisis in the classroom. The religious studies courses I taught included "Evil," "Death and Dying," "Populism," and "Conspiracy Theories/Disinformation." The theoretical approaches taught in these courses were no longer analyzing the broad historical and religious topics normal to such survey courses, they were the reality that both my students and I were experiencing.

As QAnon, Pizzagate, COVID-19 hoax theories, the Great Reset, and the topics of freedom, liberty, and religious persecution became the headlines of media sources and the content of social-media memes and posts, the theoretical became reality. Teaching courses about these topics amid a worldwide crisis had changed both my pedagogy and my interactions with my students. The crisis facing the world, were developing into a crisis in the pedagogy of religious studies, as I grappled with how to impart the skills to contextualize the world through various religious lenses, and how this understanding can and does impact the political and being empathetic to what we were all witnessing and living through. Throughout the pandemic my syllabi had become more of a possible roadmap, with an understanding that there will always be forks in the road where we—instructor and students—will leave the chosen path and venture into the reality of what is occurring outside of the classroom walls. Both I and my students learned about each other on a very emotional plane. As they asked questions about rising populism, moral panics, and death and dying, I felt I'd become a real-life version of Ms. Frizzle from the television series *The Magic School Bus,* leading the students on field trips through the magic of headlines, social media, insurrections on Capitol Hill, anti-COVID-19 lockdown protests, conspiracies, and politics.

In essence my approach to the subject matter I taught had to be adapted to address what was occurring in the world outside of the classroom, but I had to be cognizant that the learning process was not one only being undertaken by my students. Throughout the crisis of the world outside of my locked down existence, I was granted two new post-doctoral positions, both researching conspiracies, disinformation, social media, and right-wing extremists.

Simultaneously, my work had transitioned. As a scholar of conspiracies and Christian apocalyptic thought, my work, at times, had been marginalized as "salacious" or a topic that was not be considered serious academia. Yet, as the topics of my research became mainstream, I was called upon as an "expert" in the media. This new form of public intellectualism brought with it a greater realization of the anger, frustration, and animosity that the public was articulating through their conspiracies, protests, and social-media warrior tactics. I found myself in the crosshairs of their vitriol, as angry emails, direct messages, and social media posts began to arrive.

Each of my courses addressed topics which are difficult but must be part of the public discourse. Moral panics, conspiracy theories, and populism thrive on racism, anger, fearmongering, and notions of perpetual disaster. Moral panics create a foundation for two possible outcomes: an establishment response that soothes public fears by allowing experts and institutions to guide, lead, and resolve the situation; or a populist response that encourages the public to focus on the spectacle of the crisis and suggest it is irresolvable without populist input. With the COVID-19 pandemic the public's justifiable sense of fear was heightened and transformed into a moral panic through the non-establishment mechanics of social and non-traditional media. In this case, the populist response eclipsed the establishment response, and the ensuing moral panic led to citizens taking sides in a battle—not against the virus, but against opposing elements of society representing the moral divide of a country.

The pandemic, combined with the mainstreaming of conspiracy theories and extremism, provided a means of linking the historical to the contemporary. Bruce Lincoln, in "Thesis on Method," noted that understanding the system of ideology within one's own society can prove difficult, because our own consciousness is ingrained with, and a product of, that very system, rendering it as the "natural" order (Lincoln 2013, 165–167). Yet, here as I taught the history of moral panics, one was raging within the academic institution itself, as public battles regarding critical race theory were waged against academia. As we, as educators were accused of inculcating "self-hatred" and "guilt" into our students, the classroom was dissecting the topic in real time. Simultaneously, populism was rising across North America, with clear articulations of the very institutions of society being the "deviants" or group dismantling the moral fiber of society. Discussions of deep-state actors, politicians beholden to foreign entities, and the limitations of rights and freedoms—including religious persecution due to COVID-19 preventative measures—all leapt from social media feeds and headlines and mingled with the historical and theoretical in lectures. As the morality and values of society were questioned across the political spectrum, we discussed moral panics in our virtual classrooms.

Moral panics are comprised of a scare or a perceived threat from what are deemed "deviants" or a group who are characterized as engaging in evil practices. This group, or the deviants, are blamed for attacking a society's culture or value systems. The moral panic is often out of proportion to the actual threat. There too, exists a measurement of delusion as some of these threats are often imaginary, although some threats may indeed be real. Historically, moral panics have erupted only within certain components of society, leaving others unmoved or not impacted by the perceived threat. The panic is often supported by the media, as they play a significant role in its creation. A typical component is sexuality or sexual acts. The morality, or fears associated with the sexual sphere, impose a status of wrongdoing or abnormality to the "other" (Goode and Nachman 2010, 33). These notions of fears, and the bewilderment that those outside of the affected group feel, make linking moral panics to conspiracy theories an easy task.

Conspiracy theories, while often portrayed as being tied to socio-economic position or education, are used as a narrative for expressing injustice and an articulation of fears both real and imagined, which are then propagated as the basis for some social movements. Conspiracies are one among many tools utilized for mobilization. The use of conspiracy theories as a lens to interpret the political, and as a motivational tool for populist and militia movements, has played a significant role in the history of the United States. To illustrate moral panics and conspiracy theories, normally the comic book moral panic from the 1950s is used, but this time in my lectures QAnon was the example. QAnon is a bricolage of far-right conspiracy theories that at the center holds that former president Donald Trump is leading a secret war against an international group of satanic pedophiles. QAnon at its essence brings together religion, far-right politics, conspiracy theories, and radicalization to propel some individuals to acts of violence and criminality. The FBI has also named QAnon as a possible security threat in their report on the increasing influence that anti-government, identity based, political fringe groups may have via the internet to expose individuals who lean towards extreme behavior to enact these violent actions.

Fundamentally QAnon allows for individuals to interpret and create theories about the conspiracy that can allow some adherents to create an alternative history and an alternative reality. From its beginning, QAnon has been linked to politics and the "demonization" of those in power positions in the Democratic Party and of liberals as a whole. Beginning with symbology and coded words in John Podesta's emails, the Pizzagate conspiracy was born. Then on October 28, 2017, the QAnon conspiracy emerged on the pages of 4chan's politically incorrect page. Q's first announcement was that secretary of state Hillary Clinton would be arrested on a specific date and time. From there, Tracy Diaz, a YouTube vlogger, used her considerable influence with her significant subscriber base to discuss the "crumbs" (i.e., clues) left by Q, launching the conspiracy theory from the pages of 4chan.

QAnon links together contemporary politics, racist tropes, and religion. They are social heroes rising against "the Cabal" whose singular goal is to undermine American democracy to empower themselves through their nefarious agenda. In essence, the Cabal ultimately seeks to destroy American freedom and subjugate the citizens to their will. Mixed within the conspiracy are the moral taboos of pedophilia, Satanism, and human sacrifice. In the end, the adherents believe the oppressed will be free when "The Storm" comes to arrest and destroy the oppressors.

Traditionally conspiracies have been within the realm of those who are marginalized, yet with QAnon, the then president of the United States was supporting and expressing his own conspiracies from the pulpit of the White House. His vocal battles with the government agencies and institutions such as the FBI supported the notion that he is the leader who will defeat the Deep State. With this supposed or interpreted support from the highest of political positions, QAnon has spread to being not just a belief within the borders of the country. QAnon has spread to other countries including the United Kingdom and Canada. The conspiracy, much like apocalyptic thought, can provide people with a sense of purpose and control in the face of disenchantment and fear in their present reality. Most importantly it can provide a conduit to belonging within a community of patriots, fighting for God, country, and family. As scholar Michael Barkun argues regarding apocalyptic thought, believers gain a sense of control or meaning over what is transpiring through the discovery and interpretation of signs and symbols (Barkun 2013, 3). What is unique with QAnon is that interpretation is completely left up to the reader, as Q drops "crumbs" for them to "bake" (i.e., interpret). These crumbs allow the believer to gain enough control to corroborate their belief system with the phenomena they are facing, in the crisis-ridden world, and to allow for a coming golden era, where this crisis will have been alleviated.

In many instances, these conspiratorial ideas are linked to millennialist or apocalyptic thought. These worldviews are based upon the idea of a continuing struggle between good and evil, which will persist until the end of history, with the defeat of evil. Barkun argues that millennialists are attracted to conspiracism for two reasons. The first is because a millenarian movement without a large following or membership can blame hidden forces on its lack of popularity or social impact. The second, is because conspiracism provides someone to blame when the end of times appears to be elusive. The blame can be placed upon a conspiratorial group or the "minions of Satan." In essence, conspiracy theories provide an explanation for the failure of the group and the world at large. Further radical groups envision their values and morals as being superior to others, and in doing so develop an us-vs-them mentality. The group will rationalize violence as a way to address their problem or concern. This violence is directed at the "other," whom they have demonized or blamed for the problem. The last characteristic is the belief in the efficacy of using violence (Barkun 2013, 3).

Zwingmann and Sebastian posit that history and historical events play a significant role in the interpretation of the end times. Current events are interpreted as important signals of the coming end times. Historical and current events are dualistic in nature, when conceived through a millennialist lens. The events are interpreted as those who are just or "good" and those who are evil. There is no moral ambiguity. There are two versions of interpretation, those who see the pessimistic apocalyptic perspective, and those who have the expectation that evil will gain control in the world and that evil has to be eliminated via a catastrophe that will be brought about by God. The world as we know it will be destroyed but, in its place, will be a world of peace for 1000 years for those who are "good" or "just." This form of interpretation is called pre-millennialism, "pre" being used to explain that the return of Christ will occur before the establishment of the millennium. The secondary interpretation is an optimistic one: that the 1000 years of peace will be brought about by those "good" or "just" individuals, brought forth by following the plan of God. In essence, good humans following the directions of God will bring about a time of peace without a catastrophe being needed. This interpretation is referred to as post-millennialism, because the return of Christ will happen after the good and just believers have established the millennium (Zwingmann and Murken 2000, 18).

Belief in these end times scenarios can be brought forth by times of cultural crisis, when the world is understood as segregating, persecuting, or attacking one's social group. The millennial will provide a change in the social order and provides a conduit in which to criticize the contemporary society the adherents find themselves in. In becoming a believer of apocalyptic or millenarianism, the future is interpreted as promising and full of hope, due to their being on the side of good and just. Being on the side of good provides the believer with a special importance, a new identity of sorts. The events of the unfolding end times can seem threatening, but the believer understands them to be controlled and have a context of meaning. Every crisis or threat is understood to be a pathway for the "chosen" that will lead to their salvation, while those working on the side of evil will be punished or exterminated. Through connecting with like-minded individuals, the believer finds validation; but also, they are socially integrated and supported by their new community (Zwingmann and Murken 2000, 21).

Not all conspiracy theories lead to radicalization, nor do they spur political action or mobilization. Yet across the Americas, conspiracies can be linked to both. These theories have provided a conduit for the expression and symbolic representation of the extreme-right's fears. In defining the extreme-right and the use of fear and conspiracy for mobilization, important commonalities need to be acknowledged. Commonly, there is a trope of making their nation more ethnically homogenous and demanding a return to more traditional values. Descriptions of those in power and national institutions are seen as being under the control of elites who place internationalism before the nation. Elites, or powerful individuals, are described by the extreme-right as putting their own self-interests ahead of those they represent. This notion of fear and dread is an important component of the power of conspiracy theories, in that they can provide an "answer" or rationale as to why these fears manifest. Linked to politics, religion, and racism, conspiracy theories have served as justification for political mobilization, activism and—in some cases—violence. Politically, populism and conspiracy are usually connected.

Within this articulation of themselves and the enemy, conspiracy theories consist of a framework that argues there exists a secretive, powerful group that is manipulating the events or progressions within the social milieux of the nation. Many, if not all, conspiracy theories share an apocalyptic narrative within their structure. This narrative creates a good-versus-evil ideology. Richard Hofstadter in *The Paranoid Style in American Politics* wrote of how the right-wing extremists of his time felt dispossessed, that their America had been taken away from them. Their goal was to repossess America and to "prevent the final destructive act of subversion." Hofstadter argued that those who believed in conspiracy saw it through an apocalyptic lens. Of a typical adherent, Hofstadter wrote "he traffics in the birth and death of whole worlds, whole political orders, whole systems of human values...like religious millennialists, he expresses the anxiety of those who are living through the last days, and he is sometimes disposed to set a date for the apocalypse" (Hofstadter 2012, 5).

Barkun argues that there are different types of conspiracy theories. The most prevalent on the extreme right is what Barkun refers to as "improvisational conspiracism." This form can only exist when there are significant subcultures. Mainly rising or appearing during times of crisis, improvisational conspiracism is comprised of heterodox religion, esoteric and occult beliefs, fringe science, and radical politics; and it has a potent influence on politics within the nation (Barkun 2013: xi). In many instances these conspiratorial ideas are linked to millennialist or apocalyptic thought. These worldviews are based upon the idea of a continuing struggle between good and evil, which will persist until the end of history with the defeat of evil.

These foundations for moral panics, conspiracy theory, and extremism were easily applied to the societal events occurring throughout the time I was teaching during lockdown. The pedological approach I have is one that could be defined as "radical," in that I strive to create a community within the classroom. The topics we address—even when not in crisis—are difficult, and a measure of trust is required for discourse in the classroom. The first day of classes is spent in introductions. With students responding to a set of questions about themselves, their pronouns, and why they are interested in the subject. In addition to introducing themselves, I require that each student discuss a shared connection or pose a question to a minimum of two presentations by their fellow students. This helps to create connections and commonalities among the students and begins the process of discussions on the very first day.

As the instructor I am not removed from this process, as each student is asked to participate in an AMA ("Ask Me Anything"). The students are encouraged not to ask me about the course or assignments; this is their opportunity to engage with me as a member of our community—or "public." Questions range from specifics about conspiracies, my research on right-wing extremism and social media, to favorite baking recipes; but the AMA provides an opportunity for the students to become comfortable with me and approaching me as we tackle some difficult subject matter. This idea of creating a "public" within the classroom is developed from the work of sociologist Michael Burawoy. Burawoy has coined the term "public sociology" which he defines as an umbrella of teaching "constituting students as a potential public, engaging with them as a community with pre-existing experience that they bring into the classroom. Teaching turns this community into a public and connects it to other publics beyond the university" (Burawoy 2008, 1). Further he states there is a secondary meaning to this pedagogy of public sociology, where there is less concern or focus on the reconstitution and extension of the classroom into civil society, but using the public realm as a classroom in itself. This public sociology is what occurred in our virtual classrooms during the pandemic.

For Burawoy, critical approach to teaching begins with an assumption that the students in our classroom come "armed" with their own experiences, and that this is acknowledged through a dialogue with our students. This is a reciprocal teaching approach where the educator learns from their students, and the student learns how to "teach" their knowledge. One sees this in courses outside of the classroom, such as field studies (Burawoy 2008, 9). The classroom and the world collide in this "pedagogy of crisis" in that everything becomes a "field study" of sorts.

Teaching of public sociology is broken down into three dialogues. The initial dialogue is between the instructor and the student. The student brings to the classroom their lived experience, and the teacher takes this as their "point of departure," expanding on it through lectures and readings. So, this is where the student engages in an "internal dialogue." The course materials and the lectures become a conduit through which the students apply this dialogue in an expansion of their self-understanding. The second dialogue is among the students. The very notion of "public sociology" is that they create a public, and that this is achieved through a conversation with one another. This is where the divergent lived experiences of the students are expressed through common readings and assignments: "Every effort is made to force a common dialogue among students that also facilitates their individual expression" (Burawoy 2008, 10). Lastly the third dialogue is the idea of the students as a public among the many other publics. This includes family, those they work with, and so on; and as they interact with these other publics, they expand the notions of each group as a public themselves. The students take what they have learned in the classroom and try to share it through their involvement with these other groups or publics. This is the dialogue they have with the world around them.

There is a formal version of this in having students do placements, work co-ops, and volunteering; but this three-level dialogue became instantaneous within my classroom and the publics both the students and myself interacted with. Our classroom, in many ways, was the greater public, ourselves, and the crises we were witnessing. Our combined lived reality was what was being analyzed by the theories taught in the classroom.

One particular assignment created and supported this public within the classroom. Students were asked to post articles, news pieces, podcasts, videos, or blogs that they had encountered into discussions posts every two weeks. The topics were not constrained, other than they had to address or interact with the course material or course subject matter. The purpose of this was to allow the students to share with each other the material that they'd encountered in their real world. Many of the students enrolled in the courses had selected them as electives, and so came from a mix of numerous fields of study across the university. Computer engineering students could post about topics they encountered while doing readings or research, as could students from the health sciences. This provided a bricolage of approaches to the topics of the course, where the theories learned were provided through various lenses and mediums. Students were required to write a summary of the piece they were posting, including what new information they had learned from the piece, how it interacted with the course material, and why they had chosen it. Importantly, they also had to pose a question to the class. Each student was responsible for responding to a minimum of three posts other than their own, where they too had to pose a question.

Rarely did the students respond to the minimum required. Conversations continued well after the deadline, with students asking that I stop the "closing" of the discussion boards, so that they could continue their discussions. In fact, many of the discussions continued in my virtual office hours, via video classrooms. The students were grappling with the crises that were happening. They were scared, and some were traumatized as the violence grew. The conversations were honest and, at times emotional, as topics touched upon the death of George Floyd, the Black Lives Matter protests, the Capitol Hill events, QAnon violence, COVID fears and tensions from the virus itself, and public reactions. From those conversations, the historical material and the theories from the course syllabi were being applied to the upheaval of their society.

To accommodate students who were out of the country and in different time zones, I would hold virtual office hours at staggered times throughout the week. As this could cause time constraints, I coordinated my video office hours over all of the courses I was teaching, so there were often students from my different courses engaging in conversation with me at the same time. Many of my courses include some crossover, and the role of religion in each played a significant aspect in these talks. Similarly, the crises of society became a common topic of discussion, but from the various perspectives of each course. The conversations, then, were also varied as the theoretical and historical material from the courses were applied by the students in their discussions. Ideas of evil, conspiracy, populism, and religious response to both the death and dying due to the pandemic and the preventative measures were all discussed.

Within the course material there are ideas of evil from radicalization or political mobilization, this mobilization can be articulated through populism, which in itself depends upon conspiracy, nationalism, and racism. Current research on radicalization and violence shares many commonalities with those who are conspiracists and the theories which they believe in. Counterterrorism scholar Amanda Garry argues that conspiracy and extremist ideologies are different, but they can intersect. Garry and colleagues found that, "While conspiracy theories may not have mass radicalizing effects, they are extremely effective at leading to increased polarization within societies" (Garry et al. 2021, 154). Doosje et al argue that there are five characteristics of radical groups, the first being that the group perceives that there is a serious problem in society. Once having perceived the problem, the group is dissatisfied with the manner in which it is being dealt with by institutions. The institutions blamed are predominately the police and politicians, who are understood as not acknowledging or paying attention to the problem or as simply not doing enough to handle the issue. This lack of acknowledgement or action sows a distrust in the institutions and an understanding that the authorities are not legitimate (Doosie 2016, 80). Professor of law, Mark Fenster states that a conspiracy theory is affective when politics are interpreted through a conspiratorial lens by those individuals and groups for whom politics are inaccessible. This inaccessibility renders politics as something that is impenetrable or secret (Fenster 1999, 69). Importantly, Fenster also notes that although conspiracy theories can be wrong and appear simplistic in their presentation of "answers," they may harbor a problem or an issue that needs to be discussed or addressed. Beneath the conspiracy can be issues such as structural inequities, an unjust political order, a dysfunctional civil society, or an exploitative economic system. The conspiracy can provide a response to these issues for the adherents when society as a whole or the social safety net does not. Those who feel disenfranchised will seek out others who understand or feel the same and create a community or social group of like-minded individuals.

Conspiracy theories, while often portrayed as being based on socio-economic position and education, are used as a narrative for expressing injustice, an articulation of fears both real and imagined, which are then propagated as the basis for some social movements. Conspiracies are one among many tools utilized for mobilization. The use of conspiracy theories as a lens to interpret the political and as a motivational tool for populist and militia movements has played a significant role in the United States. Michael Barkun describes the links between religion and violence as being the use of a cosmic plan. By following or acting on behalf of this cosmic plan the perpetrators are free from any inhibitions that are imposed by laws or customs. In Barkun's research of white supremacist movements, he notes that many of them are described as political organizations, and that some do pursue political objectives, which fulfill religious beliefs. White supremacist movements have a millenarian character, unlike other right-wing groups, since white supremacist groups possess both an apocalyptic rhetoric and a paramilitary structure. In his assessment of the white supremacist movements, Barkun argues that linking or trying to understand these movements by comparison to the past is not an identical comparison. For example, American Fascism in the 1930s and 1940s had a rhetoric of violence but rarely committed violent acts. Contemporary movements, however, do engage in violent acts. As well, they not only speak about an overthrow of the government, but they also actually believe that this is possible (Barkun 1989, 416).

  This belief was apparent in the discussion posts and conversations as my students read and watched what was occurring throughout 2020 and 2021. As they discussed the realities they encountered or were or witnessing, a new public was created. In this way, they engaged in the second level of public sociology, by teaching each other and learning from each other through dialogue. The creation of this new public attempted to understand the social crises or upheavals, while I—as their instructor—continued to teach and participate in the conversation. This public also created a desire for a deeper understanding for the students, many of whom took one of the other courses they had engaged with, via the student discourse in the virtual office hours. I too learned from them. As they asked questions about QAnon, COVID-related protests, and conspiracies, I was required to articulate my research in new ways. From what I learned from their questions and my responses, I was able to change my articulation of events to the media. The third level of public sociology was quickly becoming evident. The students brought forth questions from their publics and the discussions they were having about the course material, while simultaneously, I was taking what I was learning from my discussions with them and using it to reach a larger public through my media interviews. There was a triple dialogue of "student-teacher, student-student, student-public" occurring.

  Burawoy took the idea of public sociology out of the classroom and stated that the sociologist was accountable to audiences outside of academia. No matter the framework, the "teacher" was participating in a reciprocal communication, always between the sociologist and the public. The pedagogy of teaching material linked to crises faced by society, has changed my teaching for the better. The public or communities I try to create in my classrooms has moved to new publics in new ways. My goal of having the students bring the contemporary version of the theories they are learning in the classroom, has shifted in that now the encounters are everywhere, and they are the basis for much of our classroom interaction. While my courses are based upon my areas of research, I understand the value of bringing current and perhaps incomplete research into the discussion. On a personal note, these courses helped both myself and my students to understand what was happening in the world around us. It also brought us much closer as a public and a community.

  In October of 2021, sociologist Mark Carrigan, wrote a blog post entitled "How Bad Will Things Get? The Role of Social Theory when Civilisation is Collapsing" in which he questions how our past experiences can render us blind to our present reality. As we try to understand what is occurring around us, we attempt to filter this understanding through what has happened. As the term "unprecedented" is applied as an adjective to almost every event in the last two years, Carrigan notes that "the unprecedented becomes the precedented" (Carrigan 2021). Similarly, the historical and the theoretical aspect of my research and my teaching has left the realms of the marginalized and the dismissed and come to a place where conspiracy, extremism, and populism has become mainstream, with real world implications. Barkun addressed the idea of the mainstreaming of the fringe, and unlike Fenster, does not see the rise of a political party, but the increase of violence as an outcome. In his argument, Barkun acknowledges the protection that democracies have through constitutional provisions, court decisions, and statutes; but he also notes the important role that customs, practices, and norms play in structuring daily life in democratic societies. These norms, practices, and customs include "norms of civility, ideas about toleration, ways of gathering and disseminating information, and techniques for organizing to advance social and political cause" (Barkun 1989, 441). These norms are challenged by conspiracies and ideas that are, or were considered, on the fringes of society. With the decaying of these norms, Barkun sees the potential for violence. Let us hope that the unprecedented potential for violence and political upheaval does not become the precedent, and that those of us teaching in the midst of crises are creating publics where discourse prevails. While crises in the forms of political uncertainty, global pandemics, the mainstreaming of conspiracy theories, hate speech, racism, and misogyny affect every aspect of our world, attempting to understand these crises through a pedological religious studies perspective within the walls of academia, can be challenging. These crises are not constrained by a scholar's understanding of the discipline, nor the lived experiences and worldviews of the students. Indeed, these unprecedented moments in time can be approached by a shared sociological approach that, too, is not constrained by the walls of the classroom.

Carmen Celestini is a postdoctoral fellow at Queen's University and a definite-term lecturer in religious studies at the University of Waterloo. Her research focuses on improvisational conspiracy, the overlapping belief systems of apocalyptic Christian thought and conspiracy theories, and the impact of these beliefs on the North American political system.

References

Barkun, Michael. 2013. *A Culture of Conspiracy: Apocalyptic Visions in Contemporary America*. Berkeley, CA: University of California Press.
Barkun, Michael. 1989. "Millenarian Aspects of 'White Supremacist' Movements." *Terrorism and Political Violence*, 1(4): 409–434.
Burawoy, Michael. 2008. "What Might we Mean by a Pedagogy of Public Sociology?" *Enhancing Learning in the Social Sciences*, 1(1), 1–15.
Carrigan, Mark. 2021. "How Bad Will Things Get? The Role of Social Theory When Civilisation is Collapsing." Retrieved from https://markcarrigan.net/2021/10/09/how-bad-will-things-get/amp/?__twitter_impression=true
Doosje, Bertjan, et al. 2016. "Terrorism, Radicalization and De-radicalization." *Current Opinion in Psychology* 11: 79–84.

Fenster, Mark. 1999. *Conspiracy Theories: Secrecy and Power in American Culture*. Minneapolis, MN: University of Minnesota Press.
Garry, Amanda, et al. 2021. "QAnon Conspiracy Theory: Examining its Evolution and Mechanisms of Radicalization." *Journal for Deradicalization*, 26: 152–216.
Goode, Erich and Ben-Yehuda Nachman. 2010. *Moral Panics: The Social Construction of Deviance*. Chichester: John Wiley & Sons.
Hofstadter, Richard. 2012. *The Paranoid Style in American Politics*. New York: Vintage.
Levindon-King, Robin. 2021. "Toronto Lockdown—One of the World's Longest?" Retrieved from www.bbc.co.uk/news/world-us-canada-57079577
Lincoln, Bruce. "Theses on Method." In Aaron W. Hughes (ed.), *Theory and Method in the Study of Religion*, 165–167. Leiden: Brill.
Zwingmann, Christian, and Sebastian Murken. 2000. "Coping with an Uncertain Future: Religiosity and Millenarianism." *Archive for the Psychology of Religion*, 23(1): 11-28.

Part IV

Locus

Landmarks in Religious Adaptations in the Face of "Crisis"

Chapter 13

"Social" Church and "Pragmatic" Relationship with the State

The Wager of the Roman Catholic Church in Mexico and the Orthodox Church in Russia in Response to Discourses of Crisis

Xochiquetzal Luna Morales

The beginning of the twentieth century saw two influential revolutions that deemed religion incompatible with their nation-building projects. The 1910 and 1917 Mexican and Russian Revolutions, respectively, sought to defeat religion, or at least suppress its supposedly pernicious influence, a process necessary for transformation (De la Cueva 2018, 503–505). In Mexico, the decades that followed the revolution were crucial for the survival of the Catholic Church. As an institution, the Church faced an imminent secularization process in the country that constrained its privileges while confronting a society where Catholics struggled between being loyal to their faith and being citizens of the new political regimen. In Russia, religion never entirely disappeared throughout the tenure of the communist government. It instead worked mainly underground, albeit considerably diminished. In the case of the Orthodox Church, for instance, both clergy and believers suffered persecution by the state despite the institutional support of the communist party. The state closed churches, imposed severe legal restrictions, and maximized control over spiritual life. No revolutionary leader—in Mexico or Russia—could foresee that faith among the believers and their religious institutions (i.e., the Roman Catholic Church and the Orthodox Church) would escape annihilation and re-emerged to reclaim their role in society.

Without intending to portray these two religious institutions as static and monolithic, this chapter examines how the Roman Catholic Church in Mexico and the Orthodox Church in Russia navigated two critical periods of political and social crisis during the twentieth century. Specifically, it focuses on the years at the end of the Cristero War in Mexico, and the time of *glasnost* (transparency) and *perestroika* (reorganization) in Russia. Grounded in the idea that discourses are clusters of socially constructed knowledge of some aspect of reality (Foucault 1989; Arribas-Ayllon and Walkerdine 2017),[1] this chapter analyzes how the

---

1. Although not expressly discussed in this chapter, the Foucauldian concept of discourse is intrinsically related to the notion of power. Indeed, power, understand it in its broad terms, is for Foucault what moves discourses in society, making them possible to be "seen."

prevalent discourses about crisis "move" to elicit responses from the Mexican Roman Catholic Church and the Russian Orthodox Church. It argues that these institutions have survived despite their internal fractures and divisions because they handled a "pragmatic" relationship with the government and wagered to be a "social" church. Finally, I ask if the efforts and postures these two religious institutions have taken during the COVID-19 pandemic resemble responses to previous political and social turmoil, given that, in this case, the "enemy" is not a political condition or ideology but a universal health crisis.

Cognizant of the difference in time between these two proposed historical periods—around fifty years apart—they remain suitable for examining the churches' responses to a crisis. Their similarities go beyond their revolutionary bond, where religion was deemed antagonistic to the new political regime. Both in Mexico and Russia, citizens still struggle to adjust their identity to the changing times. In Mexico, for instance, while the government encourages its citizens to embrace liberal ideals to build a robust, stable, and modern country, they also feel compelled to protect their faith against the government's rules that constrict its practice. In Russia, the endeavor for its citizens was not only to assimilate themselves into a new capitalist and democratic system, but also into a society where, suddenly, religion "became a mass phenomenon" (Pravmir 2013) and a cohesive element to rebuilding a nation. Furthermore, the current role of the Mexican Catholic Church and the Russian Orthodox Church is impossible to understand without comprehending their responses in the following years after the Cristero War and perestroika, respectively.

The chapter is divided into four sections. The first one sets the methodology and definitions in which I develop my arguments, such as *crisis* and *social church*. The second and third parts explore the prevailing approaches after the Cristero War in Mexico and perestroika in Russia that the Catholic and Orthodox Church used to navigate those difficult years. Finally, the fourth section reflects on if and how those approaches remain salient for these churches in their current responses to the COVID-19 pandemic.

A Social Church in a Time of Crisis

We have become accustomed to using the term "crisis" loosely. Practically, any situation that steps outside of what is considered "normal" may qualify as a crisis: a health crisis, a humanitarian crisis, a personal crisis, an economic crisis, a faith crisis, and so forth. It seems that crises are not only diverse but perennial in our contemporary societies. Hence, what exactly do we mean when we examine a religious tradition through the prism of a crisis? What type of answers, as scholars, are we looking for in a crisis framework?

Moffit (2015, 189) argues that one of the challenges when we label a situation as a crisis is a tendency to assume that we can accurately identify its causes. However, the author argues, a crisis is often "a loose description of a bundle of phenomena" (ibid.). For Moffit, crises "are never neutral, but must be mediated and 'performed' by certain actors" (ibid., 190). Hence, crises result from how social actors interact with each other and the discourses surrounding them. In addition, the term crisis has traditionally conveyed the notion of temporality because it is understood as a moment in time. However, Roitman warns us that crisis, once used to designate a critical moment, holds a contradiction in contemporary settings as it is constructed as an experiential, but at the same time, prolonged condition (Roitman et al. 2020, 774). For Roitman, crises are defined in time and mobilized "in narrative constructions to mark out a 'moment of truth' or as a means to think 'history' itself" (Roitman 2012). Therefore, a crisis cannot be perennial and should entail a vital decision whose choice, for Moffit (2015, 196), is so significant that it changes and delineates the course of history. I understand crisis as a critical moment in time for the state, the church and its believers in Mexico and Russia, identified by the circulation of the available discourses.

My concern is not exploring "what when wrong" after the Cristiada (Cristero War) or the perestroika that produced a "moment of truth" for the Mexican Catholic Church and the Russian Orthodox Church. Instead, I follow Roitman's approach that explores crisis not as a claim about error, but as a judgement about value (Roitman et al. 2020, 775). In other words, I explore these moments of crises by considering how the approaches used by the church and its believers to counteract the state's anti-clericalism allowed the church's survival and even, at times, revitalization.

To understand the complexities and nuances of the existing approaches at that time, I apply the following two frameworks to base my analysis:

(a) Scholars have traditionally framed narratives surrounding the church and the state under the secularization thesis. Nieuwenhuis (2012, 156) argues that the relationship between the church and the state has multiple dimensions beyond just the mere level of separation between them. The author explores this relationship in three dimensions: "religious' place in the state domain, government's role in the religious domains, and state and religion meeting together in intermediate domains" (ibid., 173). The last of these dimensions, where the church and the state meet, guide my analysis. I argue that the Roman Catholic Church in Mexico and the Orthodox Church in Russia survived after the Cristero War and perestroika because they fought to regain spaces in their countries' cultural and social life by actively engaging in the people's welfare, education, and spiritual needs. This is what I termed a "social" church: A church that seeks spaces in the public sphere to be part of people's life and, despite secular discourses, chooses to build its institutional strength from its believers. Although secularization is not an inevitable paradigm to analyze the relationship between the state and the church, it is pertinent to this chapter because it allowed specific responses from both sides.

(b) Meyer's thesis that an institutional religion can become an element of ethnic and national identity and a form of patriotism, especially in times of crisis (Meyer 1993, 712) also guides my analysis. The historian points out that in "a world of suffering and misery, [religion] it is both the comfort of the afflicted and the luxury of the poor" (ibid.). Religion, Meyer argues, is "a warrant of mental survival, dignity, and hope against the odds" (ibid., 711).

The Roman Catholic Church in Mexico after the Cristero War

1929 saw the end of one the most critical and dramatic moments in the relationship between the Roman Catholic Church and the Mexican government. The war and the ten years that followed were instrumental in the configuration of the modern nation-state of Mexico. The cristeros, peasants that did not share the culture of the elites (Meyer 1976, 181), fought to defend their faith against radical anti-clericalism. The most immediate antecedent of the war was the state's attempt in 1925 to establish a schismatic Church "to weaken the Catholic Church and destroy both the Catholic unions and the left-wing independents" (Quintanilla n.d.). However, the conflict represents the zenith of a complex relationship that started with the overwhelming influence of the Catholic Church in the "New World." According to Meyer (1976, 1), the metamorphose of the conflict traces back to three centuries of Spanish domination, where Catholicism and the Church that represented it were ubiquitous.

There are no official statistics of the number of casualties the Cristiada left; historians estimate around 250,000 civilians and military died in the turmoil (Quintanilla n.d.). The "peace agreement" that the Church and the government reached in 1929 was seen as a betrayal by the cristeros, who were not consulted about the settlement terms (Meyer 1976, 201). Moreover, the day after the peace was reached, the Mexican government began a systematic and premeditated murder of all the Cristero leaders to prevent further uprisings (ibid.). Meyer argues that the Catholic Church never led or inspired the movement, though the Vatican and the Catholic hierarchy certainly tried to avoid the violence. Nevertheless, some civil unrest was still inevitable after the agreement with the revolutionary government, which suppressed any further uprisings. In the end, after three years of armed confrontations, the Catholic Church found itself afraid to lose its popular support as some groups of Catholic militants "criticized the settlement and continued to advocate armed resistance to the government" (Reich 1995, 27). In addition, the peace agreement with the state proved to be fragile, and, in 1931, a new wave of anti-clericalism took place while groups of *guerrillas* began to appear. This will be called "the second Cristiada."

The challenge for the Catholic hierarchy in these following years was how to navigate anticlerical discourses while controlling the resurgence of armed uprisings. At the same time, the Church's internal pluralism and its necessity to coexist with a liberal government paved the way to turn to lay Catholic activism. Laity advocacy for a legal, social, and political framework where Catholicism was accepted as part of public life was not new in Mexico during the afterwar period. Before the Cristero War, a burgeoning Catholic social movement represented in

La Unión de los Católicos Mexicanos—better known as "La U"—the Caballeros de Colón, the Asociación de Damas Católicas, and the Asociación Católica de la Juventud Mexicana (ACJM) played a vital role in the attempt to heal the Mexican social question under Catholic values and principles despite their diverse, and sometimes opposite approaches on how to do it (Andes 2014, 42–49). By 1929, some of these organizations continued to function, but the Vatican and the Mexican hierarchy tried to advance a more moderate response of lay activism. The idea was to counteract the state's anti-clericalism by focusing mainly on education, catechism, and the promotion of family values (ibid., 163), working at a root level. As a result, the lay organization Acción Católica Mexicana (ACM) was founded having two essential characteristics: direct episcopal supervision of its activities and mass involvement (Reich 1995, 97). In this sense then, amidst a crisis, the Church wagered to be "social."

ACM was envisioned to grow as a grass-roots movement. Like its European counterparts, the "social Catholicism" of Pope Leo XIII's 1891 encyclical *Rerum Novarum* inspired the organization's founding (Reich 1995, 101). The Church in Mexico especially encouraged its parishes to promote involvement with Acción Católica at lower levels to exert political influence indirectly (Reich 1995, 93). Lay activists helped organize the home-school movement and "civic studies" classes to oppose the ban on religious education that the state tried to introduce in the Mexican constitution (ibid., 101–102). In 1934, the Mexican Congress approved a change of Article 3rd stating that "the education imparted by the state should be socialist, exclude all religious doctrine and combat fanaticism through the inculcation of a rational and exact concept of the universe and of social life" (Quintanilla n.d.) It was the first time that the term "socialist education" appeared in any Latin American constitution (ibid.). Indeed, the ban on religious education was a prominent discourse that triggered a response from Catholic lay activists.

It would be misleading to assert that the Church was solely responsible for the different initiatives that lay Catholic groups put in place within ACM. As some investigations suggest, lay Catholic activism "did not spontaneously generate without innovation, encouragement, or instruction from clerical leaders, but it also did not depend wholly on them to develop, propagate, or thrive" (Boylan 2000, 19). In Mexico, the Catholic Church understood that its lay activists could reach those places and groups where clergy were banned due to the state's legal restrictions. Barranco explains that ACM had during the 1930s an extensive parish network that allowed the organization to reach the faithful, especially in rural areas, while becoming an extra social space for its members (Barranco 2011, 43). Moreover, the diversity of ACM groups imprinted their unique character, sensibility, and even religiosity to the organization (ibid., 44). Instead of an open confrontation with a government that envisions religion as an obstacle for the modern state, the Catholic Church wagered to be social by building a solid network of lay activism that supported it during these turmoil years.[2]

---

2. President Lázaro Cárdenas, for instance, had little sympathy for organized religion itself and believed that a moment spent on one's need is a moment lost to humanity (Boyle 2000, 74).

Perestroika and the Orthodox Church in Russia

The dissolution of the Soviet Union in 1991 marked not only the end of a regime and its ideology but also shifted centers of power around the world. Our modern societies passed from a bipolar international arena—capitalism vs. communism—to a multipolar world order in which new centers of power (re)emerged. The new configuration undoubtedly posed demanding challenges for the international community, which engaged in more complex and nuanced relationships. At the same time, it came with the "promise" to establish a more egalitarian and just world order.

This reconfiguration of power was also actual for religious institutions such as Orthodox Churches who, after the fall of communism, "have emerged as more independent political actors" (Banchoff 2008, 6). These churches based in Russia, Eastern Europe, and the Middle East are linked to global diasporas. They have increased in size, strength, and visibility around issues such as education and minority rights (ibid.). For the Russian Orthodox Church, two key events were instrumental in its "renaissance" to the public sphere: The millennium celebration of Kiev Rus in 1988—just three years before the end of the Soviet regime—and the new government's need of an all-encompassing ideology capable to unify the country and spur national sentiments. As Meyer eloquently describes it, the end of the Soviet era and the millennium celebration of the baptism of Rus were "the beginning of rebirth, a liberating February 1917 that no October cancels" (Meyer 2014, 413).

It would be difficult to conceive the transitional time in Russia of the fall of communism and the establishment of a democratic regime known as perestroika without accounting for the Orthodox Church's role in it. During the years that precede the disintegration of the U.S.S.R., the *politburo* faced the decision to either ignore the millennium celebration of Kiev Rus or take advantage of the historical event for its campaign on glasnost. This term was part of Mikhail Gorbachev's political reforms of "transparency (*glasnost*)—reorganization (*perestroika*)—speedup (*uskorenie*)," and it meant more transparency in the activities of state institutions and freedom of speech (Ustinov et al. 2015). Propelled by the government's need for people's support and a more solid international image, especially after the nuclear catastrophe in Chernobyl, the millennium celebration of Kiev Rus took place. Dubin argues that the thousandth anniversary of the Christianization of Rus, together with an active discussion in the press about the need for a new ideology and a Russian national idea, contributed to placing religion again in public life (Dubin 1998, 40–41).

After two to three years of the celebration, the hierarchy of the Communist Party seemed to start getting ready for the regime's change, and it began to have a more open relationship with the Orthodox Church. "We needed an ideology. And here it is, at hand. A ready-made Orthodox ideological machine with a thousand-year history" (Mel'nikov 2015). Thus, the Orthodox Church represented the much-needed cohesion to construct a new national identity and patriotism in a time of crisis. For the Orthodox Church, having a preferential place in politics while being recognized as the inherent religion of Russia meant a warrant to fight and resist the arrival of foreign religions. "Just as Russia endeavoured to reclaim its former title of superpower, the Russian Orthodox Church longed for its former glory as the faith of an empire" (Roslof 2004, 1).

Is this symbiosis between the Orthodox Church and the state a signal of "unequivocal mutual understanding"? It is impossible to deny that the Church and the state benefited from each other's support, particularly during the turmoiled years of perestroika. On the one hand, the state used the Orthodox Church as cohesion and advanced Putin's political purposes. A survey conducted in 1993 and 1994 indicated that Russians trusted the Orthodox Church above the army, the government, the media or even law courts (Knox 2004, 6). On the other hand, the Orthodox Church needed the state to re-establish its structure and operations and "protect" itself against the influx of foreign missionaries, new religions, and what the Church considered proselytism. Faced with the challenge of absolute novelty about the political and ecclesiastical situation in Russia and the world, the Orthodox Church hardened its relations against all churches, including certain Orthodox ones (Meyer 2014, 445).

Yet, a more careful revision of the relationship between the Orthodox Church and the state is needed to determine their cooperation's complexities, nuances, and dynamics. It seems that the Orthodox–Kremlin alliance could be better understood when framed in terms of pragmatism. In her study of authoritarian regimes and religion, Koesel identifies imbalances, for example, when these two institutions interact. "The state generally has the upper hand; however, the relative power balance begins to tip towards religious actors when nonmaterial resources are the currency of exchange" (Koesel 2014, 154). For Knox, if the Moscow Patriarchate struggled to build its believers a spiritual home with firm foundations in the "shifting sands of the new Russia" in the decade after the collapse of communism, recently the Church "has emerged as an independent actor, vociferous, confident, and, at times, at odds with the state" (Knox 2012, 122). Moreover, the contentious issue of returning church land and property may signify how pragmatic their relationship has been.

While the Church learned to navigate the political arena of the new era, it was equally important to develop "new ways of being involved in Russian society and culture" (Roslof 2004, 4). The Orthodox social ministry after communism was born out of a necessity to revive the Church at a grass-roots level, "the level where national identity is formed" (ibid.). Interestingly, during these early years of post-communism, individual Orthodox priests viewed social welfare as "a way to reacquaint Russians with the faith of their ancestors and thereby preserve Orthodoxy's influence in post-Soviet life" (ibid., 2). Priests created, for instance, social programs on alcoholism and to work in orphanages; they also rebuilt temples hand to hand with communities, and in general, sought the way to get involved in people's everyday life. "In Moscow, the legacy of Fr. Alexander Men influenced social work among his followers while other priests increased the church's presence in society through legislation aimed at the return of church property and the teaching of Orthodoxy in state schools" (ibid., 30). It is essential

152 • *Discourses of Crisis and the Study of Religion*

to notice that social work occurred at a parish level without being the "official" policy of the Church. The Orthodox hierarchy does not always endorse social ministry, nor do reformists and traditionalists within the Church agree on how the institution should be involved during this transitional period. However, the local examples of social ministry represent how some sectors of the Orthodox Church wagered to be "social" at a time of crisis as the best response to strengthen or rebuild Orthodox roots in society. As Knox argues, "the course of the Orthodox Church in the post-Soviet period has been one of struggle between competing visions of how to meet the challenges of post-Soviet realities" (Knox 2004, 8).

Churches' Responses to the COVID-19 Crisis: A Reflection

The Roman Catholic Church in Mexico and the Orthodox Church in Russia have responded to the current pandemic somehow similar to how they did the Cristero War and perestroika. Both churches have found the public to be one of their best allies to navigate challenging times by attending to people's needs. Nonetheless, and for obvious historical conditions, the notion of being "social" has been framed differently. After the Cristiada, the Catholic Church in Mexico sought to control and promote lay militant activism by creating its lay organization Acción Católica Mexicana and its different branches. The Church built its popular support at a grass-root level against a state's radical anti-clericalism through these groups. Acción Católica utilized what the liberal government tried to erase: religious practices and values in people's lives. I argue that these groups provided the much-needed space to preserve people's beliefs and engage with them intellectually while strengthening the Church's presence in society in a time of crisis. Indeed, Acción Católica's groups can be seen as spaces where Catholic Mexicans tried to accommodate their religious values and beliefs with their struggle to function as citizens within the liberal government. When COVID-19 spread to Mexico, the Catholic Church was able to help the masses thanks to a well-established infrastructure, organization and lay support built throughout those early years. The Church did not hesitate to be "social" and engage with the government and other Christian organizations in helping those in need. This time, despite the strict separation of spheres between the church and the state that prevails in Mexico, the pandemic seemed to soften those boundaries and allow for joint responses and initiatives. Religion was not the "enemy" to defeat this time. On the contrary, religion became spiritual, moral, and tangible support in times of crisis, an element of comfort when people needed it the most.

For the Russian Orthodox Church, the perestroika brought a profound change in the country's social, political, and cultural life. With the millennium celebration of Kiev Rus, Orthodoxy became the central element of cohesion in the country, arousing suspicion about the real place and role of the Church within the ephemeral democratic regime. Although internal discrepancies, some parts of the Orthodox clergy managed to establish social ministries that sought the revival of the Orthodox spirituality and culture among Russians. The COVID-19 crisis has demonstrated how vital it is for the Church to consolidate its social ministries to guarantee its influence on Russian society and culture. This time, the Church's efforts are run and supported from its hierarchy instead of being organized by priests on the ground. At moments, the Orthodox Church during the current pandemic did not feel threatened by other Christian denominations but rather adventured to join forces with them in helping those in need. Nevertheless, the Church still debates how close its ecumenical relationships should be to preserve its hegemony in the country.

Conclusion

There is a spectrum of different discourses that the Roman Catholic Church in Mexico and the Orthodox Church in Russia valued during the crisis years after the Cristiada and within the perestroika. In Mexico, the Church sought support in the idea that anti-clericalism could be defeated by protecting religious education, preserving family values, and avoiding any armed confrontation with the government. Indeed, one can argue that the Catholic Church, rather than aiming to access the sphere pertaining to the state and establish an open confrontation, decided to counteract the secularization process by using the domain Nieuwenhuis defined as the middle ground. This third domain, or the space where the church and the state encounter each other, was critical for the Church's survival. The intensive lay Catholic activism to regain official access to education, for instance, is a prime example of secularization's subtleties in which the Church tends to counteract secular processes.

In contrast, the Russian Orthodox Church placed value in what Nieuwenhuis tailored as the state's domain. By giving cohesion to a political regime and securing its historical place within the formation of national identity, the Orthodox Church wagered in the first place its survival during the turmoil years of perestroika. Although the Orthodox Church also valued social assistance, internal differences reframed it from building a more robust approach on this third domain during that period. Although with different intensity, the churches wager to be social, and their decision to distance from or collaborate with the government at a practical level allowed them to implement particular positions. As a result, the Catholic and Orthodox Church survived as institutions in a time of crisis and found themselves establishing pragmatic alliances with the state in what remains a complex, nuanced, and dynamic relationship.

Xochiquetzal Luna Morales is a PhD candidate at Wilfrid Laurier University. Her research takes place at the intersection of journalism and religious studies.

References

Andes, Stephen J.C. 2014. *The Vatican and Catholic Activism in Mexico and Chile: The Politics of Transnational Catholicism, 1920-1940.* Oxford: Oxford University Press.

Arribas-Ayllon, Michael, and Valerie Walkerdine. 2017. "Foucauldian Discourse Analysis." In Carla Willig and Wendy Stainton-Rogers (eds.), *The Sage Handbook of Qualitative Research in Psychology*, 110–123. London: Sage Publications.

Banchoff, Thomas. 2008. *Religious Pluralism, Globalization, and World Politics.* New York: Oxford University Press.
Barranco V., Bernardo. 2011. "Posiciones Políticas en la Historia de la Acción Católica Mexicana." In Roberto Blancarte (ed.), *El Pensamiento Social de los Católicos Mexicanos.* Cd. de México: Fondo de Cultura Económica.
Boylan, Cristina A. 2000. "Mexican Women's Catholic Activism, 1929–1940." PhD dissertation, St. Cross College, University of Oxford.
de la Cueva, J. 2018. "Violent Culture Wars: Religion and Revolution in Mexico, Russia and Spain in the Interwar Period." *Journal of Contemporary History* 53(3): 503–523.
Dubin, Boris V. 1998. "Orthodoxy in a Social Context." *Russian Social Sciences Review* 39(3): 40–51.
Foucault, Michel. 1989. *Archeology of Knowledge.* London: Routledge.
Knox, Zoe Katrina. 2004. *Russian Society and the Orthodox Church Religion in Russia after Communism.* London: RoutledgeCurzon.
Knox, Zoe Katrina. 2012. "Church, State, and Belief in Post-Soviet Russia." *The Russian Review (Stanford)* 71(1): 122–127.
Koesel, Karrie J. 2014. *Religion and Authoritarianism. Cooperation, Conflict, and the Consequences.* New York: Cambridge University Press.
Lynch, John. 1986. "The Catholic Church in Latin America, 1830–1930." In Leslie Bethell (ed.), *The Cambridge History of Latin America*, 527–595. Cambridge: Cambridge University Press.
Mel'nikov, Andrey. 2015. "Перестройка наделила Церковь правами, а обязанностями не успела." *Независимая Газета*, March 6. Retrieved from www.ng.ru/ng_religii/2015-06-03/1_perestroika.html
Meyer, Jean A. 1976. *The Cristero Rebellion: The Mexican People Between Church and State 1926-1929.* Cambridge: Cambridge University Press.
Meyer, Jean A. 1993. "Historia Política de la Religión en el México Contemporáneo." *Historia Mexicana El Colegio De México*, 42(3): 711–44.
Meyer, Jean A. 2014. *La Gran Controversia.* México, D.F.: Fábula, Tusquets Editores.
Moffit, Benjamin. 2015. "How to Perform a Crisis: A Model for Understanding the Key Role of Crisis in Contemporary Populism." *Government and Opposition*, 50(2): 189–217.
Nieuwenhuis, Aernout J. 2012. "State and Religion, a Multidimensional Relationship: Some Comparative Law Remarks." *International Journal of Constitutional Law*, 10(1): 153–174.
Pravmir. 2013. "Тысячелетие Крещения Руси в воспоминаниях." *Правамир*. July 23. Retrieved from www.pravmir.ru/tysyacheletie-kreshheniya-rusi-v-vospominaniyax/
Quintanilla, Susana. n.d. "La Educación en México Durante el Periodo de Lázaro Cárdenas 1934-1940." Retrieved from http://biblioweb.tic.unam.mx/diccionario/htm/articulos/sec_31.htm
Reich, Peter Lester. 1995. *Mexico's Hidden Revolution: The Catholic Church in Law and Politics since 1929.* Notre Dame, IN: University of Notre Dame Press.
Roitman, Janet. 2012. "Crisis: Janet Roitman." *Political Concepts: A Critical Lexicon.* Accessed August 22, 2021. Retrieved from www.politicalconcepts.org/issue1/crisis/
Roitman, Janet, Sara Angeli Aguiton, Lise Cornilleau, and Lydie Cabane. 2020. "Anti-Crisis: Thinking with and against Crisis Excerpt from Interview with Janet Roitman." *Journal of Cultural Economy*, 13 (6): 772–778.

Roslof, Lara McCoy. 2004. "The Political, Economic and Social Activities of the Russian Orthodox Church, 1991–2003, and the Reintegration of Russian Orthodoxy into Post-Soviet Russian National Identity." Master's dissertation, Miami University.

Ustinov, Georgi, et al. 2015. "Перестройка была прыщавая и слюнявая." *Коммерсантъ*, April 23. Retrieved from www.kommersant.ru/projects/perestroika

Chapter 14

Yoga's Flexibility in Brazil during the COVID-19 Pandemic

Gustavo H. P. Moura

Yoga is well known for its flexibility, which goes much beyond the exotic postures associated with it. In South Asia alone, yoga's ideas have a long history of adaptations within Hinduism, Buddhism, and Jainism. More recently these ideas have travelled widely around the world, forming a movement encompassing diverse communities linked through shared practices, values, and aspirations under today's fashionable label "yoga." Based on my field observations, I here ask how the framework of "crisis" during COVID-19 reshaped practices of yoga in Brazil and what lessons we may learn by observing such developments.

The first part of this chapter investigates the impact of the COVID-19 pandemic on the Brazilian yoga movement: Is the number of people interested in yoga increasing, and if so, why? How are instructors and practitioners coping with lockdown policies? What strategies have been deployed in the cities, in the ashrams, and within the online space? Above all, how enduring are these adaptations and in what ways could they be reshaping the yoga landscape?

The second part of the chapter then discusses the nature of this yoga movement, asking what is shared with a wider international yoga public and what is peculiar to the Brazilian situation. Also, how is the technology of communication blurring borders and contributing to the already prominent culture of hybridism in Brazil? To address this question, I apply Meredith McGuire's (2008) approach of "lived religion" with special attention to issues of individual practice and hybridity. Moreover, for the sake of highlighting the experiential nature of yoga as a system of practices, I engage Foucault's (1988) concept of "technologies of the self." Finally, I reflect on the flavor of yoga in Brazil as Indian ingredients are combined with African and indigenous ones.

Testing Yoga's Flexibility

Moments of crisis provide a rich backdrop to observe how religion and religious groups adapt and, sometimes, even thrive. History has shown that in times of political, cultural, or social distress, religion offers people alternatives to cope with crisis (Ganiel, Winkel, and Monnot 2014). At the same time, religion can be a powerful transformative force within societies. As we shall discuss, there is no scarcity of religious elements pervading the yoga movement's landscape, especially in the way it has been unfolding in Brazil. Here we start by asking how the Brazilian yoga community has been adapting and evolving in face of the COVID-19 challenges.

As with the rest of the world, Brazilians have been facing travelling restrictions and series of lockdowns since the early months of 2020 due to the COVID-19 pandemic. Interestingly, a quick look at Google Trends shows a 400 percent increase in searches for "yoga mats" ("tapete de ioga") in Brazil from April to August 2020 compared to previous years. This increased interest in yoga has been noticed by major national newspapers and magazines, with dozens of articles published in the past year (Camazano 2021; Couto 2021; Desgualdo 2020; Martucci 2021; Natulini 2021; Neves 2020; Nações Unidas Brasil 2020). Furthermore, an important national survey with over twelve thousand participants was conducted by the Oswaldo Cruz Foundation, a renown scientific institution for research and development in biological sciences located in Brazil (OBSERVAPICS 2021). Aimed at improving public health policies, this study reveals that during the pandemic more than half of the Brazilian population (61.7 percent) resorted to meditation, herbal medicine, reiki, aromatherapy, homeopathy, and yoga among other techniques approved by the Brazilian healthcare system (SUS) since 2018. My fieldwork in Brazil from October 2020 to January 2021 also confirms these findings through a combination of interviews, participant observation, and informal conversations.

It is clear, therefore, that interest in yoga among Brazilians has increased considerably during the pandemic. When asked why, people I met during my fieldwork explained that yoga was helping them to stay heathy—both physically and mentally—during these "strange times." In fact, the link between calamities and religion has been well established in scholarly literature, not only for crises in general, but for the COVID pandemic more specifically (Pew Research Center 2021; Meza 2020). It was predictable, therefore, that people would turn to yoga for physical and mental support when they are prevented from going to the gym and are experiencing higher levels of stress due to social isolation and uncertainty. And yet, one may wonder about the depth and persistence of this phenomenon. Is this only a trivial and short-lived trend or can we expect something more enduring and complex?

Of course, it is too early to answer this question based on data, but previous research on religion and crises suggests long-lasting results. In a volume titled "Religion in Times of Crisis," the editors state:

> Even advocates of the secularization thesis acknowledge that crises and rapid social changes like these can temporarily motivate the popularity of religion ... But religious responses to crisis are enduring—not fleeting. Religious responses are complex—not straightforward. Religion is also dynamic—moving across boundaries of geography and identity, and changing in form.
> (Ganiel, Winkel, and Monnot 2014, 2)

This assessment also matches the perception of several yoga instructors I met. They sense that the pandemic has transformed yoga practice for good. Indeed, there is a consensus among teachers and practitioners that online yoga will continue even after the restrictions are lifted. This is because teaching yoga virtually is not just a temporary solution for times of social distancing and as such is unlikely to be abandoned once the pandemic is over. Rather, the popularization of video conferencing platforms like Zoom has inadvertently enabled a paradigm shift, opening a new range of possibilities for the practice and the study of yoga.

Following lockdown policies, yoga instructors had to find alternatives to in-person sessions. Many who were teaching yoga part-time decided to suspend their activities, but full-time yoga teachers whose income was depending on their classes were forced to seek creative solutions. Thus, the common pattern I found is that instructors either stopped their activities altogether due to the pandemic or they adapted and now have a much greater number of students. Adaptations include teaching yoga online, conducting yoga sessions outdoors, organizing yoga retreats in ashrams located in the countryside, and offering online courses.

Of course, teaching yoga remotely has its shortcomings. Some of the teachers I spoke with explained the challenges of making postural adjustments on the students when you teach online and how this often leads to a simplification of the postures presented. On the other hand, internet-based yoga goes much beyond being a poor substitute for in-person sessions: it enables people to access yoga even if they live in remote areas—or live in a city but have a hard time commuting to the nearest yoga school.

Another solution I have seen is the proliferation of yoga sessions conducted outdoors: on the beach, in a park, or leaving the urban areas for a few days to participate in a retreat in some ashram. During the three months I spent researching in Brazil, every weekend I was invited to one of such retreats. As expected, they took measures to keep safe distance between participants. For instance, visitors were requested to wear masks in common areas, they would serve meals in the room to avoid conglomeration in a dining hall, and all group meetings would take place in open areas. Despite these difficulties, in the retreats I attended the atmosphere was always vibrant and one could perceive the enthusiasm animating all people involved.

Another expression of this enthusiasm, which was triggered by the pandemic and made possible by the internet, is the proliferation of online courses. There is a growing offer in studies of classical texts like the Yoga Sutras and the Bhagavad Gita, as there are now online yoga teacher training courses, seminars on yoga Nidrā, meditation, and much more. For instance, Brazilian Vedanta teacher Jonas Masetti reaches hundreds of thousands of students with his online courses on yoga, Vedanta, Sanskrit, etc. On Ayurveda, Matheus Macêdo has an even larger following. And in July 2020, yoga teacher Márcia de Luca launched an online community (Comunidade do Despertar) for the study of yoga and Ayurveda. These are but a few relevant examples of these online developments.

Furthermore, my own Sanskrit course offered in Portuguese through a newly developed app called Yoga Culture has attracted a higher number of students during the past year even though I hardly invested time advertising it due to my current PhD commitments. For those yoga teachers who did invest on their internet presence, they saw an increase of hundreds and thousands of followers in their social media platforms and in paid courses as well. This seems to indicate a deeper engagement with the philosophical dimension of yoga as people seek for answers, meaning, and comfort in times of uncertainty.

These adaptations in Brazil indicate an increased interest in self-care. Indeed, the COVID-19 crisis sparked a renewed fascination with yoga as an answer to people's physical, emotional, intellectual, and spiritual needs. At the same time, the situation triggered a rapid development and popularization of the technologies needed for making these teachings and activities not only feasible, but also more widely available during these challenging times. Next, we shall consider the religious dimension of yoga and reflect on how the online teaching may be blurring borders and contributing to an already prominent culture of hybridism in Brazil.

Flavors of Brazilian Yoga

Several authors have identified the religious elements of modern postural yoga, even in its most "secular" expressions (De Michelis 2004; Jain 2015). Their analyses certainly apply to the Brazilian situation but require contextualization to local historical and cultural specificities. Of course, my aim here is not to trace the history of yoga in Brazil. This has been done already to a good extent by Brazilian scholars (Gnerre 2018; Simões 2018) and here I present a synopsis. The guiding question in this part of the chapter is how the adaptations happening in face of the COVID-19 crisis could potentially transform yoga practices and understandings in Brazil from now on.

Initially, it should be acknowledged that the establishment of yoga in Latin America since the 1940s followed a different trajectory from what happened in North America, having no direct influence of Indian gurus during its early stages. As Roberto Simões (2018) explains, this seems to have happened mostly due to language barriers delaying the establishment of "legitimately Indian yogic institutions in the region." And yet, he continues, this "did not prevent proto-Yoga from spreading. On the contrary, it produced beliefs and enabled masters to arise and yogic schools to fuse with native and Catholic religious elements" (Simões 2018, 310). Thus, by tracing the historical formation of yoga in Latin America, Simões reveals the roots of a movement characterized by unique values and symbolic exchanges. These include a strong emphasis on the therapeutic value of yoga coupled with approximations to Christianity and Amazonian shamanism (ibid., 291). Additionally, physical yoga in Brazil was never associated with the image of fakirs and similar "degradations" as perceived by Max Müller and other European Indologists (Singleton 2010; Gnerre 2018). In brief, the reception of yoga in Brazil followed its own trajectory relatively independent from processes happening in North America and Europe.

Another interesting factor is the long affinity between Brazil and India since colonial times through a bridge created by Portuguese missionaries and traders (Freyre 2000). Although to this day the number of Indian immigrants in Brazil is negligible, the cultural affinity remains strong, even if in a romanticized manner.

By this I mean that there is general appreciation for Indian culture which reflects on Brazilian music, TV series, and of course, on the reception of yoga. This is reinforced by a marked culture of religious syncretism.

The syncretism, which, according to historians and anthropologists (such as Gilberto Freyre and Darcy Ribeiro) is a traditional feature of Brazilian religiosity, can be considered a cultural element that contributes to the ongoing process of accepting spiritual elements of yoga within our society (Gnerre 2018).

Curiously, this eagerness in accepting the "spiritual elements of yoga" occurs side by side with a discourse of secularization. In my interactions with yoga teachers and practitioners in Brazil for over a decade, so often I have heard them describing yoga as a secular practice. Indeed, this is a position defended by some of the most influential teachers in the country (Simões 2019, 67). But often, what Brazilians mean by "secular" is that "Yoga is not a religion. Yoga may be practiced by people of all religions" (Kupfer 2010). This quote comes in an interesting context: an influential yoga teacher justifying the propriety of an article about the connections between yoga and Ayahuasca that he decided to post on his website. Responding to some adverse comments, he defends that the circulation of Ayahuasca ideas as propagated by the Santo Daime religious group is appropriate in yoga circles as much as any other religious ideas.

This episode illustrates how in Brazil people are not expected to leave their religious understandings behind when they come to the yoga studio. Indeed, by saying "secular" they do not mean a neutral space free of religious symbols, practices, and discourses. Rather, they mean a space where people of all religions may feel welcome and comfortable sharing the elements of their faith. And as already mentioned, over and above these associations with Brazilian religious cultures, there is a clear appreciation for and engagement with Eastern religious elements to an extent that is unique to Brazil.

Looking at the yoga movement from a lived religion perspective as proposed by McGuire (2008) allows special attention to be given to issues of individual practice and hybridity. In fact, people's religious lives rarely conform to the compartmentation of religion as done in institutional and academic settings, especially in a place like Brazil with a long history of religious syncretism. I should mention that regarding the negative connotations of the word syncretism, McGuire argues that "all cultural groups are fundamentally syncretic" (McGuire 2008, 190). Also, Peter Beyer writes that "Pure [cultural and religious] forms are but previous and legitimated syncretizations" (quoted in McGuire 2008, 190). But despite this hybridization process being so natural, the term syncretic has been used as if to indicate "inauthentic" religions, thus revealing hidden power dynamics and a failure to acknowledge the syncretic history of one's own religion.

What we then see happening on the ground is that Brazilians are coming together in these yoga spaces where they embrace Indian ideas of yoga, Vedanta, and Bhakti side by side with New Age, Shamanic, African, and Indigenous understandings. Some of these people are actively practicing their religion and adopting Indian elements in a syncretic manner. Others are disengaged from institutionalized religion and adopt yoga itself as their religion (Gnerre 2018).

Let me try to illustrate this with a few examples from my fieldwork, which includes online interviews, participant observation, and informal conversations with teachers and practitioners in Brazil from October 2020 to January 2021. I attended a yoga retreat near São Paulo conducted by a Roman Catholic Benedictine oblate of the World Community for Christian Meditation. Many years ago, he visited a Christian monastery at Shantivanam, India. Without compromising his Catholic commitments, he has been teaching traditional hatha-yoga classes for over two decades along with practices of Christian meditation based on the method developed by the Roman Catholic priest and Benedictine monk John Main.

Another place I visited is an Umbanda center near Porto Alegre. I spent a week with them and observed how they study the Bhagavad Gita, chant Sanskrit mantras in the morning, and practice yoga—all the while maintaining a strict routine of Umbanda ceremonies and services to the local community. Due to their Indian connections, they have adopted a vegetarian diet and a commitment to ahimsa, or non-violence, which implies no animal sacrifices in their premises, as often done in other Umbanda centers.

I also visited the Flor das Águas community in Cunha, a place between Rio de Janeiro and São Paulo whose founder's background is in Evangelical Christianity, but who has adopted yoga, Ayahuasca, and even elements of Catholicism. Differently from the Umbanda terreiro described above, where they have separate areas dedicated to the Indian and African based practices, the temple in this Ashram has all under a single roof: images of Jesus, Saint Francis of Assisi, Shiva, Durga, Ganesha, and Mestre Irineu, the founder of the Ayahuaca religion Santo Daime.

All these places and many more that I visited in the south, southeast, and northeast regions of Brazil—including Hare Krishna communities and Kardecist Spiritism centers—are locations where people are practicing and teaching postural yoga. Therefore, adopting a lived religion approach allows us to see the complex integration of all these elements instead of assuming that Catholic, Evangelical, Umbanda, Kardecist, or Hare Krishna practitioners will remain limited to the orthodoxy and orthopraxy of their respective religious institutions.

Looking at the virtual space, Jonas Masetti—who presents himself as an acharya, or traditional Vedanta teacher—has recently started a podcast on Telegram titled Saberes Ancestrais dos Povos Originários ("ancestral knowledge of the original peoples") in which he discusses similarities between the Indian, African, and Indigenous Brazilian traditions (Masetti 2021). Considering his affiliation with a Vedanta lineage coming from Shankara via Swami Dayananda, the ease with which he compares Hindu devatas with Umbanda orixás and ritual practices on both sides can only be explained by his typical Brazilian worldview.

One may wonder, however, about the logic behind these borrowings and adaptations. In a conversation with the founder of the yoga ashram Flor das Águas in Cunha (mentioned above) he told me that practices of prayer, meditation, mantra recitation and so on as taught in various religious traditions are essentially different kinds of "spiritual technologies" meant to connect us to the divine. He then offered an example to clarify: "If I try to contact you through email but you are not answering, I may send you a text message on WhatsApp."

His point resonates with Foucault's "technologies of the self," defined as techniques that allow individuals to transform their own lives in the quest for happiness, wisdom, and other types of perfection (Foucault 1988). Indeed, Brazilian practitioners often use mantra, asana, pranayama, or meditation techniques just as they use laptops and smartphones. This shows a very pragmatic approach that pervades the yoga landscape in Brazil, where one does not feel compelled to stick to the resources of one tradition alone.

While portraying my fieldwork observations of the yoga movement in Brazil, I am in no way suggesting that these phenomena are happening only after the COVID-19 crisis. The point I want to make is that the changes caused by the pandemic are acting as a catalyst to promote even more these already prominent syncretic practices. This is happening due to the popularization of communication technologies and due to renewed interest in spirituality that people feel while facing so much isolation and uncertainty. On the one hand, yoga is now accessible to marginalized populations and to those living in remote areas in Brazil (Desgualdo 2020; Antonio 2019). On the other hand, the yoga public in Brazil has been engaging with much more than physical postures. People are studying Vedanta, Ayurveda, Vedic Astrology, and classical texts like the Bhagavad Gita and the Yoga Sutras. All these developments are happening as a kind of grassroots movement, based on people's needs and interests but with no hard institutional organization behind it.

Conclusion

In response to quarantine practices during the COVID-19 pandemic, expanded uses of communication technologies has made yoga much more accessible and pervasive. As discussed above, online yoga is much more than a temporary response to the "crisis" of lockdown; it has triggered a paradigm shift in the practice and teaching of yoga which is acting as a catalyst to the already pronounced syncretic assimilations of yoga and other elements of Indian thought in Brazil.

A question arises regarding the nature and future developments of this yoga movement. Should we think of yoga in Brazil as a new religious movement (NRM) in the making? Or should we understand yoga as just one kind of "technology of the self" among many other practices that people are engaging with in a contemporary religious scenario that has been evolving in a continuous dialogue with the East (Albanese 2007; Goldberg 2010)?

While sharing many features common to NRMs (Guerriero 2006), yoga lacks a single founder, it has no predetermined canon of sacred books, and no hard institution behind it. What we do have is a practice that links to shared values and, perhaps, a distinct worldview, all of which gets transmitted through networks of practitioners. Thus, we can think of the spreading of yoga as a process of capillarity, which flows in narrow spaces without the assistance of, or even in opposition to institutions and authorities. The pressure imposed by the COVID-19 crisis only expands even more these capillary ramifications.

Since this is but an exploratory chapter on these recent developments, I suggest that further investigations be made on the yoga movement's developments in Brazil and beyond. Perhaps the dynamics of Indian religious movements like Bhakti and Tantra could provide significant insights in this regard. I propose that we are dealing with a kind of soft institution that allows for the capillary diffusion of practices and understandings in a way that perhaps could be compared to the Indian guru-śiśya paramparā, or master-disciple transmission. Whatever the case may be, I highlight how the yoga movement thrived in Brazil during the COVID-19 pandemic and how its flexibility provides an example of a living tradition capable of adapting to ever new situations.

Gustavo H. P. Moura (PhD, Wilfrid Laurier University) is a scholar of religion with academic training and lived experience in South Asian traditions. His research interests include yoga, Vedanta, Sanskrit, Bhakti, and especially Kirtan, the practice of chanting mantras and devotional songs.

References

Albanese, C. L. 2007. *A Republic of Mind and Spirit: A Cultural History of American Metaphysical Religion*. New Haven, CT: Yale University Press.
Antonio, Tainá. 2019. "Yoga Marginal—democratizando a prática do yoga." Retrieved from https://youtu.be/eT7mq7D5hd4.
Camazano, Priscila. 2021. "Projeto criado na pandemia leva aula online de ioga para mulheres negras." Retrieved from www1.folha.uol.com.br/equilibrioesaude/2021/08/projeto-criado-na-pandemia-leva-aula-online-de-ioga-para-mulheres-negras.shtml.
Couto, Camille. 2021. "Procuta pela Meditação e Técnicas de Relaxamento Disparou na Pandemia." Retrieved from www.cnnbrasil.com.br/saude/procura-pela-meditacao-e-tecnicas-de-relaxamento-disparou-na-pandemia/.
De Michelis, Elizabeth. 2004. *A History of Modern Yoga: Patanjali and Western Esotericism*. New York: Continuum.
Desgualdo, Paula. 2020. "Ioga para tod@s." Retrieved from https://saude.abril.com.br/fitness/ioga-para-tods/.
Foucault, Michel. 1988. *Technologies of the Self: A Seminar with Michel Foucault*. Luther H. Martin, Huck Gutman, and Patrick H. Hutton (eds.). Amherst, MA: Massachusetts University Press.
Freyre, Gilberto. 2000. *China Tropical*. Brasília: Global.
Ganiel, Gladys, Heidemarie Winkel, and Christophe Monnot. 2014. *Religion in Times of Crisis*. Leiden: Brill.
Gnerre, Maria Lucia Abaurre. 2017. "Yoga heritage in Brazil: History and culture in the Development of a Brazilian Yoga." *International Journal of Indic Religions*, 1(1). Retrieved from https://digitalcommons.shawnee.edu/indicreligions/vol1/iss1/2/
Goldberg, P. (2010). *American Veda: From Emerson and the Beatles to Yoga and Meditation How Indian Spirituality Changed the West*. New York: Harmony/Rodale.
Guerriero, Silas. 2006. *Novos Movimentos Religiosos*. Sao Paulo: Paulinas.

Jain, Andrea. 2015. *Selling Yoga: From Counterculture to Pop Culture*. New York: Oxford University Press.

Kupfer, Pedro. 2010. "Santo Daime ou Yoga." Retrieved from www.yoga.pro.br/santo-daime-ou-yoga/.

Martucci, Mariana. 2021. "Dia mundial do yoga: dicas para encontrar a prática perfeita para você." Retrieved from https://exame.com/casual/dia-mundial-da-yoga-dicas-para-encontrar-a-pratica-perfeita-para-voce/.

Masetti, Jonas. 2021. "Saberes Ancestrais dos Povos Originários." Retrieved from https://t.me/jonasmasetti.

McGuire, Meredith. 2008. *Lived Religion: Faith and Practice in Everyday Life*. Oxford: Oxford University Press.

Meza, Diego. 2020. "In a Pandemic Are We More Religious? Traditional Practices of Catholics and the COVID-19 in Southwestern Colombia." *International Journal of Latin American Religions*, 4: 218–234.

Nações Unidas Brasil. 2020. "ONU destaca poder da ioga para ajudar a aliviar estresse na pandemia." Retrieved from https://brasil.un.org/pt-br/92020-onu-destaca-poder-da-ioga-para-ajudar-aliviar-estresse-na-pandemia.

Natulini, Júlia. 2021. "Cresce a procura pela prática de Yoga durante a pandemia." Retrieved from www.terra.com.br/vida-e-estilo/saude/cresce-a-procura-pela-pratica-de-yoga-durante-a-pandemia,9007d4f73a5fb9bd83eb6cd475e2dd59kbhdmxaz.html.

Neves, Marília. 2020. "Ioga on-line se adapta para novo público durante pandemia." Retrieved from https://g1.globo.com/bemestar/viva-voce/noticia/2020/05/11/yoga-on-line-se-adapta-para-novo-publico-durante-pandemia.ghtml.

OBSERVAPICS. 2021. "PICS Cuidam do Bem-estar de 61,7% dos Brasileiros Durante a Pandemia." Retrieved from http://observapics.fiocruz.br/boletim/.

Pew Research Center. 2021. "More Americans than People in Other Advanced Economies Say COVID-19 Has Strengthened Religious Faith." Retrieved from www.pewresearch.org/religion/wp-content/uploads/sites/7/2021/01/01.27.21_covid.religion.report.pdf

Simões, Roberto. 2018. "Early Latin American Esoteric Yoga as a New Spirituality." *International Journal of Latin American Religions*, 2: 290–314.

Simões, Roberto. 2019. "O Yoga Brasileiro: Conversando Com Yogues E Cientistas." *Yoga Dharma: Revista de Estudos sobre o Yoga Antigo e Moderno*, January: 55–86.

Singleton, Mark. 2010. *Yoga Body: The Origins of Modern Posture Practice*. New York: Oxford University Press.

Chapter 15

Compounded Crises

How the Principle of Subsidiarity Informs Catholic Responses to Critical Issues in North America

Ben Szoller

Fifty years ago, in May of 1971, Pope Paul VI convened a synod of bishops in Rome to confront growing social concerns around economic disparity, urbanization, the rights of women and racialized communities, and the environment. The synod was titled *Justitia in Mundo*, or *Justice in the World*. That same year, the pope released an encyclical, *Octogesima Adveniens*, to mark the 80th anniversary of Pope Leo XIII's *Rerum Novarum*, the hallmark document within Catholic social teaching (CST). Paul VI's efforts marked a dramatic ideological shift towards social and economic solidarity for the Church. Just over a decade after their release, in 1984, theologian and sociologist Gregory Baum highlighted the role Canadian bishops played in the process, arguing that a conception of social utopia has been embedded within the Canadian brand of Catholic social theory ever since. This newfound economic and political posture, as it turns out, was far from popular.[1] According to Baum, society would thenceforth be "viewed as being made up of dominant structures and countervailing trends" (Baum 1984, 27), defined more along structures of opposition than by organic adaptations. While social structures (along with their own epistemologies and methodologies) were becoming ever more compartmentalized—for Luhmann (1984), "functionally differentiated social systems"—so might the external forces be seen as increasingly compounded and, to a certain extent, oppositional. Crises were as complex as the structures that sought to alleviate them.

This chapter examines what the principle of subsidiarity, developed within Catholic social thought, reveals about the Church's expanding conception of the social "crisis" in North America since the Second Vatican Council. First, it considers how in Canada and the United States, Catholic bishops incorporated a national and global outlook into their public messaging, largely informed by the economic crisis of the 1980s. Second, it looks briefly at rural organization as a lens through which we might examine critical issues in North America today, particularly in

---

1. "Many Catholics were disturbed by the social teaching of their bishops," Baum wrote, regardless of the disparate views around Canadian clerical authority beforehand (Baum 1984, 19).

light of recent Catholic documents. Catholic teaching around complex and often overlapping social, economic, and environmental concerns has been particularly salient in the rural context. Third, this chapter considers how revelations around Catholic-run residential schools in Canada elicit important questions about how the Church responds to crisis and the suitability of subsidiarity mechanisms. Evaluating how Catholic groups rendered the principles of subsidiarity and solidarity in recent decades might help those interested in religion and society understand the growing concern around globalization within Catholic thought and how the Church develops and scales substantive social responses today. Moreover, looking at compounded critical issues through the lens of religious moral praxis (such as Catholic social teaching) helps to assess how religious frameworks continue to shape public discourses in North America.

Signs of the Times and Crisis within Catholic Social Thought

Today, "crisis" is ubiquitous. Discourse within and around the Catholic Church is no different: recent titles highlight the crises surrounding Catholic education, Catholic sexual morality, clerical abuses, and economic decline. The title *Crisis* has even been claimed by a monthly magazine for lay Catholics: "Every generation," its mission states, "has its moment of crisis—the moment when it must decide" (see https://crisismagazine.com). But the emergencies keep coming and, naturally, *Crisis* has remained in print for four decades. Such commentaries are not unique, however, and Janet Roitman (2014, 2) poses the dilemma of applying such language without careful qualification: "But can one speak of a state of enduring crisis? Is this not an oxymoron?" Still, where discourse around crisis is increasingly common, the Roman Catholic Church's social teaching has consistently viewed social crises not as a series of discrete external events, but as indicators of an equally existential moral crisis brought to light by the industrial revolution and continued today through the "technocratic paradigm" (Francis 2015). For the Catholic Church, economic, social, and ecological concerns are indivisible. To this, the reforms of Vatican II and the 1971 synod were conclusive. Thereafter, Baum writes, there existed "a single mission of the Church, uniting faith and justice, which proclaims the gospel message of new life and supports the struggle against domination" (Baum 1984, 60).[2] Catholic social action was still rooted in a moral ontology but was increasingly informed by a global worldview.

The shifts in Catholic social thought and Catholic action that Baum identified are indicative of wider trends brought about by modernization. In his book, *The*

---

2. Baum attributes this hybridization to the reforms of Vatican II: "While the Church's primary mission was spiritual, supernatural, and related to the order of salvation, the secondary mission, guided by Catholic social teaching, was earthly, natural, and related to secular society. The two missions remained distinct. What has happened at the Vatican Council (1962–1965), and more especially since the early Seventies, is that under the impact of the new religious experience of faith-and-justice, the Catholic Church has begun to define its mission in terms that include both salvation and earthly liberation" (Baum 60).

Crisis Paradigm, Andrew Gilbert (2019) writes about the development of crisis narratives in the eighteenth century "when there was a growing consciousness that the future could not be reliably predicated on the past, and human actions in the present were transforming the future in ways that were not fully foreseeable" (Gilbert 2019, 209–210). Crises seemed to be coming faster and more frequently. Still, Catholic social teaching itself remained relatively reluctant in its use of crisis language, and papal documents, bishops' statements, and local efforts responded to specific "signs of the times" in varied ways, themselves products of their times. Accordingly, popes often take on particular themes within their tenure. Most recently, for instance, Pope Francis has consistently drawn attention to the plight of immigrant populations, ecological devastation, and the missionary posture of the Church.

Understanding how Catholic theologies, leaders, and individuals respond to the signs of the times requires an attention to public discourse more broadly. What are the big issues for the Church today, and how are they similar to or different from public narratives? At the same time, we should heed Gilbert's scrutiny over the proliferation of "crisis ontology" within academic discourse: "This is a concern for sociology, where the construction of "society," the object of its investigation, has itself been explained into existence by reference to a "crisis" which affects it" (Gilbert 2019, 13).[3] These questions are not foreign to those that study how religious movements shape the worldviews of its members—Pope Francis and sociological critiques alike recognize the power and limitations of *paradigms*.[4] We might use Gilbert's model to consider how religion specifically is a viable sociological lens to define and understand the reciprocal relationship between the state (i.e., predicate) and specific issues (i.e., objects) of crisis. Gilbert's critique may also be helpful to evaluate religious participation in the public sphere, for example, where institutions (secular or otherwise) regularly employ crisis language to "legitimize" and advance their position in public action.

Subsidiarity: Understanding Tensions for Catholic Agency within the Local and Global Contexts

The principles of *solidarity* and *subsidiarity* within CST are essential to understanding how the Catholic Church articulates its participation in the public sphere. Quantifying them, however, is tricky. For example, we might struggle to map how

---

3. Gilbert remarks that "the idea of 'the crisis' worked as a kind of semantic anchor, around which a plurality of political narratives competed for discursive space" (Gilbert 2019, 2). Crisis, as a discursive topic, functions as a "legitimation device" (Gilbert 2019, 45–47) even while escaping the critique of its *a priori* status.

4. Mark Shiffman evaluates Francis' use of *technocratic paradigm*: "The use of the term "paradigm" to describe the basic structural principles of a whole way of seeing, thinking, and acting." Shiffman is careful to point out that Francis's use of the term is deliberate: "Pope Francis only ever uses the word "paradigm" to refer to the deep structure of the relationship to nature he is criticizing." So, within "Laudato Si'," a paradigm of life is oppositional to the dominant technocratic paradigm.

a local parish weighs papal teaching on the environment, particularly given the unique challenges within its jurisdiction, for instance, diminished industry or mounting civil unrest. How do regional religious communities orient themselves within the geographic and cultural expanses of a state, nation, or the world? Within Catholic social thought there is a unifying principle of solidarity on one hand, and, on the other, the organizational principle of subsidiarity (I often argue that subsidiarity is the lesser known and lesser understood partner to solidarity). Put simply, subsidiarity warrants that action should be taken at the most local level possible and, when necessary, deferred to a higher level (Annett 2019, 30). This privileges agency (and thus promotes human dignity) but also provides support through organizational structures. According to the Compendium of the Social Doctrine of the Church, "[t]he principle of subsidiarity protects people from abuses by higher-level social authority and calls on these same authorities to help individuals and intermediate groups to fulfil their duties" (Pontifical Council for Justice and Peace 2006, §187). Cooperation among parishes, dioceses, or bishops, for example, may therefore be necessary in order to meet local needs, such as may be the case with food shortages. At the same time, subsidiarity calls the Church to consider and strategize with other stakeholders—including the state—in order to meet social needs. As a result, solidarity and subsidiarity are always and necessarily in tension as Catholic communities at all levels navigate their place in civil society.

However, where examples of local, regional, and international solidarity movements are widely available (for example, in the efforts of Catholic bishops and organizations around industry and workers' rights in Canada, the United States, and Mexico), mechanisms of subsidiarity are somewhat more opaque. Baum's analysis, for instance, draws explicit attention to the principle of solidarity without explicitly addressing its correlative, subsidiarity. Baum argues that, while firmly embedded in "reformist impulses," the Canadian bishops' response to financial crisis promoted solidarity through its emphasis on "the organic unity of society, on cooperation, on shared values and on respect for authority. The struggle for justice had to take place within this social context" (Baum 1984, 22). Still, Baum implies the tension between subsidiarity and solidarity, particularly in the context of globalizing challenges brought about by modernization: nuclear threat, increased migration, advances in social communication, and most prominently, transnational economic structures:

> On the global scale, Justitia in Mundo perceives an expanding system of dependency and oppression, which draws the smaller nations, especially the former colonies, into greater subservience to the large economic corporations. It also acknowledges the struggles of peoples, groups and classes to free themselves from domination and assume responsibility for themselves.
> (Baum 1984, 25–26)

José Casanova's (1994) theory around deprivatization and religious participation in the public sphere lends further insight into subsidiarity within the CST tradition. For instance, the Compendium cautions that subsidiarity entails "striking a balance between the public and private spheres, with the resulting recognition of the social function of the private sphere" while also supporting "appropriate methods for making citizens more responsible in actively 'being a part' of the political and social reality of their country" (Pontifical Council for Justice and Peace 2006, §187). While the principle may have emerged in part in response to political structures that undermined the intrinsic dignity of the human person at the turn of the twentieth century (communism, fascism, and increasingly, capitalism, are perennial concerns within Catholic social and economic thought), it took a new dimension in the years following Second Vatican Council. According to Hollenbach (2002, 226), the "social vitality" of local communities was a necessary antidote to the "forces of globalization." At times, subsidiarity seems to lie at the heart of political/prophetic tensions that guide Catholic organization itself, such as the case with liberation theology.

More recently, Pope Francis has employed the concept of *integral ecology* to illustrate that "everything is connected"—both good and bad. As a social document prompted by ecological crisis, "Laudato Si'" (Francis 2015) highlights the connection between the health of the planet and human dignity. The connection between an option for the poor and an option for the earth lends itself to the language of deprivatization because it confronts functional systems that inhabit the public sphere, for example, trade regulations, global conflict, migration, capitalist ownership and subsistence. In doing so, "Laudato Si'" expands its call to all levels of human organization, Catholic and non-Catholic, and "argues that all elements of our society—international organizations, national and local governments, businesses, civil society actors, religions, and ordinary individuals—have their own role to play in identifying and implementing solutions."[5] In his most encyclical, *Fratelli Tutti*, Pope Francis goes to some length to unpack the tension between global and local:

> It should be kept in mind that "an innate tension exists between globalization and localization. We need to pay attention to the global so as to avoid narrowness and banality. Yet we also need to look to the local, which keeps our feet on the ground. Together, the two prevent us from falling into one of two extremes. In the first, people get caught up in an abstract, globalized universe... In the other, they turn into a museum of local folklore, a world apart, doomed to doing the same things over and over, incapable of being challenged by novelty or appreciating the beauty which God bestows beyond their borders." We need to have a global outlook to save ourselves from petty provincialism.
>
> (Francis 2020, §142, citing *Evangelii Gaudium*)

---

5. For Annett, it is not a coincidence that the document was released in 2015, a major year for international Sustainable Development and the Paris Agreement. Because of its international and public scope, "Laudato Si'" is explicit in calling on multiple "levels of action." It appeals on the *supranational level*, or "the level of the international community" (31); the *domestic political level* (for example, countries must report on Sustainable Development Goals every 5 years); the *business level*, and Francis notes that business should be a "noble vocation."

This tension permeates Catholic communities. Just a year before *Fratelli Tutti* was released, a synod of South American bishops highlighted the importance of localized Indigenous knowledge to protect the communities and ecologies of the Amazonian region (see Francis, *Querida Amazonia*, 2020). Still, within the framework of modern CST, local challenges in Amazonian communities remained symptomatic of other universalizing trends, such as transnational migration, asymmetrical economic structures, and climate change. In Catholic social thought, local crises are always concomitant with global ones.

Considering Catholic Responses to Compounded Crisis through a Rural Lens

The Amazon Synod was a timely reminder that rural issues have often been at the heart of Catholic social thought. Notably, Leo XIII's *Rerum Novarum* responded primarily to issues brought about through industrialization, including rural flight and agricultural mechanization. Eighty years later, Pope Paul VI echoed the perennial concern around the "weakening" of the agrarian way of life in his encyclical *Octogesima Adveniens*. The document again stressed the expanding divide between rural and urban societies first identified in *Rerum Novarum*: "This unceasing flight from the land, industrial growth, continual demographic expansion and the attraction of urban, centers bring about concentrations of population" (Paul VI 1971, §8). Rural flight notably preceded all other overlapping social concerns developed within the document: workers' rights, women's roles, racial discrimination, employment, social communication (i.e., mass media), and—in the context of growing ecology—the environment. In all these issues, Paul VI writes, there exist two complementary orientations, "the aspiration to equality and the aspiration to participation, two forms of man's dignity and freedom" (ibid., §22). Here, equality and participation as expressions of human dignity and freedom, respectively, underscore the tensions between solidarity and subsidiarity in public Catholic organization.

Bishops (along with Catholic organizations) are essential to the Church's public response to social crises. In many regards, bishops represent the political agency of the Church and in the last 50 years regional bishops' associations have assumed a heightened role in the political and social advocacy in public and political arenas (Casanova 1996). This seems especially true for ruralized communities. For example, in 1989 Catholic bishops in Ontario penned *The People and the Land* to call attention to the social, economic, and environmental consequences of the recent recession. The Great Depression of the 1930s may not have seemed all so distant at the time, but the response of the bishops was new: *The People and the Land* exemplifies the social shift diagnosed by Baum just years earlier. South of the border, the United States Conference of Catholic Bishops (USCCB) has been consistently vocal in addressing America's agricultural position. In 2003 the USCCB released *For I Was Hungry & You Gave Me Food: Catholic Reflections on Food, Farmers, and Farmworkers*, a handbook dedicated to Catholic agricultural social thought. The document is explicit in how it associates human dignity with the rural experience:

> Agriculture is different because it touches all our lives, wherever we live or whatever we do. It is about how we feed our own families, and the whole human family. It is about how we treat those who put food on our table and those who do not have enough food. It is about what is happening to food and farming, rural communities and villages, in the face of increasing concentration, new technology, and growing globalization in agriculture.
>
> (United States Conference of Catholic Bishops 2003, 1)

Here, the American bishops weave together pastoral considerations, Catholic theology, and empirical evidence to confront the crisis facing American farmers. Again, the crisis is symptomatic of broader economic and environmental concern.

In fact, Catholic bishops in Canada and the United States have often organized around rural communities in order to call attention to broader social concern. David Bovée's (2010) history of the National Catholic Rural Life Conference (NCRLC) presents a Catholic organization that was not only ahead of the environmental curve, but also instructive to the Church's broader ecological and economic teaching. According to Bovée, although the Catholic Church pursued environmental issues vigorously in the 1990s, the NCRLC had a longstanding, proto-environmentalism mandate rooted in social concern.[6] The NCRLC provides a helpful example of the deprivatization in action: even as the NCRLC became "Americanized," so were the United States' agricultural and economic policies *Catholicized* by the religious organization (Bovée 2010, xi). Not only would NCRLC programs educate rural Catholics, but they also educated urban Americans (Catholic and non-Catholic) about the benefits of rural life.

Canada's Antigonish Movement was perhaps the greatest example of a programmatic Catholic social teaching in North America and was rooted in the rural experience. Organizing through St. Francis Xavier University's Extension Department, Fathers Moses Coady and Jimmy Thompkins advocated tirelessly for rural, Maritime communities. But their role as *priest-professors* uniquely equipped them to mediate the needs of their community into secular, economic terms (Dodaro and Pluta 2012). As a result, even while the "Antigonish way" established itself as a local movement, sponsored and inspired by local clergy, but with a global, secular appeal.[7] Both the NCRLC in the United States and the Antigonish Movement in Canada had international impact. Following the release of *Mater et Magistra* in 1961, the NCRLC made several global missions and pleaded for America (and its farmers) to help international communities, for example, by supporting displaced Polish immigrants. In doing so, the Conference effectively

---

6. For the NCRLC, the most longstanding environmental issue was soil conservation, beginning with a 1947 resolution and "[s]oil conservation was one of the motives behind the NCRLC's promotion of organic (or biological) farming" as far back as the 1930s.

7. Fay speaks briefly to the expansive reach of the program: "Although primarily committed to Nova Scotians and the Nova Scotian community, Coady and the Antigonish Movement spread to struggling fishing and agricultural communities in Central and South America, Asia, India, and Africa. Jamaica, Puerto Rico, Trinidad, San Domingo, and Dominica among others sent people to study the Antigonish Movement."

worked "for the abolition of the national origins quota system," which Bovée even credits with catalyzing American immigration reform in the 1960s (Bovée 2010, 191)! Within Casanova's framework then, the NCRLC mirrors the distinctive trajectory from "the 'social Catholicism' of the interwar period to the new form of 'public Catholicism' that emerged in the 1980s."

Today, increased ecological concern and, most recently, the threat of COVID-19 both highlight the organizational challenges faced by social institutions to confront global crises through regional, national, and international programs. In some ways, these crises test not only the currency of the Church's social teaching for Catholic communities in North America, but also the Church's salience as guiding praxis to the other social structures. Examining the principles of subsidiarity and solidarity through the lens of Casanova's theory on the deprivatization of religion helps examine the relationship between the scale and scope of religious social programming and its mobility in the public sphere. Further, the Church's articulation of globalization as a force that "compresses time and space" intersects with other social mechanisms, such as public health and human rights policies, which also work to identify systemic and structural roots of crisis and at the same time establish effective plans of action at the local level.

Critical Issues Today

This year, Canadian Catholics faced the greatest organizational and moral crises since the abuse scandals of the 1990s. In May 2021, the Tk'emlúps te Secwépemc First Nation reported the discovery of hundreds of unmarked graves on the grounds of the former Kamloops Residential School in British Columbia (Potenteau 2021). In the months that followed, news outlets reported on dozens of Church burnings. Most, but not all, were Roman Catholic; many were on Indigenous land. Vandalized churches became symbolic markers of a public wrestling with the religious participation in the *Colonial Project*. News outlets and commentators struggled with how to portray these events: were they reactionary acts of vandalism, or timely declarations of an ever-more secular society? Catholics publicly and privately struggled to reconcile the Church's role in colonial oppression and Canadians *en masse* continued to ferret out the role of religion in social structures—discussions around religious freedom and discrimination had just been reignited once again by the passing of a bill banning religious symbols in public positions in the province of Quebec. Furthermore, these sites have become physical and symbolic landmarks of where various crises intersect: the Church's role in the Colonial Project is inseparable from rural and remote development that shapes the North American landscape but also shapes how its citizens understand environmental policy, international trade, and—at least in Canada—the very notion of sovereignty.

Since Kamloops, numerous more reports of unmarked graves at former Residential Schools have surfaced, and estimates are in the thousands. There have been dozens of cases of Church vandalism reported. The impacts on Catholic membership and on public attitudes on religion in Canada are still unknown. Yet this crisis was firmly rooted on the experience of Indigenous communities who suffered centuries of colonization: one crisis seemingly sparked instantaneously, and the other a steadily burning ember, a half-millennium marked with perennial flames of protest and action. Perhaps what was most surprising about the coverage surrounding the church vandalism was what remained absent. Where was the centering of Indigenous Catholic voices? Should there be public discussions about what it might mean to be Indigenous *and* Catholic in Canada? Where was the coverage of the CCCB and regional bishops? No mention was made to the Amazonian Synod, convened just three years earlier to address parallel concerns around colonization, ecological devastation, and the place of the Church in South America.

Although publicity around these gravesites was new, the local knowledge around them was not. The last 50 years especially have witnessed Indigenous leaders pleading their case to both government and Church. In May of 2018, in the wake of the Truth and Reconciliation Commission (TRC) into church- and state-run residential schools, members of parliament in Canada's House of Commons voted for a motion demanding that the pope apologize for the Catholic Church's role in the schools (Ballingall 2018). If nothing else, the process was a fascinating elucidation of the Church's public subsistence in Canadian civil society. The official statement from the CCCB in response to the TRC begins: "The Catholic community in Canada has a decentralized structure. Each Diocesan Bishop is autonomous in his diocese and, although relating to the Canadian Conference of Catholic Bishops, is not accountable to it" (CCCB n.d.). Here, the principle of subsidiarity limits responsibility to the participating parish and thereby insulates much of the institutional Church from moral and—potentially—civil liability. While this chapter argues that rural Catholic subcultures signaled a shift towards economic, ecological, and moral solidarity, it should also highlight where these principles have been called to question in the public sphere.

Over the past two years, COVID-19 has reminded the world that everything is indeed connected. The pandemic has compounded pre-existing crises, disproportionately affecting our poorest communities while benefitting many of the world's richest companies, all in the midst of an ongoing environmental upheaval. Those interested in the life of the Catholic Church—and religion in society more broadly—must consider how modern understandings of crisis, and the current penchant for "crisis language" informs religious activity, particularly in the public sphere. As Gilbert's points out, identifying the proliferation of crisis narratives may highlight underlying political agendas. Moreover, we ought to examine the impact for religious groups that find themselves in a constant state of crisis. Certainly, the study of religion, while rooted in the social sciences, has a unique position as it considers attitudes and actions situated within distinctly ontological and teleological narratives. This may be especially true given how modernization seems to catalyze crises or, at the very least, discourse surrounding them. The public reckoning around graves at residential schools may also act as a heuristic springboard to consider how religions respond to global crises in the public sphere. To this, Grace Davie (2007) suggests we examine what religion does (or does *differently*) when an existential crisis becomes the new "everyday."

For Davie, such moments are instrumental, and sociologists of religion "need to be attentive to episodes, whether individual or collective, in or through which the implicit becomes explicit." Those studying the Catholic church ought to consider not only its interior pastoral role, but also the position of the Church within other functional systems, legitimations, or simply, as coparticipant with secular mechanisms (civic organizations, labor unions, governments, etc.) that respond to such crises. To this, rural communities are an important venue: they are understudied, but they are also longstanding examples of how critical issues compound and, sometimes, compete.

Conclusion

The Church's use of solidarity and subsidiarity as organizational expressions of its value on human dignity and participation, as Baum notes, is essential to understanding its response to crises. Here, crisis is not simply, as Roitman cautions, "a narrative device." So, what comes next? I suggest that we are in the midst of yet another shift in Catholic teaching. Where Baum responded to the financial and social crisis of the 1970s, this one is wholly embedded in the Church's reluctant confrontation with its colonial past in Canada and North America especially. Baum's prognosis for the Church four decades ago gives us a language to help explain how the Catholic Church—and its leaders especially—envisage its participation in the public sphere. It should also call us to examine how the Church might mediate structures of opposition without defaulting back to a passive organic adaptation, relegated to the private realm or, alternatively, further entrenched within oppressive structures. Those interested in the life of the Catholic Church might heed Davie's caution and follow Baum's example by watching to see if and how the Church changes its posture and exercises subsidiarity in a profoundly new way, particularly in *relationship with* Indigenous communities.

Ben Szoller is a PhD candidate in the Department of Religious Studies at the University of Waterloo. Ben's research interests include agricultural ethics and the relationship between religious organizations and government policy. His current research examines how Catholic communities across Canada advocate for social and ecological justice through land-based agricultural training programs.

References

Annett, Anthony. 2019. "Our Common Responsibility for Our Common Home: The Activist Vision of Laudato Si'." In F. Pasquale, *Care for the World: Laudato Si' and Catholic Social Thought in an Era of Climate Crisis*. New York: Cambridge University Press.
Ballingall, Alex. 2018. "House of Commons makes 'historic' call for residential school apology from Pope Francis." *The Toronto Star*, May 1. Retrieved from www.thestar.com/news/canada/2018/05/01/house-of-commons-makes-historic-call-for-residential-school-apology-from-pope-francis.html
Baum, Gregory. 1980. *Catholics and Canadian Socialism*. Toronto: Lorimer.

Baum, Gregory. 1984. "Chapter 2: The Shift in Catholic Social Teaching." In G. Baum and D. Cameron (eds.), *Ethics and Economics: Canada's Catholic Bishops on the Economic Crisis*. Toronto: Lorimer.

Bovée, David. 2010. *The Church and the Land: The National Catholic Rural Life Conference and American Society, 1923-2007*. Washington, DC: Catholic University of America Press.

Canadian Conference of Catholic Bishops (CCCB). "Indian Residential Schools and TRC." Retrieved from www.cccb.ca/indigenous-peoples/indian-residential-schools-and-trc (accessed August 31, 2021).

Casanova, José. 1994. *Public Religions in the Modern World*. Chicago, IL: University of Chicago Press.

Casanova, José. 1996. "Global Catholicism and the Politics of Civil Society." *Sociological Inquiry*, 66(3): 356–373.

Davie, Grace. 2007. *The Sociology of Religion: A Critical Agenda*. London: Sage.

Dodaro, Santo, and Leonard Pluta. 2012. *The Big Picture: The Antigonish Movement of Eastern Nova Scotia*. Montreal: McGill-Queen's Press.

Francis. 2015. "Laudato Si'." Encyclical letter. Retrieved from www.vatican.va/content/francesco/en/encyclicals/documents/papa-francesco_20150524_enciclica-laudato-si.html

Francis. 2020. "Querida Amazonia." Apostolic exhortation. Retrieved from www.vatican.va/content/francesco/en/apost_exhortations/documents/papa-francesco_esortazione-ap_20200202_querida-amazonia.html

Francis. 2020. "Fratelli Tutti." Encyclical letter. Retrieved from www.vatican.va/content/francesco/en/encyclicals/documents/papa-francesco_20201003_enciclica-fratelli-tutti.html

Gilbert, Andrew Simon. 2019. *The Crisis Paradigm: Description and Prescription in Social and Political Theory*. Basingstoke: Palgrave Macmillan.

Hollenbach, David. 2002. *The Common Good and Christian Ethics*. Cambridge: Cambridge University Press.

Leo XIII. 1891. "Rerum Novarum." Papal encyclical. Retrieved from www.vatican.va/content/leo-xiii/en/encyclicals/documents/hf_l-xiii_enc_15051891_rerum-novarum.html

Luhmann, Niklas. 1984. "The Self Description of Society: Crisis Fashion and Sociological Theory." *International Journal of Comparative Sociology*, 25 (1–2): 59–72.

Paul VI. 1971. "Octogesima Adveniens." Apostolic letter. Retrieved from www.vatican.va/content/paul-vi/en/apost_letters/documents/hf_p-vi_apl_19710514_octogesima-adveniens.html

Pontifical Council for Justice and Peace. 2006. "Compendium of the Social Doctrine of the Church." Retrieved from www.vatican.va/roman_curia/pontifical_councils/justpeace/documents/rc_pc_justpeace_doc_20060526_compendio-dott-soc_en.html (accessed September 25, 2024).

Potenteau, Doyle. 2021. "Grief, Sorrow after Discovery of 215 Bodies, Unmarked Graves at Former B.C. Residential School Site." *Global News*, May 28. Retrieved from https://globalnews.ca/news/7902306/unmarked-graves-kamloops-residential-school/

Roitman, Janet L. 2014. *Anti-Crisis*. Durham, NC: Duke University Press.

Szoller, Ben. 2021. "The Amazon Synod Revisited: Rural Solidarity, Canadian Catholic Communities, and COVID-19." *Critical Theology*, 3(4): 7–11.

United States Conference of Catholic Bishops. 2003. *For I Was Hungry & You Gave Me Food: Catholic Reflections on Food, Farmers, and Farmworkers*. Washington, DC: United States Conference of Catholic Bishops.

Part V

Locution
Upending the Discipline

Chapter 16

World Society: Upended?

Adrian Hermann

Rhetoric of crisis is nothing new to the study of religion (see Cahill 1982; Lipner 1982; Engler and Stausberg 2011; Hughes 2017; Davidsen 2020). But in 2020 and 2021, crisis became the modus operandi of the world as a whole. At least this is the popular description that 2021 AAR president Marla Frederick adopts in "Religion, Poverty, and Inequality," the essay on her presidential theme, when she claims that "Covid-19 has upended our world" (Frederick 2021). But what exactly does this mean? In this short text, I want to explore what "world" could refer to in this context and provide some reflections on what such upending could (or could not) mean from the perspective of a sociological theory of society.

If one begins with the basic hypothesis of *world society theory*—that today "there is only one societal system on earth," primarily defined by a "plurality of functionally specified systems" which are interconnected but notably characterized by a "lateral, non-hierarchical organization" (Stichweh 2019, 515, 520, 522)—the statements formulated by sociologist (and leading world society theorist) Rudolf Stichweh in a short newspaper article published in Germany on April 7, 2020 (in the first months of the COVID-19 pandemic) were quite surprising. He claimed that the functional differentiation of society, in which no single societal area (politics, science, religion, the economy, the law, etc.) can assert primacy for itself, might have been temporarily suspended by the events of the pandemic (Stichweh 2020a).[1]

If we look at these statements in more detail, what could Stichweh have meant by this? World society theory assumes, on the basis of sociological differentiation theory and primarily the theory of society produced by Bielefeld sociologist Niklas Luhmann, that the structure of modern society is no longer primarily defined by a hierarchy of social subsystems (estates, strata, etc.; that is: peasants, clergy, and nobility), as it was until the eighteenth century (see Luhmann 2012, 2013). Rather, the theory suggests, the structure of modern society is characterized by the simultaneity and, in principle, equal ranking of a number of so-called *function systems* of society (Luhmann 2013, 87–108). Lists of such systems usually include

---

1. The article "Simplifikation des Sozialen" first appeared in the *Frankfurter Allgemeine Zeitung* on April 7, 2020. It was republished together with the postscript "Ein soziales Immunsystem für Pandemien" as Stichweh (2020a). An English version was published online as "Simplification of Social Life" (Stichweh 2020b).

politics, religion, science, education, economy, law, art, sports, and mass media, but also the healthcare system and the system of intimate relationships and families. All of these function systems have a certain relevance for modern society, but none of them can, from a sociological point of view, claim an importance that fundamentally exceeds that of the others and enforce this primacy society-wide. Or rather: a determining importance of certain function systems (the economy with its markets, for example) is of course repeatedly asserted by certain social actors, it just cannot actually be realized in modern society. In Luhmann's systems theory, this societal order is described as the "primacy of functional differentiation" (Luhmann 2013, 108), which represents the constitutive structural form of modern society. And this modern society, according to Luhmann and the sociologists that adopt this perspective, is best understood as a single social system spanning the entire planet: *world society*. (Luhmann 2012, 83–99).

Social and individual life in modern society is thus characterized by every social actor's partial and temporary participation in a variety of these function systems. According to systems theory, in modernity every situation takes place in the context of a plurality of communicative possibilities, which are always available and must be taken into account (Nassehi 2011, 134). Politics, religion, science, the economy, etc.: all these are communicative contexts whose communications are held together by symbolically generalized communication media (like power, belief, truth, money, etc.) that create higher likelihoods of continuing communication within each function system (ibid., 132). This is what, according to sociologist Armin Nassehi, is meant by "differentiation" in systems-theoretical world society theory. Stressing the "operative, empirical, eventful character" (ibid., 130) of these differentiations, he writes: "The shape of functionally differentiated society therefore is not simply characterized by a static, stable existence of function systems, but rather by the *operative* connective routine of communications that result in the emergence of different systemic contexts which thereby can remain indifferent to each other" (ibid., 131, emphasis in the original).[2] As societal structures, function systems continuously have to "prove" themselves in the present (ibid., 136). Rather than as "superstructures," they exist only as series of communicative events that constantly re-stabilize themselves (Nassehi 2006, 252). In Peter Beyer's (2006, 12) words: "Social subsystems are ... structures of boundary creation and boundary maintenance ... ways of continuously regenerating certain kinds of boundaries of meaning." Understood in this way, functional differentiation as the main structure of world society is always contested and only exists as it is reproduced in each present moment on the basis of prior communications. Its stability is not guaranteed by anything beyond the autopoietic logic of its operations (Nassehi 2011, 137).

---

2. "Die Gestalt der funktional differenzierten Gesellschaft ist also nicht einfach durch die feststehende, stabile Existenz von Funktionssystemen gegeben, sondern durch die *operative* Anschlussroutine von Kommunikationen, die unterschiedliche Systemzusammenhänge emergieren lassen und sich dadurch füreinander indifferent halten können" (Nassehi 2011, 131).

As a social actor in world society, one participates in a variety of functional contexts sequentially and at the same time, even if it may seem to the individual at times as if he or she primarily "lives" in one of these function systems (e.g., when teaching or research days seem endless again). The decisive characteristic of modern societal order is that we always participate in a multitude of function systems, i.e., we are "included" in (and sometimes "excluded" from) them (Stichweh 2021, 28). Stichweh has repeatedly pointed out that in a certain sense, as a complementary development to the structure of *functional differentiation*, the other "revolutionary invention" of modernity is the *individual* as the intersection of the various inclusions into these systems. We are loosely linked to all (or at least most) of these function systems at particular times and "individualize" ourselves precisely through this combination of involvements (Stichweh 2020c; Stichweh 2021, 22–23, 28). This situation, which replaces the premodern singular inclusion of persons in one of the strata of society, originated in the "inclusion revolutions" of the last few centuries (Stichweh 2021, 19–22), as a result of which—at least in principle—every individual can potentially participate in or is addressed by each of the function systems.

A crucial point about world society theory, moreover, is that each of the function systems operates according to its own logic, and thus the communication that takes place within them, as well as the roles individuals assume in them, cannot be transferred directly to other function systems. They have to be "translated" (if they can be transferred at all) into the logic of other systems, sometimes with considerable friction. Leaving aside the—quite interesting—problem of "corruption," as well as the general question of links and connections between systems (see Luhmann 2013, 108–124), the position of an individual in one system does not directly impact their position in another system. Just because you are a mayor, i.e., you hold a certain position in the political system, does not automatically mean that you will be treated differently at the supermarket checkout or at the hairdresser. Nor can you take those positions with you to another system: a scientific article written by a mayor will not be treated differently in a peer review process than one written by a part-time cab driver. Each of the function systems operates according to its own logic—politics is about decisions, science is about publications, economics is about payments—at least according to sociological systems theory (Nassehi 2011, 141–147).[3]

So, in light of all of this, what can we say about the "upending of the world" described by 2021 AAR president Marla Frederick? As mentioned above, in April 2020 Stichweh writes that the structure of world society has been, at least to a certain extent, temporarily suspended as a result of the COVID-19 pandemic. He

---

3. All of this does not exclude the possibility of corruption, of course (see Luhmann 1995; Hiller 2010). It only points to the systems-theoretical conviction that most everyday communication in world society operates according to this logic of functional differentiation. This implies questions of "boundary maintenance," which is a central point of contention in regard to the theoretical proposals of systems theory and differentiation theory in general (see Nassehi 2011, 141–147).

describes this as a theoretical challenge in the following words: "Regarding the corona crisis, an essential sociological question is whether and how it temporarily puts modern social order into question and what this means for the development of society in the long term" (Stichweh 2020b).

In a sense, he subsequently answers this question in the affirmative in his short article. Not only does he see the function systems of healthcare, politics, and science in a special "leading role" in the pandemic, but, perhaps relevant in the context of the AAR's presidential theme, he describes religion as the "actual loser" of the pandemic situation, since—he claims—physical co-presence in time and space during religious rituals is a main characteristic of many forms of religion (ibid.). In addition, he asserts, religious interpretations of the COVID-19 crisis have not taken on much relevance anywhere in the world, a point that I cannot explore here further (but see Meyer 2020; Borsch et al. 2020; Pezzoli-Olgiati and Höpflinger 2021). Stichweh (2020b) continues: "It is this triad of extremely narrowly conceived functional references [healthcare, politics, science, A.H.] that has, in the past few weeks, almost completely dominated our daily lives and the way we deal with information. Never before has our life been so simple and never again, after these few weeks are over, will it be this simple."

So far, so good. If we follow this interpretation, the COVID-19 pandemic has—sociologically speaking—fully upended our world, as it has managed to call into question the main characteristic of modern world society: the primacy of functional differentiation. Only three months later, in June 2020, however, Stichweh sounds quite different in a second text. He writes: "The functional differentiation of world society has in no way been challenged, no function system will disappear, and no new function system will be added, not in this case and not on this occasion" (Stichweh 2020a, 204).[4] Rather, Stichweh claims, new "institutional complexes" will emerge orthogonally to the structure of the function systems. Their task will be to observe relevant events in other function systems and present them in the context of their own system, increasing the chances for successful reactions to complex society-wide problems (Stichweh 2020a, 205). No upending of the world, then? In retrospect it must be said, especially in view of the longer quotation above, that Stichweh's focus had perhaps been somewhat unclear in the first text and that even in April 2020 he was actually more interested in the *temporary* standstill of societal dynamics, and less in questioning the primacy of functional differentiation per se.

Against Stichweh, or at least against the Stichweh of April 2020 and perhaps then again with the Stichweh of June 2020, I therefore suggest that we understand the dynamics of the COVID-19 pandemic not so much as an upending, but rather as a confirmation of the functional differentiation of modern world society. The question of an upending of the world as the result of an alleged crisis—as is being argued by various contributors to this book—is therefore always a matter

---

4. "Die funktionale Differenzierung der Weltgesellschaft steht in keiner Weise in Frage, es wird kein Funktionssystem verschwinden und auch kein neues Funktionssystem hinzukommen, nicht in diesem Fall und nicht aus diesem Anlaß" (Stichweh 2020a, 204).

of perspective. My claim here, then, is not so much that the COVID-19 pandemic *is not a crisis*, or that particular worlds *have not been upended*, but rather that one of the important questions we as critical scholars should ask about the rhetoric of crisis is the following: *whose world is being described as upended by whom, and for what reason?*

This is what we should ask ourselves when we read the 2021 AAR president's text claiming that "*our* world" has been upended, "laying bare the real human costs of poverty and the inequalities that undergird *our* social systems" (Frederick 2021, my emphasis). In sociological terms, if we follow the systems-theoretical description I have presented, *world society*—that is: functional differentiation as the central structure of modern society—has *not* been upended. And to adopt this theoretical perspective might allow us to better describe those contexts where there is no doubt that some worlds have ended and that others are disrupted almost beyond recognition as a result of the COVID-19 pandemic. These crises, however, are then to be described in contrast to the continuation of other—more general?—structures of our contemporary societal context.

In Germany for example, especially at the end of 2021 where reports of rapidly increasing COVID-19 infections hint at the situation being more and more out of control, this silent continuation of the functionally differentiated structure of society is becoming increasingly obvious. The difference between science and politics, for example, and the challenges resulting from a societal structure in which no one actor can declare one of these systems to now be in charge of the others, can be observed again and again at the moment. This has actually been *our* reality all year—the un-upended continuation of *our* world—not the least because of the general elections for the German *Bundestag* and chancellorship that took place in September 2021, which made sure that the internal logics of politics would trump the logics of science in political discussion at many moments throughout the year. In looking at things from this perspective, then, the internal logics of the political system continue to dominate political action and political discussion, rather than being replaced by a simple "implementation" of scientific recommendations or advice into political activity.

Coming back to the fate of religion over the last two years, Stichweh's early claim that religion could be considered the "actual loser" of the COVID-19 pandemic points us to the ways in which religious institutions have reacted to these events. Not so much in an attempt at understanding how religion can help us navigate the various crises in which people find themselves, as suggested by the AAR's 2021 president—not that these are unimportant in themselves, by any measure—, but rather in order to understand the *stability* of religion despite the "upending of worlds." In what ways has "religion"—as a societal function system—been able to continue as before, or rather has shown a remarkable resilience in asserting itself as one of the "essential" aspects of society—or even as of "systemic importance" (*systemrelevant*, as one has learnt to say in German)? And how has it re-invented itself by transferring existing communication and activity into virtual spaces? This directs us, for example, to all the attempts to supplement or recreate the meaning of physical co-presence in ritual through forms of virtuality (see e.g.,

Bukovec and Volgger 2021; Cooper 2021; Kühle and Larsen 2021; Neumeier 2021).

To underscore this point: recently, the sociologist David Kaldewey (2022) has provided an analysis of the use of the semantics of *Systemrelevanz* during the COVID-19 pandemic (that something is or is not of systemic importance) as an aspect of the contemporary "politics of knowledge." The term has a particular history in German sociological theory since the 1960s and is a category that can also be related to the prominent labels in Anglophone countries of "essential workers" and other societal "essentials" that allegedly became more visible during the pandemic (as also argued by the 2021 AAR president; see Frederick 2021). Kaldewey (2022) suggests that such semantics (of "systemic relevance" or "essential workers") might stick around in the future as popular "folk" categories of sociological analysis. Despite the fact that distinctions between "essential" and "inessential" aspects of society—or between things of systemic and not of systemic importance—might not provide much theoretical insight (especially in the context of the systems-theoretical perspective on modern society presented above, in which a central claim is that there is no clear hierarchy of societal systems), they might prove to be attractive in the future as part of political programs and other popular descriptions of society.

From this perspective, Stichweh's remark about religion as the "actual loser" of the pandemic, can be reformulated as a question about all the ways in which religious groups and institutions have been successful in defining and defending themselves as "essential" and as therefore exempt from many general regulations (see Floyd-Thomas 2022; Movesian 2022; Storslee 2022).

But where do we go from here? In his already mentioned "Postscript" of June 2020 (which expands on his earlier short article), Stichweh himself sees the development of a "social immune system for pandemics" as the decisive societal task of the foreseeable future (Stichweh 2020a, 205). As a sociologist, he is interested in all the institutional and structural projects and developments that might be undertaken to achieve better societal preparedness, especially as far as they relate to the aforementioned problems of "coordinating" multiple function systems in a reliable way (Stichweh 2020a, 204–205).

This question could probably also be discussed with reference to the future relevance of the networked infrastructure of "planetary-scale computation" that sociologist and philosopher Benjamin Bratton described as "the Stack" in his book on the topic in 2015 (see Bratton 2015). In his more recent essay *The Revenge of the Real: Politics for a Post-Pandemic World* (Bratton 2020), he describes a societal "sensing layer" that exists in most nation states and regions of the world but, he argues, is not sufficient in its current form as the COVID-19 pandemic has shown. He sees this layer's expansion, and a clear recognition that nation states critically require the information it provides, as the precondition of a successful post-pandemic politics (ibid., 41–46). In this context, he also suggests a positive understanding of bio-politics (against Giorgio Agamben's writings on the COVID-19 pandemic, see ibid., 109–119) as part of what he calls an "epidemiological view of society" (ibid., 33–40). He describes the societal "sensing layer" as follows: "all of the ways in which a society is able to sense what is going on at both granular and holistic levels so as to make a model that it may use to act back upon itself and thereby govern itself" (ibid., 42). Consisting of multiple regimes of testing and of a large variety of sensor arrays, among other things, the sensing layer includes "many different kinds of technologies, different kinds of encounters" (ibid., 42). While all of them contribute to the "valid models" society attempts to make of the world, "[s]ome of them may be quite intimate, some quite visceral, some quite distantiated, some non-tactile, some immediate, some highly mediated" (ibid., 42–43). In sum, this structure of connected digital networks, platforms, and technological "forms of sensing" in contact with "the world" through a multiplicity of "sensors" (ibid., 43, 42) appears at least to Bratton—in light of the COVID-19 pandemic—as the central prerequisite for meaningful policy-making in the future. In his view, this applies in particular to "grand challenges" (Kaldewey 2018) like climate change or future pandemics, but beyond that is necessary for sensible everyday governance as well. Starting from a different theoretical perspective, but coming to the same conclusion as Stichweh above, for Bratton (2020, 46) the sensing layer can be understood as an important "instantiation of a collective immune system" and represents an aspect of a "larger epidemiological and biopolitical stack" by which society understands and constructs itself. In regard to the upending of certain worlds and the continuing stability of others, these questions therefore also connect the ongoing digitalization of society with the possible futures of the functional differentiation of world society (on this topic see also Priester 2021).

In closing, I want to mention one more point in connection with what it might mean to claim that "our world" has been radically upended. What does this perspective leave out? And in what ways does it restrict our thinking? This relates to the striking lack of utopian perspectives we have been witnessing in most spaces in 2020 and 2021. And the possibly radically different claim that we have seen no upending. Nowhere.

Without in any ways negating all the suffering and devastation that the COVID-19 pandemic has created for a large number of people, I want to argue that one of the problematic results of speaking of an upending of "our world" is also visible in the dearth of publicly visible utopian thinking during the pandemic. Much of the political debate, even after the pandemic years, was primarily an expression of a search for a return to an imagined "normality," as expressed, for example, in the statements of German Christian Democratic Party politician (and now newly elected party leader) Friedrich Merz in September 2020 that people must be careful not to "all [get] used to the idea that we can live without work" (Tagesspiegel 2020). Teachers in particular, he argues, are called upon to maintain the social significance of the "school system" even in "corona times" (ibid.).

Little was and is still to be heard in these words (and in many similar assessments) of the refreshing forms of utopian thinking that appeared possible in the first weeks of March 2020. In the words of literature and ecocriticism scholar Patrícia Vieira:

> During the Covid-induced lockdown, it became clear that radical changes in the current way of life are well within our reach: traffic almost stopped; flights were grounded; people stayed home with their families or roommates; there was a drastic decrease in air and water pollution—think of the famous images of shoals of fish roaming through the usually murky canals of the Venice lagoon—, and so on. This does not mean that all transformations brought about by the pandemic were positive. The inability to socialize with friends and with some family members left many struggling with loneliness and other psychological problems. And confinement at home led to a sharp increase in violence against those who are more vulnerable … What was positive about the crisis was that it opened up a whole horizon of possibilities. It showed us that another world is possible …
>
> (Vieira 2020, 430)

In the same vein, I remember discussions questioning the previous significance of (many forms of) (gainful) employment for our individual and social coexistence. I also remember debates that used the sudden changes of the early pandemic situation as an occasion for discussing what role, for example, schools and universities can and should play in our lives, especially in an increasingly digital society. The quick disappearance of utopian thinking in the months since—making many exchanges of early 2020 now feel like the distant past—also affects many universities. Here, it often seems like both the administration and significant parts of the faculty continue to reflect on the current and future role of online teaching mostly based on the premise of a return to a previous status quo (see also Hermann 2021). In Germany this leads to the consequence that, due to the dynamics of the fourth wave of the COVID-19 pandemic, in the winter term of 2021/22 it was once again necessary at many universities to return to partial or fully online teaching in an unstructured and somewhat chaotic process. In contrast, thinking about the future of the university—both on site and online—beyond a "deficit perspective" in regard to the digital, the development of hybrid forms of collaboration, and an innovative and creative imagining of forms of teaching and research specifically conceived as online from the beginning was and still is urgently needed (see also the essays collected in Hermann 2021). Considering the predominant agreement on the "normality" of teaching in person, which most institutions quickly returned to, as far as university campuses are concerned, the COVID-19 pandemic does therefore not signify a radical upending of "our world," but rather points to how little "we" have—or have been—allowed to let the events of 2020 and 2021 upset "our" academic worlds.

What could be the alternative? I can't go into much detail here, but I just want to mention one "utopian" context, which has done so much for my own sanity during the COVID-19 pandemic, especially as some worlds around me might have been transformed. This is the field of *analog games* (see Torner et al. 2016) transferred into a digital space. In particular, the incredibly dynamic design space of independent tabletop and live action role-playing games (Hedge and Grouling 2021; Lowthian 2021; Hermann and Reininghaus 2021). Such games provide not only a fascinating—and pandemic compatible—leisure activity, but also can serve as inspirations in regard to what would be possible when using digital technology in research and teaching. Especially the ways in which some role-playing games designed specifically for an online environment—so-called live action online games (LAOGs)—experiment with and explore various forms of online communication could inspire new ways of thinking about making use of the now ubiquitous Zoom classroom (see Reininghaus and Hermann 2021).

One way of dealing with the current crisis, then, is to not give up looking for the utopian—in our work, but also in the everyday. And, lastly, we might find such (maybe temporary) utopian refuge also in fictional, but maybe no less real, worlds (see Gabriel 2020), until some of the multiple worlds around each one of us might actually become upended.

Adrian Hermann is full professor of religion and society and director of the Department of Religion Studies at Forum Internationale Wissenschaft, University of Bonn. His work focuses on the global history of the concept of "religion," the use of non-fictional media in contemporary religious movements, and the religious history of the globalized world. He is the author of *Unterscheidungen der Religion* (Göttingen: Vandenhoeck und Ruprecht, 2015) and is currently working on a monograph on Philippine independent Catholicism around 1900. Recently he has begun to also contribute to the emerging field of analog game studies.

References

Beyer, Peter. 2006. *Religions in Global Society*. London: Routledge.
Borsch, Anne, Merijn ter Haar, Inken Prohl, and Vera Schaer. 2020. "Corona and Religion." Retrieved from https://religionswissenschaft.zegk.uni-heidelberg.de/veroeffentlichungen/veroeffentlichungen/Religion%20and%20Corona.pdf.
Bratton, Benjamin. 2015. *The Stack: On Software and Sovereignty*. Cambridge, MA: MIT Press.
Bratton, Benjamin. 2020. *The Revenge of the Real: Politics for a Post-Pandemic World*. London: Verso.
Bukovec, Predrag, and Ewald Volgger (eds.). 2021. *Liturgie und Covid-19: Erfahrungen und Problematisierungen*. Regensburg: Friedrich Pustet.
Cahill. P. Joseph. 1982. *Mended Speech: The Crisis of Religious Studies and Theology*. New York: Crossroad.
Cooper, Levi. 2021. "Kaddish During COVID: Mourning Rituals During a Pandemic." *Contemporary Jewry* 41, 39–69. https://doi.org/10.1007/s12397-021-09395-x.
Davidsen, Markus A. 2020. "Theo van Baaren's Systematic Science of Religion Revisited: The Current Crisis in Dutch Study of Religion and a Way Out." *NTT Journal for Theology and the Study of Religion* 74(3), 213–241. https://doi.org/10.5117/NTT 2020.3.002.ALTE.
Engler, Steven, and Michael Stausberg. 2011. Crisis and Creativity: Opportunities and Threats in the Global Study of Religion\s." *Religion* 41(2), 127–143. https://doi.org/10.1080/0048721X.2011.591209.
Floyd-Thomas, Stacey M. (ed.). 2022. *Religion, Race, and COVID-19: Confronting White Supremacy in the Pandemic*. New York: New York Univ. Press.
Frederick, Marla. 2021. "Presidential Theme for the 2021 Annual Meeting: Religion, Poverty, and Inequality: Contemplating Our Collective Futures." Retrieved from https://aarweb.org/AARMBR/Events-and-Networking-/Annual-Meeting-/Presidential-Theme-for-the-2021-Annual-Meeting.aspx.

Gabriel, Markus. 2024. *Fictions.* Cambridge: Polity.
Hedge, Stephanie, and Jennifer Grouling (eds.). 2021. *Roleplaying Games in the Digital Age: Essays on Transmedia Storytelling, Tabletop RPGs and Fandom.* Jefferson, NC: McFarland.
Hermann, Adrian (ed.). 2021. *Experimente mit digitaler Lehre: Überlegungen und Modelle jenseits einer Defizitperspektive.* Bonn: Forum Internationale Wissenschaft. https://doi.org/10.48565/bonndoc-3.
Hermann, Adrian, and Gerrit Reininghaus. 2021. "Beyond the Character Sheet: 'Character Keepers' as Digital Play Aids in the Contemporary Indie TRPG Community." *Japanese Journal of Analog Role-Playing Game Studies* 2: 31–50. https://doi.org/10.14989/jarps_2_31.
Hiller, Petra. 2010. "Understanding Corruption: How Systems Theory Can Help." In Gjalt de Graaf, Patrick von Maravić, and Pieter Wagenaar (eds.), *The Good Cause: Theoretical Perspectives on Corruption,* 64–82. Leverkusen: Barbara Budrich.
Hughes, Aaron (ed.). 2017. *Theory in a Time of Excess: Beyond Reflection and Explanation in Religious Studies Scholarship,* Sheffield: Equinox.
Kaldewey, David. 2018. "The Grand Challenges Discourse: Transforming Identity Work in Science and Science Policy." *Minerva* 56, 161–182. https://doi.org/10.1007/s11024-017-9332-2.
Kaldewey. David. 2022. "Was bedeutet Systemrelevanz in Zeiten der Pandemie?." *Berliner Journal für Soziologie* 32(1), 7–33.
Kühle, Lene, and Tina Langholm Larsen. 2021. "'Forced' Online Religion: Religious Minority and Majority Communities' Media Usage during the COVID-19 Lockdown." *Religions* 12(7), 496. https://doi.org/10.3390/rel12070496.
Lipner, Julius. 1983. "Theology and Religious Studies: Thoughts on a Crisis of Identity." *Theology* 86(711), 193–201. https://doi.org/10.1177/0040571X8308600306.
Lowthian, Declan. 2021. "10 Tabletop RPGs That Changed The Hobby Forever." CBR.com. December 28. Retrieved from www.cbr.com/tabletop-rpgs-changed-hobby-forever/.
Luhmann, Niklas. 1995. "Kausalität im Süden." *Soziale Systeme* 1(1), 7–28.
Luhmann, Niklas. 2012. *Theory of Society,* vol. 1. Stanford, CA: Stanford University Press.
Luhmann, Niklas. 2013. *Theory of Society,* vol. 2. Stanford, CA: Stanford University Press.
Meyer, Birgit. 2020. "Studying Religion in Times of Corona." *TRAFO: Blog for Transregional Research.* https://trafo.hypotheses.org/23783.
Movsesian, Mark. 2022. "Law, Religion, and the Covid Crisis." *Journal of Law and Religion,* 37(1), 9–24.
Nassehi, Armin. 2006. *Der soziologische Diskurs der Moderne.* Frankfurt am Main: Suhrkamp.
Nassehi, Armin. 2011. *Gesellschaft der Gegenwarten: Studien zur Theorie der modernen Gesellschaft II.* Berlin: Suhrkamp.
Neumaier, Anna. 2021. "Wann macht es Klick? Über digitale Kirche in Corona und was man schon aus Prä-Corona-Zeiten lernen kann." *Communicatio Socialis,* 54(1), 106–115. https://doi.org/10.5771/0010-3497-2021-1-106.
Pezzoli-Olgiati, Daria, and Anna Höpflinger (eds.). 2021. *Religion, Medien und die Corona-Pandemie: Paradoxien einer Krise.* Baden-Basen: Nomos.
Priester, Stefan. 2021. "Plattformsoziologie." *FIW Working Paper* 15. Bonn: Forum Internationale Wissenschaft. Retrieved from www.fiw.uni-bonn.de/publikationen/fiw-working-paper/fiw-working-paper-no.-15.
Reininghaus, Gerrit, and Adrian Hermann. 2021. "*Live Action Online Games* (LAOGs) als Impulsgeber für die digitale Lehre." In Adrian Hermann (ed.), *Experimente mit digitaler Lehre: Überlegungen und Modelle jenseits einer Defizitperspektive,*

108–118. Bonn: Forum Internationale Wissenschaft. https://doi.org/10.48565/bonndoc-3.

Stichweh, Rudolf. 2019. "World Society." In Ludger Kühnhardt and Tilman Mayer (ed.), *The Bonn Handbook of Globality*, 1: 515–526. Cham: Springer.

Stichweh, Rudolf. 2020a. "Simplifikation des Sozialen." In Michael Volkmer and Karin Werner (eds.), *Die Corona-Gesellschaft: Analysen zur Lage und Perspektiven für die Zukunft*, 197–206. Bielefeld: transcript. https://doi.org/10.1515/9783839454329-020.

Stichweh, Rudolf. 2020b. "Simplification of Social Life." Retrieved from https://zif.hypotheses.org/740.

Stichweh, Rudolf. 2020c. "Unablässige Prozesse: Inklusion, Exklusion und die Differenzierungsdynamik der modernen Gesellschaft." *Forschung und Lehre*, 4/2020, 298–300.

Stichweh, Rudolf. 2021. "Individual and Collective Inclusion and Exclusion in Political Systems," In Anna L. Ahlers, Damien Krichewsky, Evelyn Moser, and Rudolf Stichweh (eds.), *Democratic and Authoritarian Political Systems in 21st Century World Society, Vol. 1: Differentiation, Inclusion, Responsiveness*, 13–38. Bielefeld: transcript. https://doi.org/10.14361/9783839451267.

Storslee, Mark. 2022. "COVID-19, Neutrality, and the Free Exercise of Religion." *Journal of Law and Religion* 37(1): 72–95. https://doi.org/10.1017/jlr.2021.81.

Tagesspiegel. 2020. "Merz warnt vor Gewöhnung an 'Leben ohne Arbeit'." *Der Tagesspiegel*, September 21. Retrieved from www.tagesspiegel.de/politik/cdu-politiker-zum-alltag-in-der-coronakrise-merz-warnt-vor-gewoehnung-an-leben-ohne-arbeit/26204686.html.

Torner, Evan, Aaron Trammell, and Emma Leigh Waldron. 2016. "Reinventing Analog Game Studies: Introductory Manifesto." In Aaron Trammell, Evan Torner, and Emma Leigh Waldron (eds.), *Analog Game Studies*, 1: 1–5. Pittsburgh: ETC.

Vieira, Patrícia. 2020. "Utopia, Dystopia and the Future of Homo Sapiens in the Wake of Covid-19." *Esboços: Histórias em Contextos Globais*, 27(46), 426–433. https://doi.org/10.5007/2175-7976.2020.e77772.

Chapter 17

Competing Economies in Studies of Identity and Religion

K. Merinda Simmons

Anxiety within and about "the profession" has ramped up over recent years among academics looking to address our place both in scholarly and societal worlds. A variety of factors play into this phenomenon: the moral panic that conservatives have manufactured about the academy as an ideological initiation zone; the increasing reliance upon contingent, contract labor to fill teaching lines; the administrative de-emphasis on curricular requirements in the humanities; the gaping maw of student loan debt; post-pandemic pedagogical constraints; and so on. All of these factors—at least inside a North American context—are predicated on a capitalist framing of higher education, along with the economic inequality and wealth disparity that continues to grow ever more extreme. Thus, discourses of "crisis" in the academy are necessarily economically inflected, whether or not we overtly attend to them as such.

Offered within the context of a roundtable on "Class, Identity, and Religion"—and as part of a larger program on "Discourses of Crisis and the Study of Religion—my brief comments here concern the roles that considerations of class play in identity studies more broadly. Specifically, I discuss how identitarian claims (so frequently invoked in crisis-rhetoric) too often foreclose the intersectional approaches those claims nominally advance. This foreclosure occurs, I suggest, when the former employs analyses of specific economies of meaning to the exclusion of specific economies of capital. Intersectionality, however, demands active attention to the structural apparatuses constituting both economies simultaneously. Different and more interesting work becomes possible when those modes of economy are neither conflated nor dichotomized.

In an attempt to offer a conceptual framework for this conversation, my fellow roundtable participants and I agreed to organize our respective thoughts around two points of provocation. Here are mine:

1. Identitarianism and intersectionality are co-extensive but mutually exclusive.
2. Anxiety (as a byproduct of precarity) is the engine of ontological truth claims.

I do not offer either of these as some kind of settled conclusion. On the contrary, I want instead to think about what conversations are made possible if we use them as starting points. There are many examples one might use to test out these claims, but, just to offer one example, I will focus on the fault lines between identitarian and class-based approaches within Black studies before offering a glance at helpful scholarship that presses the implications of intersectionality in relation to a particular identity category. The latter approach is one that would assist, too, in discourses on crisis, inasmuch as that concept is inevitably a nexus wherein identity and institutionality meet.

Class-based analyses within Black studies have rightly or wrongly become characterized—perhaps caricatured—by work by scholars like Adolph Reed Jr.,[1] Kenneth Warren,[2] and Walter Benn Michaels.[3] All of them prestigious scholars in their own rights, they have also long appeared for many as gadflies in the larger field because of their critiques of from ascriptive, identitarian analyses of race, as well as their unapologetic critiques of neoliberalism and the political left. Because of their respective insistences on keeping dynamics of capital and labor at the fore, their work often ends up looking like critiques of antiracism as much as of white supremacist power structures. As Reed has suggested, "antiracism is not a different sort of egalitarian alternative to a class politics but *is* a class politics itself: the politics of a strain of the professional-managerial class whose worldview and material interests are rooted within a political economy of race and ascriptive identity-group relations...[a politics] that naturalizes the outcomes of capitalist market forces so long as they are equitable along racial (and other identitarian) lines" (Reed 2016). This insight resonates with my first point of provocation above: In many instances, an identitarian standpoint epistemology is easily confused with an intersectional one. The co-extensive nature of self-identification and structural habitus, however, gets collapsed when the former is invoked at the cost of the latter. Reed in particular discusses race in a way religious studies scholars should find familiar. Just as many of us in NAASR would balk at an account of religion as a self-evident phenomenon in the world, Reed suggests the following about race:

> It makes sense that race can be an object of study and an object for study. [T]he problem ... is when we use race as a category of analysis, what we're doing is employing the notion that presumes an abstraction to be a real thing that has impact in the world.
>
> (Reese 2021)

---

1. For just a couple of examples, see *Renewing Black Intellectual History: The Ideological and Material Foundations of African American Thought* (Reed and Warren 2010) and *Class Notes: Posing as Politics and Other Thoughts on the American Scene* (Reed 2000). He is also a contributor to a number of online venues, such as Common Dreams and The New Republic, and he hosts the recently launched Class Matters podcast.
2. See *What Was African American Literature* (Warren 2011) and his pieces for sites like nonsite. org and Jacobin—representative among them, "Reparations and other Right-Wing Fantasies" (Warren 2016), as well as "'Blackness' and the Sclerosis of African American Cultural Criticism" (Warren 2019).
3. See *The Shape of the Signifier* (Michaels 2004) and *The Trouble with Diversity: How We Learned to Love Identity and Ignore Inequality* (Michaels 2006).

In this way, the abstraction and the real thing are co-extensive, but mutually exclusive.

The response to such critiques, even when sympathetic, can easily grate against the perceived tone they take. To folx like Reed who have described antiracist identitarianism as "shrill" (Reese 2021), one might be tempted to invoke The Dude from *The Big Lebowski* when he chastises his bombastic and opinionated friend: "You're not *wrong*, Walter. You're just an asshole." And to be fair, the popular discourse on class often serves a smoke screen for ignoring race dynamics. For example, after Donald Trump was elected, cable news outlets and political pundits were quick to explain his voting constituency in terms of economic disenfranchisement and poverty instead of continued and pervasive racism. Those elements are not necessarily incompatible, of course, but the emphasis of one over and against the other risks perpetuating a sensibility comforting to many—namely, one that imagines white supremacists as people belonging to isolated fringe groups brandishing confederate flags and carrying torches rather than as people who fail or refuse to take structural stock of white privilege.

That said, however, what I read scholars like Reed as trying to do (whether or not with quite as much tact as we might like) is to confront identity theorists with the consequences of framing class and race as rhetorical tools wielded to the exclusion of each other. When a focus on race forecloses or precludes substantive renderings of class dynamics, what often results are relational formulations of antiracism at the expense of more difficult, and more mundane, structural ones. The relational approach continues to have a great deal of purchase, as evidenced by the widespread success and popularity of, as just one example, Robin DiAngelo's *White Fragility* (2018), despite numerous critiques that followed on the heels of its publication. Appealing to change in hearts and minds does not have to stand in for appealing to change in policy, of course, but internal affirmations of good intentions prioritize identity over intersectionality and are thus more easily managed than is the time-consuming work of community organizing that requires attention be paid to multiple systems of oppression operating simultaneously. In other words, while we talk a big game about intersectionality, we fail to take it seriously when we insist on an approach that attempts to move race to the head of the class, so to speak, or to class off from structural discussions of race.

When members of this roundtable formulated our ideas with a conversation ahead of the NAASR meeting, Dennis LoRusso prompted my thinking about this particular point—that sloppy understandings of intersectionality often amount to assuming identity categories all work in the same way at the same level and are thus interchangeable. Those faulty construals, then, allow for discourse about just one category even while invoking others (i.e., "A conversation about race demands a reckoning with gender and class! Now about 'the white vote'..."). Or, as Jeremy Posadas suggested in relation to this phenomenon, class and identitarian categories are often used as *alibis* for each other in order to suit the purposes of a particular project. Put simply, when we try to put everything on the same level, we end up collapsing difference and erasing contextual and historical nuance.

Religion and Black studies scholar Joseph Winters asks the generative question, "What happens to intersectional approaches when gender, class, and citizenship concerns are overshadowed by the Black/Human non-relationship?" (Winters 2017). I'm generalizing, of course, but too often the answer is "not much." In too many cases, as long as we land on "the right side" of history and ontology, we forgo structural analysis of either, consequently trafficking in the same affective identitarian logics that contribute to the social realities which force us into a defensive position in the first place. Kenneth Warren has discussed this phenomenon in terms of racecraft:

> Races are not simply "there" to be represented. Rather, as Karen E. Fields and Barbara J. Fields have argued, races are conjured through discursive and social practices (... "racecraft") that transform "racism into race, disguis[e] collective social practice as inborn individual traits...[and] entrench...racism in a category to itself, setting it apart from inequality in other guises." Particularly noteworthy...is that those committed to social justice are often as likely to contribute to racecraft as are those who are happy with the world inequality has made.
>
> (Warren 2019)

Recent work in the broader domain of identity studies provides some possible answers regarding what analyses committed to intersectional logic might look like. One example is Judith Butler's discussion of religiously inflected campaigns against so-called "gender ideology." In a 2019 essay, they talk about anxieties created by wealth acquisition and systematic removal of social/welfare services—anxieties which fuel a compulsion to load an empty ideological container of "gender" with threat. Specifically, Butler suggests "that we understand the historical formulation of neoliberalism and financialization ... not as the cause of the anti-gender ideology movement, but as part of the complex scene of heightened conflict where nationalism, racism, and heightened militarism ally with anti-gender ideology propaganda" (Butler 2019). I would suggest the same is true on the progressive side of the same identitarian coin: that political and social structures of capital have everything to do with our investments in gender and race as ontological realities to safeguard. This is what I'm getting at with that second point of provocation: Anxieties borne of a lack of proximity to structural safety can, in many ways, drive truth claims about identity. Sometimes that looks like fierce, conservative resistance to "gender ideology"—and, as we've seen even more recently in the U.S., to a specific rendering of critical race theory. Sometimes, however, that looks like progressive embraces of identitarianism in the name of coalition-building. I am *not* suggesting that each has the same effect or holds the same implications, but I *am* suggesting that the ontological framework and identitarian logics upon which each relies warrant skeptical examination.

Class analyses can usefully direct us to nuanced considerations of the idea of "economy"—namely, that the concept is always and only ever simultaneous in its signifying power, implicating both financial systems of global capital and what have been called within our own professional class "economies of meaning." Lee Edelman directs us away from ontological identity claims with that latter invocation. His own concept is "queerness," which for him "refers, to whatever figures, in a given social order, a disruption in the economy of meaning, even if such figures of disruption are required for that economy to survive" (Edelman 2019). The challenge then becomes mitigating our anxieties by taking intersectionality seriously enough to accept and even pursue the occasions that it undermines identitarianism. In reference to African American literature specifically, Kenneth Warren puts it like this:

> The task at hand ... is not to try to produce an African American literature adequate to the current moment, but to recognize that any attempt to limn the contours of an African American literature—however one tries to define it—cannot escape being the incoherent, class-inflected project that such an effort has always been.
> (Warren 2019)

The same goes for our productions of gender, sexuality ... and, to be sure, religion. If and when attempting to have productive conversations about *crisis* in relation to such concepts, we must attend to the various economies—structural and symbolic alike—shaping the crucible in question.

K. Merinda Simmons is professor of religious studies at the University of Alabama. Her books include *Changing the Subject: Writing Women across the African Diaspora* (Ohio State University Press, 2014), *The Trouble with Post-Blackness* (co-edited with Houston A. Baker, Jr., Columbia University Press, 2015), and *Race and New Modernisms* (co-authored with James A. Crank, Bloomsbury, 2019). She is editor of the book series *Concepts in the Study of Religion: Critical Primers* and editor of the *Bulletin for the Study of Religion* (both with Equinox Publishing).

References

Butler, Judith. 2019. "What Threat? The Campaign against 'Gender Ideology.'" *Glocalism: Journal of Culture, Politics and Innovation*, 3. Retrieved from https://glocalismjournal.org/wp-content/uploads/2020/01/Butler_gjcpi_2019_3-1.pdf

DiAngelo, Robin. 2018. *White Fragility: Why It's So Hard for White People to Talk about Racism*. Boston, MA: Beacon Press.

Edelman, Lee. 2019. "Queerness, Afro-Pessimism, and the Return of the Aesthetic." *REAL: Yearbook of Research in English and American Literature* 1: 11–26.

Michaels, Walter Benn. 2004. *The Shape of the Signifier*. Princeton, NJ: Princeton University Press.

Michaels, Walter Benn. 2006. *The Trouble with Diversity: How We Learned to Love Identity and Ignore Inequality*. New York: Metropolitan Books.

Reed, Adolph. 2000. *Class Notes: Posing as Politics and Other Thoughts on the American Scene*. New York: The New Press.

Reed, Adolph. 2016. "How Racial Disparity Does Not Help Make Sense of Patterns of Police Violence." Retrieved from https://nonsite.org/how-racial-disparity-does-not-help-make-sense-of-patterns-of-police-violence

Reed, Adolph, and Kenneth Warren, eds. 2010. *Renewing Black Intellectual History: The Ideological and Material Foundations of African American Thought*. Paradigm Press.

Reese, Hope. 2021. "Adolph Reed Jr.: The Perils of Race Reductionism." *JSTOR Daily*, April 28. Retrieved from https://daily.jstor.org/adolph-reed-jr-the-perils-of-race-reductionism

Warren, Kenneth. 2011. *What Was African American Literature?* Cambridge, MA: Harvard University Press.

Warren, Kenneth. 2016. "Reparations and other Right-Wing Fantasies." Retrieved from https://nonsite.org/reparations-and-other-right-wing-fantasies

Warren, Kenneth. 2019. "'Blackness' and the Sclerosis of African American Cultural Criticism." Retrieved from https://nonsite.org/blackness-and-the-sclerosis-of-african-american-cultural-criticism

Winters, Joseph. 2017. "Blackness, Pessimism, and the Human." Retrieved from www.aaihs.org/blackness-pessimism-and-the-human

Afterword

Hey, What About Me?

Aaron W. Hughes

> O wad some Pow'r the giftie gie us
> To see oursels as ithers see us!
> It wad frae mony a blunder free us,
>   An' foolish notion:
> What airs in dress an' gait wad lea'e us,
>   An' ev'n devotion!
> —Robert Burns, "To a Louse"

> There's nothing more useless than a car that won't start
> It's even more useless at the end of the world
> —Bob Geldof, "The End of the World"

What follows presents my response to the previous set of chapters. But, even more than that, it also functions as a platform to respond to the immediate reaction to the oral version of my paper that was delivered virtually on November 12, 2021. While surprised by the audience's response, upon further reflection many of the comments expressed at that time expose a thorny issue in the study of religion, one that often goes unnoticed and, just as often, unacknowledged. Indeed, so problematic is it that it risks undermining the entire edifice upon which the critical study of religion sits.

Expressed in the form of a question: What happens when theorizing cuts too close to home? Framed somewhat differently, but again in the form of a question, how is it possible to theorize others, and not ourselves? This problem is endemic to the study of religion, moving as it does beyond the classic insider/outsider problem. It was there at the field's genesis in functional approaches to the religions of others (often coded as "primitives"); and it was there in the hey-day of phenomenology that sought to impose the idea of the "sacred" on others. Jonathan Z. Smith then came on the scene and talked about the importance of self-reflexivity and the often (over) active role of the scholar in creating religion, and we listened. Or did we?

This admittedly truncated history of our field is nonetheless revealing. It shows that we have always struggled with understanding others because our "selves"—our bodies, our categories, our own religious backgrounds, and so on—always get in the way. While we in the present think we have cracked the epistemological code, clearly, we haven't. We cannot claim the critical distance that theory and method afford only when it suits us and then fall back on the "experiential" when said theory and method affects us personally. That cannot be how critical scholarship works. Since NAASR prides itself on theoretical and methodological sophistication, surely such questions demand to be addressed. And I try to do precisely that here.

This is where one of my favorite stanzas from the Scottish bard comes in. In his "To a Louse," Burns begins the poem by noticing a louse—a small parasite, often referred to by the plural "lice"—on the hat of a beautiful lady named Jenny as she sits in church. Everyone stares at the louse, but Jenny mistakenly thinks they are staring at her, admiring how beautiful she is, and she coquettishly tilts her head to one side, with the intention of acknowledging everyone acknowledging her:

> O Jenny, dinna toss your head
> An' set your beauties a' abroad!
> Ye little ken what cursed speed
>   The blastie's makin!
> Thae winks an' finger-ends, I dread
>   Are notice takin!

Burns humorously laments that if we had the power to see ourselves as others see us, such ridiculous displays could be prevented.

When I initially presented my keynote address, I was surprised by the reaction that it received. Actually "dumbfounded" or "gob smacked" might be more accurate descriptors. I had spent several weeks thinking about how to craft what I hoped would be a theoretically sophisticated paper that would have broad appeal among NAASR's general membership. I had, after all, been a part of NAASR, on and off, for roughly fifteen years. I was part of its leadership that sought to differentiate it from the more theologically inflected American Academy of Religion (AAR) a few years back when it risked becoming an extension of that organization. So, when Rebekka King, its president, asked me to give a lecture devoted to "crisis," I assumed, in true NAASR-fashion, that I would theorize, historicize, and taxonomize the term and the discourses surrounding it, thereby scattering a set of talking points among the audience that I thought could be picked up in the annual meeting that commenced the following day.

Crisis, after all, is but a word, one that is used and abused in any number of often-competing contexts. Rather than produce a paper that looks at the repercussions of COVID-19—assuming that this was the reason behind the theme of the conference in the first place—I opted to look at the material conditions that operate behind the scenes whenever something is labelled as a "crisis." Everything can potentially be labelled as a "crisis" (just as any period can ostensibly be called a "golden age") and surely it would be interesting to look at how the term has been deployed in other contexts—By whom? At what point? And, perhaps most importantly, for what purposes?

The raison d'être of NAASR, I used to think, was about making more theoretical moves than many in the field make, shining the torch back a little further, and looking at the subterranean discourses and hidden assumptions that often remain hidden to the naked eye. I even joked in the beginning of my lecture that were this an AAR address, I would do something considerably different. I might, for example, address Buddhist responses to the crisis brought on by the pandemic. Or, again, how have Muslims tried to overcome the pandemic, and so on and so forth. Such a lecture, I surmised, might then involve an interfaith exploration of the world's religions and spiritual traditions, all with the aim of offering us some sort of antidote to our present crisis and, in so doing, help alleviate our collective suffering.

Such a keynote would at least address religion. But I did not want to do that given that I thought NAASR was about something a little different than providing descriptions of religious actors' lives. I was right, at least: the online audience did not want me to do that. Instead, and here is where I was baffled, they expected me to bear witness to their own personal crises. Many saw it as my job that virtual evening to declare the Trump presidency (and the whole MAGA movement) a "crisis." Well, it certainly was for some; for others, however, it was a boon. And this is precisely what I wanted to get at. A crisis is only ever a crisis for some but, at the same time, not necessarily for others. That was the whole point of the initial paper.

Someone in the audience wanted me to address the "real crisis" brought about by Trump's presidency and presumably not my own theoretical and academic musings based on my own professional standards. The whole point of my talk was that crises are subjective and here some were talking about *real* crises, presumably unaware of the rhetoric of authenticity. I did not have the heart to mention that my interlocuter's talk of a "crisis" would probably have amused his Republican neighbors. For the latter the "real crisis" was the liberal ideas being spouted by the left-leaning professorial classes! Yet others saw it as my job to acknowledge their "crises" of being overworked, burned out by online classes, and their problems with childcare, etc. That they might have tenure-track or tenured positions and had the luxury of teaching remotely during the height of the pandemic while front-line workers risked their lives daily was not brought up.

What, I think, the audience wanted from me was to listen to them as opposed to vice versa. Here, I certainly acknowledge that the "crisis" brought on by the pandemic has been burdensome for many, both inside and outside the academy. Our online meeting was, after all, one of the few times NAASR members had had a chance to meet, and my sense is that Q&A functioned as a makeshift hallway or pub. At a face-to-face meeting, no doubt, this is where people would gather and express "tea and sympathy," as my late father would have said. A keynote, however, is not about triage. And a keynote for NAASR is not—or should not be—about "feelings" or personal experiences. I have made a career of trying to show how deleterious this is for the field. I quite literally do not have the wherewithal to do this. So, I did what I do: I theorized.

This is also not to say that descriptions of crises, both historical and contemporary, cannot be interesting or useful. Suzanne Owen's analysis of the "crisis" facing the academic study of religion in the U.K. is extremely helpful in isolating some of the problems that have long beset the study of religion: its coupling with theology.

My goal, however, was not to look at specific crises, but to examine the rhetoric of "crisis." A crisis, I (re)submit, is a discourse manufactured to protect certain interests, which, by extension, is also tantamount to the subversion of others. I doubt Jeff Bezos or Elon Musk would call what we have all gone through a "crisis." They have benefitted from it and their profits have soared. They have done so, moreover, at the expense of all those underpaid front-line workers who risked their lives to feed their families. The "freedom convoy" that made its way across Canada and ended up in Ottawa, the nation's capital, in February of 2021, to use another example, was deemed a national "crisis"—so much so that Prime Minister Justin Trudeau invoked the Emergencies Act. This act allows the federal government to take extraordinary temporary measures to respond to, among other things, public order emergencies, and involves upending certain basic Charter rights (e.g., right to free assembly). This, of course, is not to deny that public order was being undermined by the convoy. That is not my point, it is that only after labelling it a "crisis" could the federal government act. Nor do I think that the Trudeau government had—contrary to the comments of his political opponents—any nefarious purposes. But, and again reinforcing my point, this is not to say that some future leader of Canada, or any other liberal democracy for that matter, might not invoke such measures whenever a "crisis" emerges.

Rather than ask what defines a "crisis," *pace* my virtual audience, we need to look at the social group claiming something to be a "crisis." How does labelling something a "crisis" create the crisis? Questions such as these, I again (re)submit, are often much more interesting than the former. To quote my lecture:

> A housing crisis, for example, is only a crisis if one does not have a house. An "adjunct labor crisis" is a crisis for those underemployed and under recompensed. In both cases the interests of the status quo, those in power, are protected. Potentially masked in calling something a crisis are the real structural problems that remain out of sight and hidden from view. I think it is important for us to draw attention to these structural issues instead of simply giving voice to them and repeating them as if they were a mantra.
>
> (This volume, page 19)

Discourses on crisis, after all, are not the same as complaining about one's actual crisis. We cannot simply theorize our data and then complain when someone theorizes us. We cannot revert to insiders once an "outsider" attempts to redescribe our own social worlds. This, as McCutcheon argues in his response to my paper, should be "rather uncontroversial for the so-called critical scholars of religion who often comprise NAASR's membership." But, he adds, "now we see that this turns out to depend upon what or whom one might be studying."

This, for me, is a real problem, one that threatens not only NAASR, but the critical study of religion more generally. Interfaith and interreligious dialogue types, after all, do not have such a double standard. They take spirituality or faith (or whatever we want to call it) "seriously" in both themselves and those they study.

They are, in other words, consistent. What does it mean for the more critical wing of religious studies to be only self-critical when studying others, but when their own self-identity is at risk revert to some other position? Such a position strikes me as not only problematic, but as duplicitous.

I do not believe I need to rehash the contents of my lecture here. A year later, it continues to speak for itself, and I still stand by everything I wrote. I do like how Dennis LoRusso adds nuance to my theoretical musings with his analysis of "the crisis of the American worker" and the "crisis of academic labor." The historical depth and breadth he brings to these discussions, while using some of my own moves, is precisely what I had wanted and indeed expected from colleagues. This is also echoed in Lauren Horn Griffin's chapter that seeks to show real crises in the modern university in general and the Humanities in particular, but that these crises emerge out of discourses. And that, because of this, the best way to examine them is through discourse analysis. This is a very "Lincolnian" move and means that we need to examine the institutionalized patterns manifest in disciplinary structures and operate by the connection of knowledge and power.

As I conclude this brief response, I would like to quote from Bruce Lincoln's "Theses on Method." This quotation should be familiar to many in NAASR, and I am sure that many of its members have also cited it in print or in the classroom. In his thesis number 4, he writes:

> The same destabilizing and irreverent questions one might ask of any speech act ought to be posed of religious discourse. The first of these is "Who speaks here?," i.e., what person, group, or institution is responsible for a text, whatever its putative or apparent author. Beyond that, "To what audience? In what immediate and broader context? Through what system of mediations? With what interests?" And further, "Of what would the speaker(s) persuade the audience? What are the consequences if this project of persuasion should happen to succeed? Who wins what, and how much? Who, conversely, loses?"
>
> (Lincoln 1996: 226)

I might tweak this here and replace his "the same destabilizing and irreverent questions one might ask of any speech act ought be posed of religious discourse" with: The same destabilizing and irreverent questions one might ask of *others* ought to be posed of *ourselves*.

Aaron W. Hughes is the Dean's Professor of the Humanities and the Philip S. Bernstein Professor in the Department of Religion and Classics at the University of Rochester. His research and publications focus on both Jewish studies and Islamic studies.

Reference

Lincoln, Bruce. 1996. "Theses on Method." *Method & Theory in the Study of Religion*, 8(3): 225–227.

Index

4chan 133
9/11 46, 116n5, 122-3

American Academy of Religion (AAR) 4-5, 11, 15, 179, 181-4, 198-9
abolition 84-5, 95, 100, 172; police 84-5, 95; theory 84; *see also* police
acculturation 69
African-American cultural forms 35, 69, 72, 80; history 70; literature 194; studies 121
agency 72, 106-8, 126, 168, 170
Amazon 170; synod 170, 173
anomaly 2-5, 88
anthropology 15-6, 18, 47, 160
anti-clericalism 147-9, 152-3
anti-essentialism 105-9, 112-3
Antichrist 64
antiracism 191-2
anxiety 36, 59, 135, 190, 193-4
apocalypse, apocalyptic 134-5; apocalyptic rhetoric 138; apocalyptic thought 130-1, 133, 135; *see also* millennialist
Aristotle 106-111
Armageddon 15
arson 70-1, 75-80, 99-100; *see also* church burnings
Asad, Talal 24-6, 28
asana 162
ashram 156, 158, 161
authenticity 35, 54n3, 125, 199
authority 3, 5, 54, 56, 82-3, 86, 88-92, 100, 121, 126, 138, 165n1, 168; hierarchy 59; Roman Church 24; regimes 151; *see also* hierarchy
Ayurveda 158, 162

Barkun, Michael 133-5, 138-40
Baudrillard, Jean 3, 6
Baum, Gregory 165-6, 168, 170, 174

Bellah, Robert 122
Benjamin, Walter 5, 63-7, 89, 92-5, 99, 115
Bergson, Henri 83, 90
Bezos, Jeff 15, 53, 114, 200
Bhagavad Gita 158, 161-2
bhakti 160, 163
biblical studies 45-6, 48, 121n18
black liberation 71; theology 99; *see also* theology
Black Lives Matter 67, 137
boundary 27, 122, 152, 180; class 38; creation 180; maintenance 180, 181n3
bourgeoisie 40, 125
Branson, Richard 114
Bratton, Benjamin 184-5
Brazil 5, 156-63
British Association for the Study of Religions, the 47-8
Brown, Wendy 119, 125
Buddhism 11, 106, 156, 199
Butler, Judith 112n9, 193

Campos-Salvaterra, Valeria 84, 87, 89, 94
Canada 16, 133, 165-6, 168, 171-4; Antigosh Movement 171; Conservative Party 14
capitalism 21, 38-9, 82, 84-5, 101, 125, 146, 150, 190-1; colonial 90n8, 94; global 82-3, 90n8; humanistic 40; and modernity 21; neoliberal 115; *see also* colonial; neoliberal
Casanova, José 168, 170, 172
category 4-5, 11, 17, 27, 57, 86-7, 89, 110, 184, 191-3, 197; of crisis 5, 63; critique of 3; construction of 4, 106; of identity 191-2; of religion 18, 25, 106-7; of self 12; of violence 83
Catholic 1-3, 47, 145-6, 148-9, 152-3, 159, 161, 165-74; hierarchy 148;

Indigenous 173; Mexican 3, 146–9, 152–3; Roman 3, 145, 147–9, 153, 166–7, 171–4; social teaching 165–72; solidarity 165–8, 170, 172–4; subsidiarity 165–8, 170, 172–4; theology 167, 171
chaos 70, 73–4, 186
Chernobyl 150
Christian 14, 18, 28–9, 45–7, 78–9, 90n8, 99–100, 106, 125, 150, 152–3, 159, 161, 185; apocalyptic 130–1, 140; Evangelical 161; Protestant 14; Christian theology 16–7
church burning 70, 76, 79, 99, 172; see also arson
civil rights 38–9; movement 71, 73, 77, 99
classification 3–4, 22, 25, 30, 36, 55–6, 63, 94, 124; act of 3, 37; crisis of 4, 22, 52
colonialism 16, 18, 19, 67, 82, 83–5, 90n8, 159, 172–4; and capitalism 90, 94
communism 145, 150–1, 169
consciousness 66, 73, 131, 167; black 71; collective 22; self 4, 51, 97
conspiracy theories 27, 130–40
construction 3–6, 35, 38, 83, 97, 106–8, 124, 145, 147, 150, 167, 185; of categories 4, 106
coup 55–7, 91; see also classification
COVID-19 4, 11, 16, 18, 27, 37–8, 41, 53, 57–8, 63, 65–7, 80, 98, 130–2, 137, 139, 146, 152, 156–7, 159, 162–3, 172–3, 179, 181–6, 198
Cristero War, the 145–8, 152–3
critical race theory 23, 132, 193
culture 6, 21–6, 28–32, 35, 38, 45–7, 51, 69–70, 72 79, 90n8, 95, 97–8, 114–7, 122, 126–7, 132, 134, 147–8, 151–3, 156, 158–60; war 23–4, 26, 30, 32

data 4–5, 22, 27, 41, 47, 54, 99, 120, 157, 200
Davis, Angela 85
decarceration 84
Deep State, The 133
Derrida, Jacques 82–95, 100, 112
diaspora 69, 150
disenfranchisement 72–4, 88n6
dissent 22, 32
divinity 27, 29, 45, 161
dogma 69

Douglas, Mary 122
Drucker, Peter 39–40
duality 69, 134
Durkheim, Émile 16

economy 14, 38–40, 53, 65–6, 71–2, 91–2, 94–5, 100, 114–8, 123, 125, 138, 146, 165–6, 168–71, 173, 179–81, 191–4; economic inequality 4; neoliberal 36, 39, 115; socio-economic issues 15, 132, 138; see also neoliberal
Edelman, Lee 31, 193–4
Eliade, Mircea 122
Elliott, Scott 115, 119–21, 123–4, 126
encyclicals, papal 149, 165, 169
epidemiology 27, 184–5
esotericism 69, 135
essentialism 105–13
ethnography 15, 18, 57
ethos 115n4, 121
extremism 2, 130–1, 135–6, 138; right-wing 131, 135–6

faith 14, 48, 65, 69, 73, 82–3, 90–2, 100, 118n10, 145–6, 148, 151, 160, 166, 200; crisis of 82, 100
Fanon, Frantz 23
fascism 139, 169
FBI 75–7, 132–3
financial crisis 50–51, 98, 117–8, 126
First Amendment, the 25
Floyd, George 83, 101, 137
Foucault, Michel 22, 32n1, 118n13, 145, 156, 162
Frazer, James George 17
Frederick, Marla 179, 181, 183–4
Freud, Sigmund 16
Friedman, Milton 117–9
functional differentiation 179–83, 185
functionalism 16

Geertz, Clifford 122
gender 1, 19, 25, 29, 38, 48, 65, 100, 118n12, 121, 124, 192–4; studies 27, 29; see also violence
genealogy 12, 14, 19, 36, 65, 92
Germany 21, 179, 183–4, 186
glasnost 145, 150
globalization 39, 83, 117, 166, 169, 171–2

Goldman Sachs 100
Gorbachev, Mikhail 150
governance 59, 115, 117n8, 185
Great Depression, The 170
Great Recession, The 41
Great Reset, The 130
Gulf War, the 3

habitus 191
Hare Krishna 161
Harman, Willis 40
Harvey, David 40, 118
Hayek, Friedrich 116-7, 125
Hegel, Georg Wilhelm Friedrich 64n3, 83n2, 90n8, 111
hegemony 28, 90n8, 153
Heidegger, Martin 83n2, 90n8, 93, 111-2
Heraclitus 111
hierarchy 59, 115n4, 125, 148-50, 152-3, 179, 184; *see also* authority
Hinduism 110, 156
historiography 64, 67, 98
Hofstadter, Richard 135
homogeneity 82, 124, 135
Hoover, Edgar J. 70, 75-6
humanities/humanist 21-23, 25-32 40, 48, 54, 121-3
hybridism 156, 159-60, 166n2, 186

identitarianism 190-4
identity 5, 82, 86, 89, 92, 97, 115, 124, 132, 134, 146, 157, 190-3; category 191-2; crisis 120; group 59; national 147, 150-1, 153; politics 123-4; protestant 28; self 57, 87, 111, 201
ideology 3, 12-3, 24-30, 39, 52, 114-5, 118, 125-6, 131, 135, 138, 146, 150, 165, 190, 193; nationalist 21; neoliberal 115, 119, 125-6; *see also* neoliberal
India 156, 159, 161-63, 171n7
Indigenous 93, 156, 160-1, 170, 172-4; African 156, 160-1; culture 46-7; religion 47
industrialization 170
insider/outsider 122, 125, 197, 200
intersectionality 190-4
ISIS 126
Islam 3, 14, 123, 126; studies 46, 116n5, 123

Jainism 156
January 6, 2021 130
Jesus 71, 134, 161
jihad 126
Jim Crow 36, 71-2
Johnson, Robert 35-8, 42
Jones, William R. 69
Judaism 19, 86, 88, 90n8, 100

Kant, Emmanuel 83n2, 87-8, 90n8, 114
Kaplan, Mordecai 19
Kardecist 161
Kennedy, John F. 70, 77
Kennedy, Robert F. 76
Keynes, John Maynard 40, 116, 125
Kiev Rus 150, 152
King Jr, Martin Luther 70-1, 73, 75, 78-79
Klee, Paul 114, 127
Klein, Naomi 118n14
Koselleck, Reinhart 5, 63-7, 99
Ku Klux Klan 72-3, 77

Latin America 117, 149, 159
Laudato Si 167n4, 169
law 52, 56-7, 59, 71, 82-95, 101, 117, 119, 138, 151, 179-80; enforcement 77, 82-6, 92-5, 100-1; force of 86; Jim Crow 72
legitimacy 22, 38, 67, 85-6, 88, 123, 138, 159, 167n3, 174
liberalism 32, 47, 75, 82n1, 84-6, 88, 92, 101, 116, 118n10, 119n15, 133, 146, 199-200; Christian 28; enlightenment 82n1; government 148, 152; Keynesian 40; secular 28
liminality 36, 43
Lincoln, Bruce 4-5, 55, 131, 201
lived religion 156, 160-1
Locke, John 23, 82n1 108-9, 111
Luhmann, Niklas 165, 179-81
lynching 69-70, 79

MAGA 199
Marxism 14
masculinity 1-2
Maslow, Abraham 40
Masuzawa, Tomoko 90
materialism 64n3
Mauss, Marcel 16

Mayes, Benjamin E. 71, 78
McCutcheon, Russell 5, 12, 22, 24, 32, 54, 56, 120, 123–4, 200
McGuire, Meredith 156, 160
mediatization 3
meditation 157–8, 161–2
messianism 63–4
metaphysics 83, 100, 109–12; substance 105, 109–12
method 5, 18, 46, 53–5, 74, 121–2, 131, 146, 161, 165, 169, 198, 201; and theory 4, 116, 120–3, 127, 198; *see also* theory
Mexico 3, 5, 117, 145–9, 152–3, 168; *see also* Catholic
Meyer, Jean 147–8, 150
Middle East, the 56, 150
millenarian 133–4, 138; *see also* apocalypse
millennium 134, 150, 152
ministry 45–6, 151–2
modernity 21, 24, 67, 166, 168, 173, 180–1; crisis 66–7
monotheism 18
moral 31–2, 39, 83, 93, 112, 125–6, 131–4, 152, 166, 172–3; panic 131–2, 135, 190; violence 89, 92n10
Müller, Max 16
Musk, Elon 114, 200
mystical foundation of authority 82–7, 90–2
myth 35, 37–8, 57, 93, 125; making 124–6

NAACP 72
NAASR 2, 4, 11, 15–6, 18–9, 35–6, 50, 54–5, 59, 120–1, 191, 198–201
Nadir of Race Relations, the 5, 69–70, 79, 99
NAFTA 117
narrative 3, 6, 12, 17, 19, 23, 28, 31, 51, 123, 132, 135, 138, 147, 167, 173–4
nationalism 21, 118, 138, 193
nativism 118
neoconservative 125
neoliberal 36, 39–41, 43, 115–20, 123–7, 191, 193; capitalism 115; economy 36, 39, 115; ideology 115, 119, 125–6
Neusner, Jacob 121n19
new religious movements 121, 162
Nietzsche, Friedrich 67
nihilism 67

Nixon, Richard 39–40
North America 4–5, 14, 46, 52, 58, 82, 87–8, 132, 140, 159, 165–6, 171–2, 174, 190
nostalgia 31

Obama administration 55, 117
occult 135
oligarchy 114
ontology 64, 90, 105, 110–2, 166–7, 173, 190, 193
Orientalists 16, 19
origin 16, 30, 35, 48, 83, 89, 91–2, 94, 106, 116; story 36
Orsi, Robert 1–3, 54
Orthodox Church, the 145–7, 150–3
orthodoxy 40, 161
Other, the 82–3, 86–95, 132, 134, 197; repugnant 2
Otto, Rudolph 16

pandemic 4, 11, 15, 27, 36–7, 41–2, 50, 53–4, 57–8, 66, 98, 114, 130–1, 136, 138, 140, 146, 152–3, 157–8, 162, 173, 179, 181–6, 199
paradigm 14, 83, 105, 107, 147, 167; shift 120–1, 158; technocratic 166; *see also* world religions paradigm
Parmenides 109
Pascal, Blaise 90–1
patriarchy 94, 125
pedagogy 130, 136, 139, 190
perestroika 145–7, 151–3
phenomenology 16, 18, 46, 121, 197
philology 18
philosophy 22–3, 26–9, 47–8, *82*, 85–6, 90n8, 100, 105, 109, 111, 121n18, 159
Pizzagate 130, 133
Plato 107–10
police 70, 73, 75, 79, 83–5, 89, 92–5, 100–1, 138; abolition 84–5, 95; violence 83–5, 92–3, 100–1; *see also* abolition
politburo, the 150
Pope Francis 167, 169
Pope Leo XIII 149, 165, 170
Pope Paul VI 165, 170
populism 56, 117, 123, 130–2, 135, 137–8, 140
postcolonial analysis 109

poststructuralism 109, 112
power 3, 13, 19, 24, 28, 31, 38, 40, 42, 83, 85, 92–3, 99, 112, 114–5, 133, 135, 145n1, 150–1, 160, 167, 180, 191, 193, 200–1; systems of 27, 31, 73
pragmatism 84, 146, 151, 153, 162
pranayama 162
privatization 24, 27–29, 31, 119
Protestant 14, 101; Christianity 14; identity 28; *see also* identity
proto-Yoga 159
Putin, Vladimir 151

QAnon 130, 132–3, 137, 139
queer identity 123, 194

racecraft 193
racism 5, 38, 69–72, 78–9, 101, 131, 133, 135, 138, 140, 191–3
Reagan, Ronald 117
Reconstruction 69, 99
reductionism 16, 36, 53, 122
Reed Jr., Adolph 191–2
reform 41, 46, 85, 150, 166, 172
revolution 67, 85, 95, 98, 146, 181; 1910 Mexican Revolution 145, 148; 1917 Russian Revolution 145; business 39; industrial 166; sexual 39
rhetoric 2, 14, 22, 24, 26–7, 29, 31–2, 36, 54–56, 58, 63–4, 66, 79, 99, 118, 192, 199; apocalyptic 138; crisis 2, 5, 31, 36–41, 51–2, 57, 64, 67, 69, 97–8, 179, 183, 190, 200; violence 139
Ribeiro, Darcy 160
right-wing movements 130–1, 135–6
ritual 57, 161, 182–3
rock 'n' roll 35–38
Robinson, Jackie 70, 77
Roman Catholic Church, the 3, 145, 147–9, 153, 166–7, 171–4
Roosevelt, Franklin D. 51, 117n8
Russia 3, 5, 145–7, 150–3
Russian Orthodox Church 145–7, 150–3

sacredness 14, 25, 27, 31, 57, 91, 121n18, 162, 197
sacrifice 73, 83n2, 133, 161
Sanskrit 158, 161
Santo Daime 160–1

Satan 132–3
Saussure, Ferdinand de 111–2
schism 78, 148
secular 11–2, 14, 18, 24, 26–31, 57, 122, 124, 145, 147, 153, 159–60, 166n2, 167, 171–2, 174; study of religion 48, 121n18, 124; theory 147, 157
segregation 71, 73, 75, 77, 79, 134
semantic shifts 12, 66, 167n3, 184
sexuality 25, 118, 132, 194
Shantivanam 161
Shiva 161
Smart, Ninian 46, 122, 125
Smith, Jonathan Z. 124, 197
socialism 116, 125, 149
social media 1–3, 30, 114, 124, 126–7, 130–2, 136, 159
Socrates 107–9, 111
solidarity 165–8, 170, 172–4
Soviet Union, the 150
statecraft 118
subsidiarity 165–8, 170, 172–4; *see also* Catholic
suffrage 72, 74
symbol 59, 117n6, 133–4, 159–60, 172, 180
syncretism 69, 160, 162
systemic changes 40–1, 43, 75, 98, 118n10, 172, 180, 183–4

Tantra 163
taxonomy 5, 27, 198
technology 3, 156, 171; digital 2, 127, 185–6; internet 2, 132, 158–9
terrorism 69–70, 72–3, 76–9, 99
theology 15–8, 37, 45–9, 64–6, 69, 71–2, 74, 78–9, 99–100, 115–6, 120–4, 198, 200; black liberation 99; Catholic 167, 171; liberation 99, 169; social-political 75, 78–9
theory 5, 50, 57, 86, 105, 109–12, 119, 122–4, 130, 132, 137–9, 168, 172, 184–5, 192, 197–201; abolition 84; Catholic social 165–72; conspiracy 130–5, 138, 140; crisis 5, 11n1, 53, 65, 97–8; critical race 23, 132, 193; economic 116–8; of essentialism 106–7; justice 82, 86n5, 92, 95; framework 5; lesbian dance 23; and method 4, 116, 120–1, 123, 126, 198; neoliberal 125–6; social

15, 53; world society 179–83; *see also* method; neoliberalism
totemism 16–7
Trans-Atlantic Trade, 69
Trudeau, Justin 200
Trump, Donald 29–31, 51–3, 125, 132, 192, 199
Trumpism 123
truth claims 30, 55, 71, 91, 180, 191, 193
Turner, Victor 122
turning point 13, 97–98
Tylor, E. B. 16–7
typology 84, 97

Umbanda 161
United States, The 5, 56, 70, 99, 101, 132–3, 138, 165, 168, 171
universal 24, 27, 38, 83, 86, 87–8, 146, 170
uskorenie 150
utilitarian 23, 26
utopia 36, 100, 165, 185–7

Vatican, the 148–9; Second Vatican Council 165–6, 169

Vedanta 158, 160–2
Vedic astrology 162
Victorian Era, the 16
violence 2–3, 37, 69–75, 79, 82–5, 89, 91–5, 100, 118n12, 132, 134–5, 137–8, 140, 148, 186; category of 83; economic 94, 100; gender 67, 95; Jihadi 126; moral 89; police 83–4, 92–3, 100–1; racial 69–75, 79, 83–4, 95; rhetoric of 139
virtue 30, 107–9, 111–2

Warren, Kenneth 191, 193–4
Western civilization 23, 28–31, 125
white supremacy 37, 71–4, 138–9, 191–2
world religions paradigm, the 46, 105–7, 112–3; *see also* paradigm
world society theory 179–83
World War II 40

yoga 156–63; Yoga Sutras, the 158, 162

Zapatista 117

www.ingramcontent.com/pod-product-compliance
Lightning Source LLC
Chambersburg PA
CBHW062028220426
43662CB00010B/1517